Struts Survival Guide

Basics to Best Practices

Srikanth Shenoy
with
Nithin Mallya

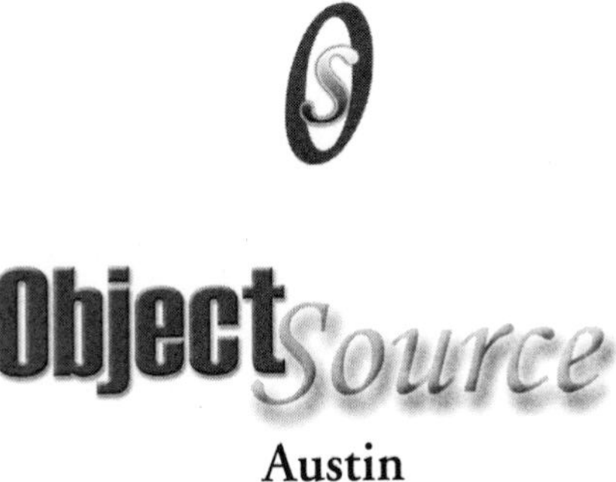

Austin

ObjectSource LLC books are available for bulk purchases for corporations and other organizations. The publisher offers discounts when ordered in bulk. For more information please contact:

Sales Department
ObjectSource LLC.
2811 La Frontera Blvd., Suite 517
Austin, TX 78728

Email: sales@objectsource.com

Published by
ObjectSource LLC
2811 La Frontera Blvd., Suite 517,
Austin TX 78728

Printing
RJ Communications
51 East 42nd Street, Suite 1202,
NewYork NY 10017

Cover Design
Matt Pramschufer
Budget Media Design
Pleasantville, New York

Library of Congress Catalog Number: 2004100026

ISBN: 0-9748488-0-8 (paperback)

Printed in the United States of America

Table of Contents

Preface

I started using Struts in late 2000. I was immediately drawn to its power and ease of use. In early 2001, I landed in a multi-year J2EE project, a large project by any measures. Struts 1.0 was chosen as the framework for the web tier in that project. Recently that project upgraded to Struts 1.1. I did the upgrade over a day. It cannot get any easier!

This book makes no assumptions about your Struts knowledge. It starts with the basics of Struts, teaches you what is important in Struts from a usage perspective and covers a lot of practical issues all in a short 200-page book. No unnecessary explanations. Concise, Clear and straight to the topic.

I am a consultant, not an author by profession. Hence my writing also tends to reflect my mindset that got shaped by the various assignments I have undertaken in the past. Large projects and their inbuilt complexities excite me. In large projects, decoupling layers is a big thing. Also minor decisions during architecting and designing (probably without the complete knowledge of the framework used) can impact the project in a big way down the line. Clearly understanding the strengths and shortcomings of a framework and minor customizations to the framework go a long way in making the applications cleaner. In that perspective, I have attempted to give a practical face to this book based on my experience. Chapters 4, 5, 6, 9 and 10 will be extremely valuable to all those wishing to use Struts effectively in J2EE projects.

Chapter 9 is based on my article originally published in IBM developerWorks in May 2002 on Best practices in EJB Exception handling (http://www-106.ibm.com/developerworks/java/library/j-ejbexcept.html). This chapter borrows some of the core concepts from that article and extends and improvises them to specifically suit the needs of a Struts web application.

I have enjoyed a lot writing this book. Even though I knew Struts well, there were some crevices that I had not explored and have made me that much better. If you are a beginner, this book is your fastest track to master Struts. There are a lot of best practices and strategies related to Struts that makes this book valuable to even experienced developers and architects.

Acknowledgements

I owe countless thanks to my parents and my wife for patiently putting up with me when I was working evenings and weekends on the book and also editing the book. Special thanks also go to Sandeep Nayak for being a beta reader and pointing out the problems in the initial two chapters. Likewise I am indebted to booksjustbooks.com, for making their book on Publishing basics available freely online without which this book wouldn't have been a reality. Thanks to RJ Commucations for printing this book. Many thanks to Matt Pramschufer from Budget Media Design for the cover design. Finally thanks to God through whom all things are made possible.

Srikanth Shenoy
December 2003

Our upcoming book

J2EE Web Project Survival Guide

Architecting the web tier

ISBN: 0-9748488-1-6 (paperback)

Wish you had designed your last J2EE project better?

Do you have questions?

- What framework to choose for view generation and web-tier?
- How to use Component Discovery mechanism to design a decoupled system?
- How to control web application flow when the user bookmarks the page or uses browser back button?
- How to handle exceptions in the system?
- How to secure the web application and provide Single Sign-on?
- How to integrate various open source frameworks and get a solid working application?
- How to use Maven instead of Ant?
- How to automate and run unit tests?
- How to effectively package classes in the EAR and utilize the J2EE class loading mechanism?
- How to run various tests and measure the performance of the system?
- How to collect metrics about the system resource utilization?
- How to monitor the production system and provide support?

This book has answers.

Chapter 1

Getting Started

In this chapter:

1. You will learn about Model1 and Model 2 (MVC) and their differences
2. You will understand the shortcomings of Model 1
3. You will understand the problems with Model 2 – The Fat Controller Anti pattern
4. You will learn how to overcome the problems in Model 2 by using Model 2 with a configurable controller
5. You will see how Struts fill the gap by providing the configurable controller and much more to boost developer productivity
6. You will look at installing Tomcat and Struts on your computer

What is Struts?

Struts is a Java MVC framework for building JSP based web applications on the J2EE platform.

That's it! As you can see, a whole lot of buzzwords appear in the above sentence. In this chapter let us dissect this sentence word by word to get a complete picture of what Struts is and why it is required. Struts is primarily used in JSP based web applications, but you can use it in template based (non-JSP) web applications such as Velocity. Although you know how to develop and deploy J2EE web applications, let us start with a quick overview J2EE and JSP before moving on to more interesting buzzwords in the above sentence.

J2EE Platform

As you might be already knowing J2EE is a platform for executing server side Java applications. Before J2EE was born, server side Java applications were written using proprietary vendor APIs. Since each vendor has his own APIs and architectures, developers and architects could not reuse the lessons learnt in the trenches. Consequently there was a huge learning curve (and hence cost) for Java developers and architects alike to learn and program in each of these API sets.

Consequently the entire Java developer community would be fragmented into islands isolated and stunted thus making it next to impossible to build serious enterprise applications in Java.

Fortunately the introduction of J2EE and its adoption by the vendors has resulted in standardization of its APIs thus reducing the learning curve for server side Java developers. J2EE specification defines a whole lot of interfaces and a few classes. Vendors (like BEA and IBM for instance) have provided implementations for these interfaces thus creating application servers, as they are called which adhere to the J2EE specifications.

The J2EE application servers provide the infrastructure services such as threading, pooling and transaction management out of the box. The application developers can now concentrate on implementing business logic and user interfaces that are important for the business.

J2EE specification defines containers for managing the lifecycle of server side components. There are two types of containers - Servlet containers and EJB containers. Servlet containers manage the lifecycle of web applications and EJB containers manage the lifecycle of EJBs.

J2EE web application

Any web application that runs in the servlet container is called a J2EE web application. The servlet container implements the Servlet and JSP specification. It provides various entry points for handling the request originating from a web browser. There are three entry points for the browser into the J2EE web application - Servlet, JSP and Filter. You can create your own Servlets by extending the `javax.servlet.http.HttpServlet` class and implementing the `doGet()` and `doPost()` method. You can create JSPs simply by creating a text file containing JSP markup tags. You can create Filters by implementing the `javax.servlet.Filter` interface.

The servlet container becomes aware of Servlets and Filters when they are declared in a special file called *web.xml*. Each J2EE web application has exactly one *web.xml* file. The web application is deployed into the servlet container by bundling it in zipped archive called Web ARchive – commonly referred to as *WAR* file.

JSPs

JSPs are servlets in disguise! So, if JSPs are servlets, why do you need JSPs anyway? The answer lies in the separation of concerns that exist in real J2EE projects. Back in the days when JSPs didn't exist, servlets were all that you had to build J2EE web applications. They handled requests from the browser, invoked middle tier business logic and rendered responses in HTML to the browser. Now that's a problem. A Servlet is a Java class coded by Java programmers. It is okay to handle browser requests and have business and presentation logic in the servlets since that is where they belong. HTML formatting and rendering is the concern of page author who most likely does not know Java. So, the question arises, how to separate these two concerns intermingled in Servlets? JSPs are the answer to this dilemma.

The philosophy behind JSP is that the page authors know HTML. HTML is a markup language. Hence learning a few more markup tags will not cause a paradigm shift for the page authors. At least it is much easier than learning Java and OO! JSP provides some standard tags and java programmers can provide custom tags. Page authors can write server side pages by mixing HTML markup and JSP tags. Such server side pages are called JSP. JSPs are called server side pages because it is the servlet container that interprets them to generate HTML. The generated HTML is sent to the client browser.

We just said JSPs are server side pages. Server side pages have to be parsed every time they are accessed. This is expensive. A way to get around the expensive parsing is by generating Java class from the JSP. The first time a JSP is accessed, its contents are parsed and equivalent Java class is generated and subsequent accesses are fast as a snap. Here is some twist to the story. The Java classes that are generated by parsing JSPs are nothing but Servlets! In other words, every JSP is parsed at runtime (or precompiled) to generate Servlet classes.

Presentation Logic and Business Logic – What's the difference?

The term Business Logic refers to the middle tier logic – the core of the system usually implemented as Session EJBs. The code that controls the JSP navigation, handles user inputs and invokes appropriate business logic is referred to as Presentation Logic. The actual JSP – the front end to the user contains html and custom tags to render the page and as less logic as possible. A rule of thumb is the dumber the JSP gets, the easier it is to maintain. In reality however, some of the presentation logic percolates to the actual JSP making it tough to draw a line between the two.

Model 1 Architecture

Model 1 architecture is the easiest way of developing JSP based web applications. It cannot get any easier. In Model 1, the browser directly accesses JSP pages. In other words, user requests are handled directly by the JSP.

Let us illustrate the operation of Model 1 architecture with an example. Consider a HTML page with a hyperlink to a JSP. When user clicks on the hyperlink, the JSP is directly invoked. This is shown in Figure 1.1. The servlet container parses the JSP and executes the resulting Java servlet. The JSP contains embedded code and tags to access the Model JavaBeans. The Model JavaBeans contains attributes for holding the HTTP request parameters from the query string.

In addition it contains logic to connect to the middle tier or directly to the database using JDBC to get the additional data needed to display the page. The JSP is then rendered as HTML using the data in the Model JavaBeans and other Helper classes and tags.

Problems with Model 1 Architecture

Model 1 architecture is easy. There is some separation between content (Model JavaBeans) and presentation (JSP). This separation is good enough for smaller applications. Larger applications have a lot of presentation logic. In Model 1 architecture, the presentation logic usually leads to a significant amount of Java code embedded in the JSP in the form of scriptlets. This is ugly and maintenance nightmare even for experienced Java developers. In large applications, JSPs are developed and maintained by page authors. The intermingled scriptlets and markup results in unclear definition of roles and is very problematic.

Application control is decentralized in Model 1 architecture since the next page to be displayed is determined by the logic embedded in the current page. Decentralized navigation control can cause headaches when requirements keep changing.

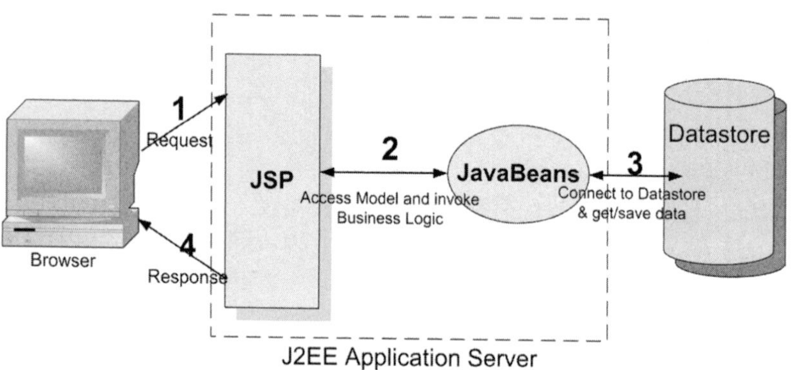

Figure 1.1 Model 1 Architecture.

Model 2 Architecture - MVC

Another important buzzword in our initial statement was MVC. MVC stands for Model View Controller. MVC originated in SmallTalk and has since made its way into Java community. The Model 2 JSP architecture is actually MVC applied to web applications and hence the two terms can be used interchangeably in the web world. Figure 1.2 shows the Model2 (MVC) architecture.

The main difference between Model 1 and Model 2 is that in Model 2, a controller handles the user request instead of another JSP. The controller is implemented as a Servlet. The following steps are executed when the user submits the request.

1. The Controller Servlet handles the user's request. (This means the hyperlink in the JSP should point to the controller servlet).
2. The Controller Servlet then instantiates appropriate JavaBeans based on the request parameters (and optionally also based on session attributes).
3. The JavaBeans talks to the middle tier or directly to the database to fetch the required data.
4. The Controller sets the resultant JavaBeans (either same or a new one) is set in one of the following contexts – request, session or application.
5. The controller then dispatches the request to the next view based on the request URL.
6. The View uses the JavaBeans from Step 3 to display data.

Note that there is no presentation logic in the JSP. The sole function of the JSP in Model 2 architecture is to display the data from the JavaBeans set in the request, session or application scopes.

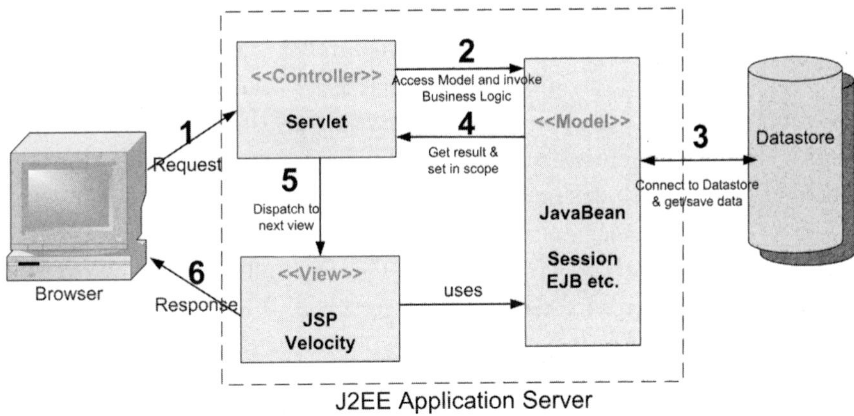

Figure 1.2 Model 2 Architecture.

Advantages of Model 2 Architecture

Since there is no presentation logic in JSP, there are no scriptlets. This means lesser nightmares. [Note that although Model 2 is directed towards elimination of scriptlets, it does not architecturally prevent you from adding scriptlets. This has led to widespread misuse of Model 2 architecture.]

With MVC you can have as many controller servlets in your web application. In fact you can have one Controller Servlet per module. However there are several advantages of having a single controller servlet for the entire web application. In a typical web application, there are several tasks that you want to do for every incoming request. For instance, you have to check if the user requesting an operation is authorized to do so. You also want to log the user's entry and exit from the web application for every request. You might like to centralize the logic for dispatching requests to other views. The list goes on. If you have several controller servlets, chances are that you have to duplicate the logic for all the above tasks in all those places. A single controller servlet for the web application lets you centralize all the tasks in a single place. Elegant code and easier to maintain.

Web applications based on Model 2 architecture are easier to maintain and extend since the views do not refer to each other and there is no presentation logic in the views. It also allows you to clearly define the roles and responsibilities in large projects thus allowing better coordination among team members.

Controller gone bad – Fat Controller

If MVC is all that great, why do we need Struts after all? The answer lies in the difficulties associated in applying bare bone MVC to real world complexities. In medium to large applications, centralized control and processing logic in the servlet – the greatest plus of MVC is also its weakness. Consider a mediocre application with 15 JSPs. Assume that each page has five hyperlinks (or five form submissions). The total number of user requests to be handled in the application is 75. Since we are using MVC framework, a centralized controller servlet handles every user request. For each type of incoming request there is "*if*" block in the `doGet` method of the controller Servlet to process the request and dispatch to the next view. For this mediocre application of ours, the controller Servlet has 75 *if* blocks. Even if you assume that each if block delegates the request handling to helper classes it is still no good. You can only imagines how bad it gets for a complex enterprise web application. So, we have a problem at hand. The Controller Servlet that started out as the greatest thing next to sliced bread has gone bad. It has put on a lot of weight to become a *Fat Controller*.

MVC with configurable controller

You must be wondering what went wrong with MVC. When application gets large you cannot stick to bare bone MVC. You have to extend it somehow to deal with these complexities. One mechanism of extending MVC that has found widespread adoption is based on a configurable controller Servlet. The MVC with configurable controller servlet is shown in Figure 1.3.

When the HTTP request arrives from the client, the Controller Servlet looks up in a properties file to decide on the right *Handler* class for the HTTP request. This Handler class is referred to as the ***Request Handler***. The *Request Handler* contains the presentation logic for that HTTP request. It also invokes the business logic for that HTTP request. In other words the Request Handler does everything that is needed to handle the HTTP request. The only difference so far from the bare bone MVC is that the controller servlet looks up in a properties file to instantiate the Handler instead of calling it directly.

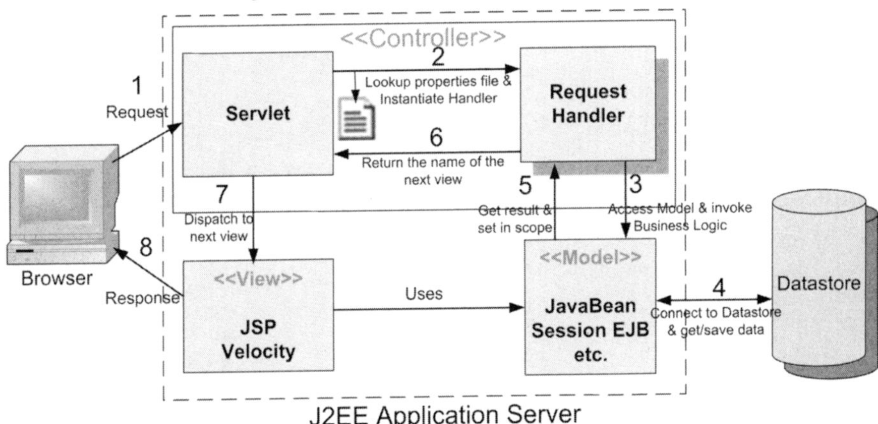

Figure 1.3 MVC with configurable controller Servlet.

At this point you might be wondering how the controller servlet would know to instantiate the appropriate Handler. The answer is simple. Two different HTTP requests cannot have the same URL. Hence you can be certain that the URL uniquely identifies each HTTP request on the server side and hence each URL needs a unique Handler. In simpler terms, there is a one-to-one mapping between the URL and the *Handler* class. This information is stored as key-value pairs in the properties file. The Controller Servlet loads the properties file on startup to find the appropriate *Request Handler* for each incoming URL request.

The controller servlet uses Java Reflection to instantiate the Request Handler. However for the servlet to generically instantiate the Request Handler, there must be some sort of commonality between the Request Handlers. The commonality is that all *Request Handler* classes implement a common interface. Let us call this common interface as ***Handler Interface.*** In its simplest form, the *Handler Interface* has one method say, `execute()`. The controller servlet reads the properties file to instantiate the *Request Handler* as shown in Listing 1.1.

The Controller Servlet instantiates the Request Handler in the `doGet()` method and invokes the `execute()` method on it using Java Reflection. The `execute()` method invokes appropriate business logic from the middle tier and then selects the next view to be presented to the user. The controller servlet forwards the request to the selected JSP view. All this happens in the `doGet()` method of the controller servlet. The `doGet()` method lifecycle never changes. What changes is the *Request Handler*'s `execute()` method. You may not have realized it, but you just saw how Struts works in a nutshell! Struts is a controller servlet based configurable MVC framework that executes predefined methods the handler objects. Instead of using a properties file like we did in this example, Struts uses XML to store more useful information.

Listing 1.1 Configurable Controller Servlet Implementation

```
public class MyControllerServlet extends HttpServlet
{
   private Properties props;

   public init(ServletConfig config) throws ServletException {
      try {
        props = new Properties();
        props.load(new FileInputStream("C:/file.properties"));
      } catch (IOException ioe) {
        throw new ServletException(ioe);
      }
   }

   public void doGet(HttpServletRequest httpRequest,
                     HttpServletResponse httpResponse)
                     throws ServletException, IOException {
     String urlPath = httpRequest.getPathInfo();
     String reqhandlerClassName = (String) props.get(urlPath);

     HandlerInterface handlerInterface = (HandlerInterface)
          Class.forName(reqhandlerClassName).newInstance();
     String nextView = handlerInterface.execute(httpRequest);
        ..
        ..
     RequestDispatcher rd = getServletContext().
                              getRequestDispatcher(nextView);
     rd.forward(httpRequest, httpResponse);
   }
}
```

First look at Struts

In the last section, you have seen the underlying principle behind Struts framework. Now let us look closely at the Struts terminology for controller servlet and Handler objects that we mentioned and understand Figure 1.4. Figure 1.4 is a rehash of Figure 1.3 by using Struts terminology. Since this is your first look at Struts, we will not get into every detail of the HTTP request handling lifecycle in Struts framework. Chapter 2 will get you there. For now, let us concentrate on the basics.

Listing 1.2 Sample ActionForm

```
public class MyForm extends ActionForm {
   private String firstName;
   private String lastName;

   public MyForm() {
       firstName = ""; lastName = "";
   }

   public String getFirstName() {
       return firstName;
   }

   public void setFirstName(String s) {
       this.firstName = s;
   }

   public String getLastName() {
       return lastName;
   }

   public void setLastName(String s) {
       this.lastName = s;
   }
}
```

In Struts, there is only one controller servlet for the entire web application. This controller servlet is called `ActionServlet` and resides in the package `org.apache.struts.action`. It intercepts every client request and populates an *ActionForm* from the HTTP request parameters. ActionForm is a normal JavaBeans class. It has several attributes corresponding to the HTTP request parameters and getter, setter methods for those attributes. You have to create your own *ActionForm* for every HTTP request handled through the Struts framework by extending the `org.apache.struts.action.ActionForm` class. Consider the following HTTP request for *App1* web application – http://localhost:8080/App1/create.do?firstName=John&lastName=Doe. The ActionForm class for this HTTP request is shown in Listing 1.2. The class `MyForm` extends the `org.apache.struts.action.ActionForm` class and contains two attributes – `firstName` and `lastName`. It also has getter and setter methods for these attributes. For the lack of better terminology, let us coin a term to describe the classes such as ActionForm – *View Data Transfer Object. View Data Transfer Object* is an object that holds the data from html page and transfers it around in the web tier framework and application classes.

The `ActionServlet` then instantiates a Handler. The Handler class name is obtained from an XML file based on the URL path information. This XML file is referred to as Struts configuration file and by default named as *struts-config.xml.* The Handler is called *Action* in the Struts terminology. And you guessed it right! This class is created by extending the `Action` class in `org.apache.struts.action` package. The Action class is abstract and defines a single method called `execute()`. You override this method in your own *Actions* and invoke the business logic in this method. The `execute()` method returns the name of next view (JSP) to be shown to the user. The `ActionServlet` forwards to the selected view.

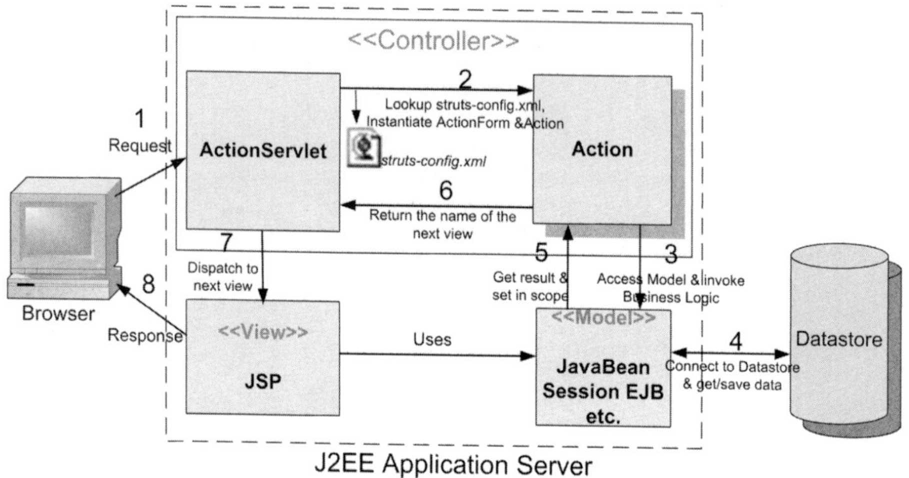

Figure 1.4 A first look at Struts architecture.

Now, that was Struts in a nutshell. Struts is of-course more than just this. It is a full-fledged presentation framework. Throughout the development of the application, both the page author and the developer need to coordinate and ensure that any changes to one area are appropriately handled in the other. It aids in rapid development of web applications by separating the concerns in projects. For instance, it has custom tags for JSPs. The page author can concentrate on developing the JSPs using *custom tags* that are specified by the framework. The application developer works on creating the server side representation of the data and its interaction with a back end data repository. Further it offers a consistent way of handling user input and processing it. It also has extension points for customizing the framework and much more. In this section, you got a bird's eye view of how Struts works. More details await you in the chapters ahead. But you have to install Tomcat and Struts on your machine to better understand the chapters ahead. Hence we will cover Tomcat and Struts installation briefly in the next section.

Tomcat and Struts installation

We will use Windows environment to develop Struts application and Tomcat servlet container to deploy and test Struts applications. Precisely we will use Tomcat-5.0.14 Beta, the latest milestone release of Tomcat. You can download Tomcat 5.0.14 from http://jakarta.apache.org/tomcat and follow the link to download. There are several binaries available – several variations of tar, exe and zip files. Choose the 5.0.14.zip file and unzip it. A folder called jakarta-tomcat-5.0.14 is created automatically. This is the TOMCAT_HOME directory. Under the TOMCAT_HOME, there are a lot of folders of which two are important – *bin* and *webapps* folders. The bin folder contains two batch files - *startup.bat*, used to start the Tomcat and *shutdown.bat*, used to stop the Tomcat. All the WAR files are dropped in the *webapps* directory and get deployed automatically.

Installing Struts is very easy. In the Struts web site, http://jakarta.apache.org/struts, go to download section and select the 1.1 Release Build. This is the latest production quality build available. Once you download the zipped archive of Struts 1.1 release, unzip the file to a convenient location. It automatically creates a folder named "*jakarta-struts-1.1*". It has three sub-folders. The *lib* sub-folder contains the *struts.jar* – the core library that you want to use and other jars on which the Struts depends. You would normally copy most of these jars into the *WEB-INF/lib* of your web application. The *webapps* sub-folder contains a lot of WAR files that can just dropped into any J2EE application server and tested.

You can test your Tomcat installation and also study Struts at the same time. Start Tomcat using *startup.bat* and then drop the *struts-documentation.war* from your Struts *webapps* folder into Tomcat's *webapps* folder. The WAR is immediately deployed. You can access the Struts documentation at the URL http://localhost:8080/struts-documentation. You should also download the Struts 1.1 source and refer to it and probably study it to get more insights about its internals. However be sure to read through this book before you dive into the Struts source code.

Summary

In this chapter, we refreshed your memory on Model 1 and Model 2 architectures for JSPs and pointed out the problems with the bare bone MVC in real life – about how it gets big and ugly. You understood how MVC with configurable controller could solve the real life problem. You also took a first look at the high level Struts architecture and saw how it matched the configurable MVC controller. You also briefly looked at Struts and Tomcat installation and warmed up for the forthcoming chapters.

Chapter 2

Struts Framework Components

In this chapter:

1. *You will learn more about Struts components and their categories – Controller and View*
2. *You will understand the sequence of events in Struts request handling lifecycle*
3. *You will understand the role of the following controller classes - ActionServlet, RequestProcessor, ActionForm, Action, ActionMapping and ActionForward in the request handling lifecycle*
4. *You will also learn about the role of Struts Tags as View components in rendering the response*
5. *You will understand the various elements of Struts configuration file – struts-config.xml*

In the last chapter, you had a cursory glance at the Struts framework. In this chapter you will dive deeper and cover various Struts Framework Components. Here is something to remember all the time.

1. **All the core components of Struts framework belong to Controller category.**
2. **Struts has no components in the Model category.**
3. **Struts has only auxiliary components in View category. A collection of custom tags making it easy to interact with the controller. The View category is neither the core of Struts framework nor is it necessary. However it is a helpful library for using Struts effectively in JSP based rendering.**

Controller Category: The `ActionServlet` and the collaborating classes form the controller and is the core of the framework. The collaborating classes are `RequestProcessor`, `ActionForm`, `Action`, `ActionMapping` and `ActionForward`.

View Category: The View category contains utility classes – variety of custom tags making it easy to interact with the controller. It is not mandatory to use these utility classes. You can replace it with classes of your own. However when using Struts Framework with JSP, you will be reinventing the wheel by writing custom tags that mimic Struts view components. If you are using Struts with Cocoon or Velocity, then have to roll out your own classes for the View category.

Model Category: Struts does not offer any components in the Model Category. You are on you own in this turf. This is probably how it should be. Many component models (CORBA, EJB) are available to implement the business tier. Your model components are as unique as your business and should not have any dependency on a presentation framework like Struts. This philosophy of limiting the framework to what is absolutely essential and helpful and nothing more has prevented bloating and made the Struts framework generic and reusable.

NOTE: Some people argue that `ActionForm` is the model component. However ActionForm is really part of the controller. The Struts documentation also speaks along similar lines. It is just *View Data Transfer Object* – a regular JavaBeans that has dependencies on the Struts classes and used for transferring the data to various classes within the controller.

Struts request lifecycle

In this section you will learn about the Struts controller classes – `ActionServlet`, `RequestProcessor`, `ActionForm`, `Action`, `ActionMapping` and `ActionForward` – all residing in `org.apache.struts.action` package and *struts-config.xml* – the Struts Configuration file. Instead of the traditional "Here is the class – go use it" approach, you will study the function of each component in the context of HTTP request handling lifecycle in Struts.

ActionServlet

The central component of the Struts Controller is the `ActionServlet`. It is a concrete class and extends the `javax.servlet.HttpServlet`. It performs two important things.

1. On startup, its reads the Struts Configuration file and loads it into memory in the `init()` method.
2. In the `doGet()` and `doPost()` methods, it intercepts HTTP request and handles it appropriately.

The name of the Struts Config file is not cast in stone. It is a convention followed since the early days of Struts to call this file as *struts-config.xml* and place it under the *WEB-INF* directory of the web application. In fact you can name the file anyway you like and place it anywhere in *WEB-INF* or its sub-directories. The name of the Struts Config file can be configured in *web.xml*. The *web.xml* entry for configuring the `ActionServlet` and Struts Config file is as follows.

```
<servlet>
  <servlet-name>action</servlet-name>
  <servlet-class>org.apache.struts.action.ActionServlet
  </servlet-class>
  <init-param>
    <param-name>config</param-name>
    <param-value>/WEB-INF/config/myconfig.xml</param-value>
  </init-param>
  <load-on-startup>1</load-on-startup>
</servlet>
```

In the above snippet, the Struts Config file is present in the *WEB-INF/config* directory and is named *myconfig.xml*. The `ActionServlet` takes the Struts Config file name as an *init-param*. At startup, in the `init()` method, the `ActionServlet` reads the Struts Config file and creates appropriate Struts configuration objects (data structures) into memory. You will learn more about the Struts configuration objects in Chapter 7. For now, assume that the Struts Config file is loaded into a set of objects in memory, much like a properties file loaded into a `java.util.Properties` class.

Like any other servlet, `ActionServlet` invokes the `init()` method when it receives the first HTTP request from the caller. Loading Struts Config file into configuration objects is a time consuming task. If the Struts configuration objects were to be created on the first call from the caller, it will adversely affect performance by delaying the response for the first user. The alternative is to specify *load-on-startup* in *web.xml* as shown above. By specifying *load-on-startup* to be 1, you are telling the servlet container to call the `init()` method immediately on startup of the servlet container.

The second task that the `ActionServlet` performs is to intercept HTTP requests based on the URL pattern and handles them appropriately. The URL pattern can be either path or suffix. This is specified using the *servlet-mapping* in *web.xml*. An example of suffix mapping is as follows.

```
<servlet-mapping>
  <servlet-name>action</servlet-name>
  <url-pattern>*.do</url-pattern>
</servlet-mapping>
```

If the user types http://localhost:8080/App1/submitCustomerForm.do in the browser URL bar, the URL will be intercepted and processed by the `ActionServlet` since the URL has a pattern **.do*, with a suffix of "*do*".

Once the ActionServlet intercepts the HTTP request, it doesn't do much. It delegates the request handling to another class called RequestProcessor by invoking its process() method. Figure 2.1 shows a flowchart with Struts controller components collaborating to handle a HTTP request within the RequestProcessor's process() method. The next sub sections describe the flowchart in detail. It is very important that you understand and even memorize this flowchart. Most of the Struts Controller functionality is embedded in the process() method of RequestProcessor class. Mastery over this flowchart will determine how fast you will debug problems in real life Struts applications. Let us understand the request handling in the process() method step by step with an example covered in the next several sub sections.

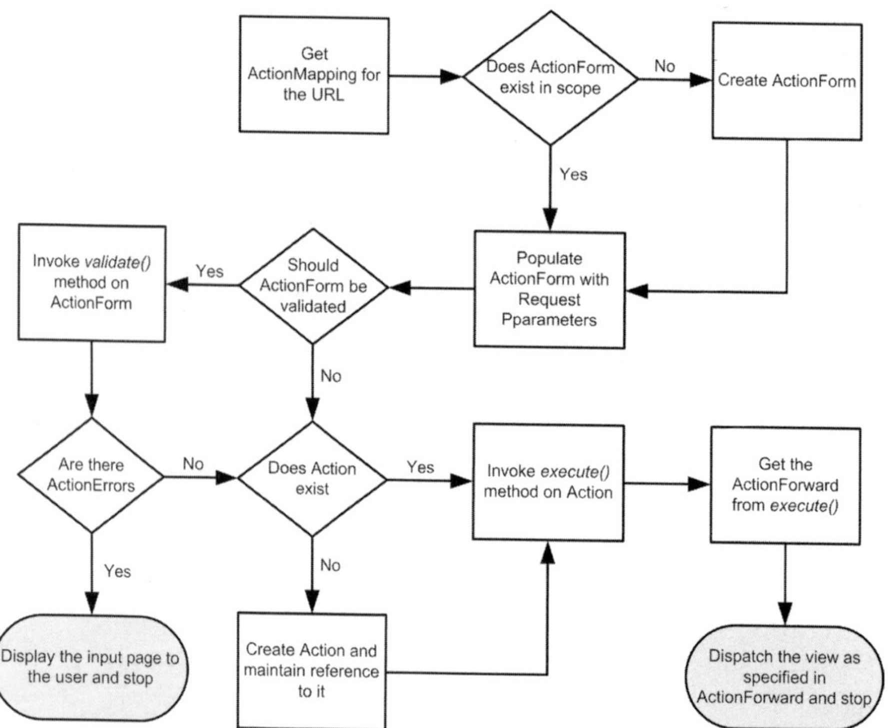

Figure 2.1 Flowchart for the RequestProcessor process method.

RequestProcessor and ActionMapping

The RequestProcessor does the following in its process() method:
Step 1: The RequestProcessor first retrieves appropriate XML block for the URL from *struts-config.xml.* This XML block is referred to as *ActionMapping* in Struts terminology. In fact there is a class called ActionMapping in org.apache.struts.action package. ActionMapping is the class that does

what its name says – it holds the mapping between a URL and Action. A sample ActionMapping from the Struts configuration file looks as follows.

Listing 2.1 A sample ActionMapping from struts-config.xml

```
<action  path="/submitDetailForm"
         type="mybank.example.CustomerAction"
         name="CustomerForm"
         scope="request"
         validate="true"
         input="CustomerDetailForm.jsp">
   <forward name="success"
            path="ThankYou.jsp"
            redirect="true"/>
   <forward name="failure"  path="Failure.jsp"  />
</action>
```

Step 2: The `RequestProcessor` looks up the configuration file for the URL pattern */submitDetailForm.* (i.e. URL path without the suffix *do*) and finds the XML block (*ActionMapping*) shown above. The *type* attribute tells Struts which Action class has to be instantiated. The XML block also contains several other attributes. Together these constitute the JavaBeans properties of the `ActionMapping` instance for the path */submitDetailForm.* The above *ActionMapping* tells Struts to map the URL request with the path */submitDetailForm* to the class `mybank.example.CustomerAction`. The Action class is explained in the steps ahead. For now think of the Action as your own class containing the business logic and invoked by Struts. This also tells us one more important thing.

> Since each HTTP request is distinguished from the other only by the *path*, there should be one and only one ActionMapping for every *path* attribute. Otherwise Struts overwrites the former *ActionMapping* with the latter.

ActionForm

Another attribute in the ActionMapping that you should know right away is *name.* It is the logical name of the *ActionForm* to be populated by the `RequestProcessor.` After selecting the ActionMapping, the `RequestProcessor` instantiates the *ActionForm.* However it has to know the fully qualified class name of the *ActionForm* to do so. This is where the *name* attribute of ActionMapping comes in handy. The *name* attribute is the logical name of the *ActionForm.* Somewhere else in *struts-config.xml,* you will find a declaration like this:

```
<form-bean name="CustomerForm"
    type="mybank.example.CustomerForm"/>
```

This form-bean declaration associates a logical name *CustomerForm* with the actual class `mybank.example.CustomerForm`.

Step 3: The `RequestProcessor` instantiates the `CustomerForm` and puts it in appropriate scope – either session or request. The `RequestProcessor` determines the appropriate scope by looking at the *scope* attribute in the same *ActionMapping*.

Step 4: Next, `RequestProcessor` iterates through the HTTP request parameters and populates the `CustomerForm` properties of the same name as the HTTP request parameters using Java Introspection. (Java Introspection is a special form of Reflection using the JavaBeans properties. Instead of directly using the reflection to set the field values, it uses the setter method to set the field value and getter method to retrieve the field value.)

Step 5: Next, the `RequestProcessor` checks for the *validate* attribute in the ActionMapping. If the *validate* is set to true, the `RequestProcessor` invokes the `validate()` method on the `CustomerForm` instance. This is the method where you can put all the html form data validations. For now, let us pretend that there were no errors in the `validate()` method and continue. We will come back later and revisit the scenario when there are errors in the `validate()` method.

Action

Step 6: The RequestProcessor instantiates the Action class specified in the ActionMapping (`CustomerAction`) and invokes the `execute()` method on the `CustomerAction` instance. The signature of the execute method is as follows.

```
public ActionForward execute(ActionMapping mapping,
                    ActionForm form,
                    HttpServletRequest request,
                    HttpServletResponse response) throws Exception
```

Apart from the `HttpServletRequest` and `HttpServletResponse`, the `ActionForm` is also available in the `Action` instance. This is what the `ActionForm` was meant for; as a convenient container to hold and transfer data from the http request parameter to other components of the controller, instead of having to look for them every time in the http request.

The `execute()` method itself should not contain the core business logic irrespective of whether or not you use EJBs or any fancy middle tier. The first and foremost reason for this is that business logic classes should not have any dependencies on the Servlet packages. By putting the business logic in the Action class, you are letting the `javax.servlet.*` classes proliferate into your business logic. This limits the reuse of the business logic, say for a pure Java client.

The second reason is that if you ever decide to replace the Struts framework with some other presentation framework (although we know this will not happen), you don't have to go through the pain of modifying the business logic. The `execute()` method should preferably contain only the presentation logic and be the starting point in the web tier to invoke the business logic. The business logic can be present either in protocol independent Java classes or the Session EJBs.

The `RequestProcessor` creates an instance of the Action (`CustomerAction`), if one does not exist already. There is only one instance of Action class in the application. Because of this you must ensure that the `Action` class and its attributes if any are thread-safe. General rules that apply to Servlets hold good. The `Action` class should not have any writable attributes that can be changed by the users in the `execute()` method.

ActionForward

The `execute()` method returns the next view shown to the user. If you are wondering what `ActionForward` is, you just have found the answer. `ActionForward` is the class that encapsulates the next view information. Struts, being the good framework it is, encourages you not to hardcode the JSP names for the next view. Rather you should associate a logical name for the next JSP page. This association of the logical name and the physical JSP page is encapsulated in the `ActionForward` instance returned from the execute method. The ActionForward can be local or global. Look again at the good old ActionMapping XML block in Listing 2.1. It contained sub elements called forwards with three attributes – name, path and redirect as shown below.

The *name* attribute is the logical name of the physical JSP as specified in the *path* attribute. These forward elements are local to the *ActionMapping* in Listing 2.1. Hence they can be accessed only from this `ActionMapping` argument in the `CustomerAction`'s `execute()` method and nowhere else. On the other hand, when the forwards are declared in the global forwards section of the *struts-config.xml*, they are accessible from any `ActionMapping`. (In the next section, you will look closely at Struts Config file.) Either ways, the `findForward()` method on the `ActionMapping` instance retrieves the `ActionForward` as follows.

```
ActionForward forward = mapping.findForward("success");
```

The logical name of the page (success) is passed as the keyword to the `findForward()` method. The `findForward()` method searches for the forward with the name "*success*", first within the *ActionMapping* and then in the *global-forwards* section. The `CustomerAction`'s `execute()` method returns the `ActionForward` and the `RequestProcessor` returns the physical JSP to the user. In J2EE terms, this is referred to as dispatching the view to the user. The dispatch can be either HTTP Forward or HTTP Redirect. For instance, the dispatch to the success is a HTTP Redirect whereas the dispatch to "failure" is a HTTP Redirect.

Difference between HTTP Forward and HTTP Redirect

HTTP Forward is the process of simply displaying a page when requested by the user. The user asks for a resource (page) by clicking on a hyperlink or submitting a form and the next page is rendered as the response. In Servlet Container, HTTP Forward is achieved by invoking the following.

```
RequestDispatcher dispatcher =
      httpServletRequest.getRequestDispatcher(url);
Dispatcher.forward(httpServletRequest, httpServletResponse);
```

HTTP Redirect is a bit more sophisticated. When a user requests a resource, a response is first sent to the user. This is not the requested resource. Instead this is a response with HTTP code "302" and contains the URL of the requested resource. This URL could be the same or different from original requested URL. The client browser automatically makes the request for the resource again with the new URL. And this time, the actual resource is sent to the user. In the web tier you can use HTTP redirect by using the simple API, `sendRedirect()` on the `HttpServletResponse` instance. The rest of the magic is done by HTTP. HTTP Redirect has an extra round trip to the client and is used only in special cases. Later in this book, we will show a scenario where HTTP redirect can be useful.

ActionErrors and ActionError

So far, we have covered Struts request handling lifecycle as a happy day scenario – from the point the user submits an html form till the user sees the next page. In reality, users of your web application may submit incorrect data or sometimes no data at all. You have to catch these as close to the user interface as possible, rather than waiting for the middle tier or the database to tell you that a column cannot be inserted in the database because it was expecting a non-null value. There are two consequences of such programming practice.

1. Server time and resources are precious since they are shared. Spending too much of server's time and resources on a request, that we know is going to fail eventually is a waste of server resources.
2. It has a negative impact on the code quality. Since one has to prepare for the possibility of having null data, appropriate checks have to be put (or `NumberFormatExceptions` have to be caught) everywhere in the code. Generally business logic is the toughest code of the system and contains enough

if-else blocks as such. More *if-else* blocks for null checks can only mean two things – bad code and maintenance nightmare. Not an elegant programming to say the least. If only you could verify the validity of the user data as close to the user, then the rest of the code only has to deal with business logic and not invalid data.

Listing 2.2 validate() method in the CustomerForm

```
public ActionErrors validate(ActionMapping mapping,
                             HttpServletRequest request)
{
    // Perform validator framework validations
    ActionErrors errors = super.validate(mapping, request);

    // Only need crossfield validations here
    if (parent == null) {
        errors.add(GLOBAL_ERROR,
                   new ActionError("error.custform"));
    }
    if (firstName == null) {
        errors.add("firstName",
              new ActionError("error.firstName.null"));
    }
    return errors;
}
```

Struts provides `validate()` method in the `ActionForm` to deal with user input validations. Let us now look at how you can validate the user input and report errors to the framework. We will postpone the discussion of how Struts reports the errors to the end user when we discuss View Components later in this chapter. As shown in the flowchart (Figure 2.1), the `validate()` method is called after the `ActionForm` instance is populated with the form data. A sample `validate()` method is shown in Listing 2.2.

In the `validate()` method, you will notice an object called `ActionErrors` is instantiated. All error checks are performed with the usual *if-else* blocks. If there are errors, then an individual `ActionError` object is created for the culprit field and added to the `ActionErrors`. Think of `ActionErrors` as a Map for the individual `ActionError` objects. You can associate one or more `ActionError` objects for each key. The form field name is generally chosen as the key and can have multiple `ActionError` objects associated with it. The `ActionError` is either specific to a field in the `ActionForm` or it is global to the entire form. When the error is specific to a form field, the field name is used as the key in the `ActionErrors`. When the error is global to the form, the key name is always GLOBAL_ERRORS. Both of the cases are shown in the Listing 2.2.

You might also notice that the `ActionError` constructor takes a rather cryptic key as the argument. This key is declared in a properties file whose value is the actual error message. The properties file is selected based on the user chosen Locale. The technical term for this properties file where the messages are externalized is ***Message Resource Bundle***. It is based on the Java's concept of Localization using the `java.util.ResourceBundle` and has a whole lot of bells and whistles. We will cover Message Resource Bundle in depth in Chapter10 on Internationalization and Localization. For now it suffices to know that the properties file also serves another purpose apart from Localization. It lets you change the messages without recompiling the code, and is quite handy while maintaining the code. An entry in the Message Resource Bundle properties file looks like:

```
error.firstName.null=First Name cannot be null
```

The `RequestProcessor` stops any further processing when it gets the `ActionErrors` object with `ActionError` objects. The `Action` instance never gets the control (and never gets a chance to return `ActionForward`). Hence the `RequestProcessor` consults the `ActionMapping` object to find the page to be displayed. Notice that the `ActionMapping` has an attribute named "*input*". This attribute specifies the physical page to which the request has to be forwarded on error. Generally this page is the original page where user entered the data since it is natural that user would want to reenter the data in the same page on error and resubmit.

That completes our overview of the working of Struts Controller components. Now, let us formally look at the Struts configuration file in detail.

Struts Configuration File – struts-config.xml

As you learnt in Chapter 1, the configurable controller is the answer to the Fat controller problem. In a Fat Controller, the programmers can code "*if*" blocks on need basis. Not so with the configurable controllers. The expressive and configuration capability is limited to what the built-in controller can support. In Struts, the built-in controller supports a variety of cases that can arise while developing web applications. It even provides points to extend the configuration capabilities. These points known as ***Extension points***, take the configuration capability to the next dimension. We will deal with extending Struts in Chapter 7. In this section, we will just look at the normal facilities offered by the *struts-config.xml.*

The Struts configuration file adheres to the *struts-config_1_1.dtd.* A Struts configuration file showing every possible element, their attributes and their description is provided in the Appendix A. Covering all of them at once would only result in information overload. Hence we will only look at the five important sections of this file relevant to our discussion and their important attributes. In fact we have already covered most of these in the lifecycle discussion earlier, but are summarizing them again to refresh your mind. The five important sections are

1. Form bean definition section
2. Global forward definition section
3. Action mapping definition section
4. Controller configuration section
5. Application Resources definition section

Listing 2.3 shows a sample Struts Config file showing all the five sections. The form bean definition section contains one or more entries for each ActionForm. Each form bean is identified by a unique logical name. The type is the fully qualified class name of the ActionForm. An interesting to note is that you can declare the same ActionForm class any number of times provided each entry has a unique name associated with it. This feature is useful if you want to store multiple forms of the same type in the servlet session.

Table 2.1 Important attributes and elements of ActionMapping entry in struts-config.xml

Attribute/Element name	Description
Path	The URL path (either path mapping or suffix mapping) for which this Action Mapping is used. The path should be unique
Type	The fully qualified class name of the Action
Name	The logical name of the Form bean. The actual ActionForm associated with this Action Mapping is found by looking in the Form-bean definition section for a form-bean with the matching name. This informs the Struts application which action mappings should use which ActionForms.
Scope	Scope of the Form bean – Can be session or request
Validate	Can be true or false. When true, the Form bean is validated on submission. If false, the validation is skipped.
Input	The physical page (or another ActionMapping) to which control should be forwarded when validation errors exist in the form bean.
Forward	The physical page (or another ActionMapping) to which the control should be forwarded when the ActionForward with this name is selected in the execute method of the Action class.

The *ActionMapping* section contains the mapping from URL path to an Action class (and also associates a Form bean with the path). The *type* attribute is the fully qualified class name of the associated Action. Each action entry in the *action-mappings* should have a unique path. This follows from the fact that each URL path needs a unique handler. There is no facility to associate multiple Actions with the same path. The *name* attribute is the name of the Form bean associated with this Action. The actual form bean is defined in Form bean definition section. Table 2.1 shows all the relevant attributes discussed so far for the *action* entry in *action-mappings* section.

Listing 2.3 Sample struts-config.xml

```
<?xml version="1.0" encoding="ISO-8859-1" ?>
<!DOCTYPE struts-config PUBLIC
 "-//Apache Software Foundation//DTD Struts Configuration 1.1//EN"
 "http://jakarta.apache.org/struts/dtds/struts-config_1_1.dtd">
<struts-config>                                  Form bean Definitions
  <form-beans>
    <form-bean  name="CustomerForm"
                type="mybank.example.CustomerForm"/>

    <form-bean  name="LogonForm"
                type="mybank.example.LogonForm"/>
  </form-beans>                                  Global Forward Definitions
  <global-forwards>
    <forward   name="logon"  path="/logon.jsp"/>
    <forward   name="logoff" path="/logoff.do"/>
  </global-forwards>                             Action Mappings
  <action-mappings>
    <action    path="/submitDetailForm"
               type="mybank.example.CustomerAction"
               name="CustomerForm"
               scope="request"
               validate="true"
               input="CustomerDetailForm.jsp">
      <forward name="success"
               path="ThankYou.jsp"
               redirect="true" />
      <forward name="failure"
               path="Failure.jsp"  />
    </action>
    <action path="/logoff" parameter="/logoff.jsp"
           type="org.apache.struts.action.ForwardAction" />
  </action-mappings>                             Controller Configuration
  <controller
    processorClass="org.apache.struts.action.RequestProcessor"
/>
  <message-resources parameter="mybank.ApplicationResources"/>
</struts-config>                                 Message Resource Definition
```

In the ActionMapping there are two *forwards*. Those *forwards* are *local forwards* – which means those *forwards* can be accessed only within the ActionMapping. On the other hand, the forwards defined in the Global Forward section are accessible from any ActionMapping. As you have seen earlier, a forward has a name and a path. The name attribute is the logical name assigned. The path attribute is the resource to which the control is to be forwarded. This resource can be an actual page name as in

```
<forward   name="logon"   path="/logon.jsp"/>
```

or it can be another ActionMapping as in

```
<forward   name="logoff"   path="/logoff.do "/>
```

The */logoff* (notice the absence of ".do") would be another ActionMapping in the struts-config.xml. The forward – either global or local are used in the `execute()` method of the Action class to forward the control to another physical page or ActionMapping.

The next section in the config file is the controller. The controller is optional. Unless otherwise specified, the default controller is always the `org.apache.struts.action.RequestProcessor`. There are cases when you want to replace or extend this to have your own specialized processor. For instance, when using Tiles (a JSP page template framework) in conjunction with Struts, you would use `TilesRequestProcessor`.

The last section of immediate interest is the Message Resource definition. In the ActionErrors discussion, you saw a code snippet that used a cryptic key as the argument for the `ActionError`. We stated that this key maps to a value in a properties file. Well, we declare that properties file in the struts-config.xml in the Message Resources definition section. The declaration in Listing 2.1 states that the Message Resources Bundle for the application is called *ApplicationResources.properties* and the file is located in the java package `mybank`.

If you are wondering how (and why) can a properties file be located in a java package, recall that any file (including class file) is a resource and is loaded by the class loader by specifying the package. An example in the next chapter will really make things clearer.

View Components

In Struts, View components are nothing but six custom tag libraries for JSP views – *HTML*, *Bean*, *Logic*, *Template*, *Nested*, and *Tiles* tag libraries. Each one caters to a different purpose and can be used individually or in combination with others. For other kinds of views (For instance, Template based presentation) you are on your own. As it turns out, majority of the developers using Struts tend to use JSPs. You can extend the Struts tags and also build your own tags and mix and match them.

You already know that the ActionForm is populated on its way in by the RequestProcessor class using Java Introspection. In this section you will learn how Struts tags interact with the controller and its helper classes to display the JSP using two simple scenarios – how FormTag displays the data on the way out and how the ErrorsTag displays the error messages. We will not cover every tag in Struts though. That is done in Chapter 6.

What is a custom tag?

Custom Tags are Java classes written by Java developers and can be used in the JSP using XML markup. Think of them as view helper beans that can be used without the need for scriptlets. Scriptlets are Java code snippets intermingled with JSP markup. You need a Java developer to write such scriptlets. JSP pages are normally developed and tweaked by page authors, They cannot interpret the scriptlets. Moreover this blurs the separation of duties in a project. Custom Tags are the answer to this problem. They are XML based and like any markup language and can be easily mastered by the page authors. You can get more information on Custom Tags in Chapter 6. There are also numerous books written about JSP fundamentals that cover this topic very well.

Listing 2.4 CustomerDetails JSP

```
<html>
  <head>
    <html:base/>
  </head>
  <body>
    <html:form action="/submitDetailForm.do">
      <html:text property="firstName" />
      <html:text property="lastName" />
      <html:submit>Continue</html:submit>
    </html:form>
  </body>
</html>
```

How FormTag works

Consider a case when the user requests a page *CustomerDetails.jsp*. The CustomerDetails JSP page has a form in it. The form is constructed using the Struts html tags and shown in Listing 2.4. The <html:form> represents the org.apache.struts.taglib.html.FormTag class, a body tag. The <html:text> represents the org.apache.struts.taglib.html.TextTag class, a normal tag. The resulting HTML is shown in Listing 2.5.

The FormTag can contain other tags in its body. SubmitTag generates the Submit button at runtime. The TextTag *<html:text>* generates html textbox at runtime as follows.

```
<input name=firstName" type="text" value="" />
```

The FormTag has an attribute called *action*. Notice that the value of the action attribute is */submitDetailForm.do* in the JSP snippet shown above. The servlet container parses the JSP and renders the HTML.

Listing 2.5 Generated HTML from CustomerDetails JSP

```
<html>
  <head>
    <html:base/>
  </head>
  <body>
    <form name="CustomerForm" action="/submitDetailForm.do">
        <input type="text" name="firstName" value="" />
        <input type="text" name="lastName" value="" />
        <input type="submit" name="Submit" value="" />
    </form>
  </body>
</html>
```

When the container encounters the FormTag, it invokes the doStartTag() method. The doStartTag() method in the FormTag class does exactly what the RequestProcessor does in the execute() method.

1. The FormTag checks for an ActionMapping with */submitDetailForm* in its path attribute.
2. When it finds the ActionMapping, it looks for an ActionForm with the name CustomerForm, (which it gets from the ActionMapping) in the request or session scope (which it gets from ActionMapping).
3. If it does not find one, it creates a new one and puts it in the specified context. Otherwise it uses the existing one. It also makes the Form name available in the page context.
4. The form field tags (e.g. TextTag) access the ActionForm by its name from the PageContext and retrieve values from the ActionForm attributes with matching names. For instance, the TextTag *<html:text property="firstName />* retrieves the value of the attribute firstName from the mybank.example.CustomerForm and substitutes as the value. If the CustomerForm existed in the request or session and the firstName field in the CustomerForm had a value "John", then the TextTag will

generate HTML that looks like this:

```
<input name=firstName" type="text" value="John" />
```

If the `firstName` field was null or empty in the `CustomerForm` instance, the `TextTag` will generate HTML that looks like this

```
<input name=firstName" type="text" value="" />
```

And thus the `ActionForm` is displayed as a HTML Form.

The moral of the story is that `ActionForms` should be made available in advance in the appropriate scope if you are editing existing form data. Otherwise the `FormTag` creates the `ActionForm` in the appropriate scope with no data. The latter is suited for creating fresh data. The `FormTag` reads the same old ActionMapping while looking for the `ActionForm` in the appropriate scope. It then displays the data from that `ActionForm` if available.

How ErrorsTag works

When dealing with ActionErrors, you learnt that the validation errors in an `ActionForm` are reported to the framework through the `ActionErrors` container. Let us now see what facilities the framework provides to display those errors in the JSP. Struts provides the `ErrorsTag` to display the errors in the JSP. When the `ActionForm` returns the `ActionErrors`, the `RequestProcessor` sets it in the request scope with a pre-defined and well-known name (within the Struts framework) and then renders the input page. The `ErrorsTag` iterates over the `ActionErrors` in the request scope and writes out each raw error text to the HTML output.

You can put the `ErrorsTag` by adding *<html:errors />* in the JSP. The tag does not have any attributes. Neither does it have a body. It displays the errors exactly in the location where you put the tag. The `ErrorsTag` prints three elements to the HTML output – header, body and footer. The error body consists of the list of raw error text written out to by the tag. A sample error display from *struts-example.war* (available with Struts 1.1 download) is shown in Figure 2.2.

You can configure the error header and footer through the Message Resource Bundle. The `ErrorsTag` looks for predefined keys named *errors.header* and *errors.footer* in the default (or specified) Message Resource Bundle and their values are also written out AS IS. In the *struts-example.war*, these are set as follows:

```
errors.header=<h3><font color="red">Validation Error</font></h3>
You must correct the following error(s) before proceeding:<ul>
errors.footer=</ul><hr>
```

For each `ActionError`, the `ErrorsTag` also looks for predefined keys `errors.prefix` and `errors.suffix` in the default (or specified) Message Resource Bundle. By setting `errors.suffix=<li>` and `errors.suffix =`

</li>, the generated HTML looks like follows and appears in the browser as shown in Figure 2.2.

```
<h3><font color="red">Validation Error</font></h3>
You must correct the following error(s) before proceeding:
<ul>
  <li>From Address is required.</li>
  <li>Full Name is required.</li>
  <li>Username is required</li>
</ul>
```

Validation Error

You must correct the following error(s) before proceeding:

- From Address is required.
- Full Name is required.
- Username is required.

Username:
Password:
(Repeat) Password:
Full Name:
From Address:
Reply To Address:
Save Reset Cancel

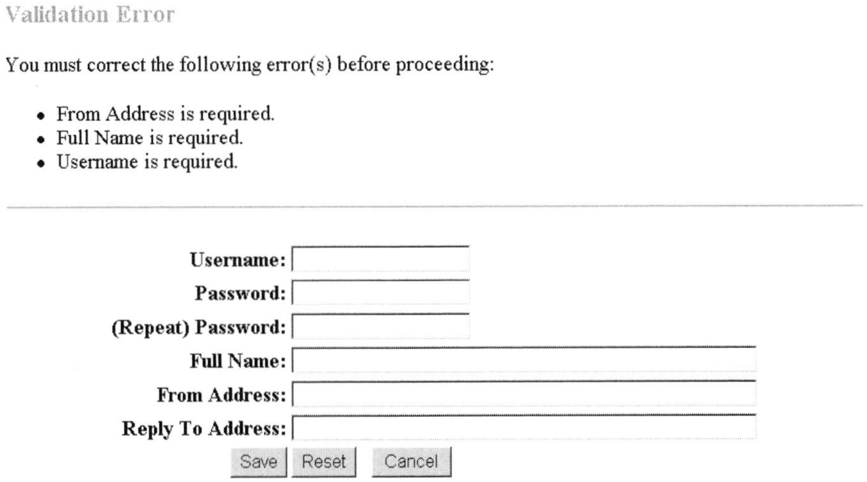

Figure 2.2 Struts error display.

Note that all the formatting information is added as html markup into these values. The bold red header, the line breaks and the horizontal rule is the result of html markup in the *errors.header* and *errors.footer* respectively.

Tip: A common problem while developing Struts applications is that <html:errors/> does not seem to display the error messages This generally means one of the following:

- The properties file could not be located or the key is not found. Set the <message-resources **null="false"**...> for debugging.
- Another reason for not seeing the error messages has got to do with the positioning of the tag itself. If you added the tag itself in the <tr> instead of a <td>, the html browser cannot display the messages even though the tag worked properly by writing out the errors to the response stream.

The View Components was the last piece of the puzzle to be sorted out. As it turns out, all the work is performed in the controller part of the framework. The View Tags look for information in the request or session scope and render it as HTML. Now, that is how a view should be – as simple as possible and yet elegant. Struts lets you do that, easy and fast.

Summary

In this chapter you learnt the Struts request lifecycle in quite a bit of detail. You also got a good picture of Struts framework components when we covered the controller and view components. You also got to know relevant sections of struts-config.xml – the Struts configuration file. Armed with this knowledge we will build a Hello World web application using Struts framework in the next chapter.

Chapter 3

Your First Struts Application

> ***In this chapter:***
>
> 1. *You will build your first Struts web application step by step*
> 2. *You will build a Web ARchive (WAR) and deploy the web application in Tomcat*

In the last two chapters you have learnt a lot about Struts. In this chapter will take you step by step in building your first Struts application and deploying it onto Tomcat.

Introduction

You can access the sample application by typing http://localhost:8080/App1/index.jsp in the browser. The *index.jsp* contains a single hyperlink. The link is http://localhost:8080/App1/CustomerDetails.jsp. On clicking the link, *CustomerDetails.jsp* is displayed. *CustomerDetails.jsp* contains an HTML Form with two buttons – Submit and Cancel. When the user submits the Form by clicking Submit, *Success.jsp* is shown if the form validations go through. If the validations fail, the same page is shown back to the user with the errors. If the user clicks Cancel on the form, the *index.jsp* is shown to the user.

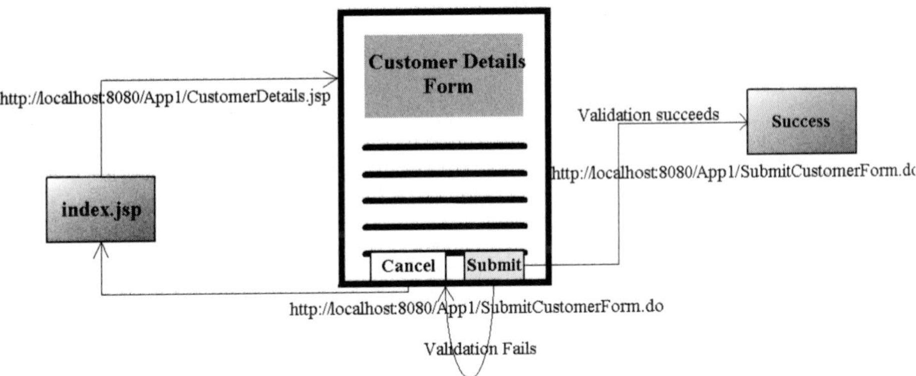

Figure 3.1 The JSP flow diagram for the Hello World Struts application.

Directory Structure overview

This is the first time you are building a sample application in this book. Hence we will introduce you to a standard directory structure followed throughout the book when developing applications. Then we will move on to the actual steps involved. Figure 3.2 shows the directory structure.

The structure is very logical. The top-level directory for every sample application is named after the application itself. In this case all the files are located under the directory named *App1*. The directory *src/java* beneath *App1* contains the Java source files (*CustomerForm.java* and *CustomerAction.java*) and also the application's Message Resource Bundle (*App1Messages.properties*). Another directory called *web-root* beneath *App1* contains all the JSPs (*index.jsp*, *CustomerDetails.jsp* and *Success.jsp*) and images (*banner.gif*). The *web-root* contains a *WEB-INF* sub directory with files *web.xml* and *struts-config.xml.*

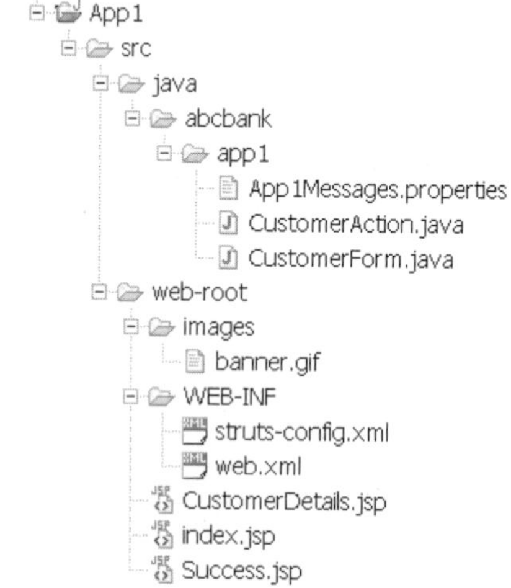

Figure 3.2 The directory structure used throughout the book for sample Struts applications.

Hello World – step by step

Here are the steps involved in creating the Struts application.

1. Add relevant entries into the web.xml
    a. Add ActionServlet Configuration with initialization parameters
    b. Add ActionServlet Mapping
    c. Add relevant taglib declaration
2. Start with a blank template for the struts-config.xml. In the struts-config.xml, add the following
    a. Declare the RequestProcessor
    b. Create a properties file and declare it as Message Resource Bundle
    c. Declare the Message Resource Bundle
    d. Declare the Form-bean
    e. Declare the ActionMapping for the Form-bean

    f. Add the forwards in the ActionMapping
3. Create the Form-bean class
4. Create the Action class
5. Create the JSP with Struts tags
6. For every `<bean:message>` tag in the JSP, add key value pairs to the Message Resource Bundle (properties file) created in Step 3b
7. Add Validation in the Form-bean
8. Define the error messages in the Message Resource Bundle
9. Create the rest of the JSPs.

Listing 3.1 web.xml for the Struts Application

```
<?xml version="1.0" encoding="ISO-8859-1"?>
<!DOCTYPE web-app
 PUBLIC "-//Sun Microsystems, Inc.//DTD Web Application 2.3//EN"
 "http://java.sun.com/dtd/web-app_2_3.dtd">
<web-app>
  <display-name>Hello World Struts Application</display-name>
  <servlet>
    <servlet-name>action</servlet-name>
    <servlet-class>
        org.apache.struts.action.ActionServlet
    </servlet-class>
    <init-param>
      <param-name>config</param-name>
      <param-value>/WEB-INF/struts-config.xml</param-value>
    </init-param>
    <init-param>
      <param-name>debug</param-name>
      <param-value>3</param-value>
    </init-param>
    <init-param>
      <param-name>detail</param-name>
      <param-value>3</param-value>
    </init-param>
    <load-on-startup>1</load-on-startup>
  </servlet>
(continued..)
```

Listing 3.1 web.xml for the Struts Application (Continued)

```
  <servlet-mapping>
    <servlet-name>action</servlet-name>
    <url-pattern>*.do</url-pattern>
  </servlet-mapping>

  <welcome-file-list>
    <welcome-file>index.jsp</welcome-file>
  </welcome-file-list>

  <taglib>
    <taglib-uri>/WEB-INF/struts-html.tld</taglib-uri>
    <taglib-location>/WEB-INF/struts-html.tld</taglib-location>
  </taglib>

  <taglib>
    <taglib-uri>/WEB-INF/struts-bean.tld</taglib-uri>
    <taglib-location>/WEB-INF/struts-bean.tld</taglib-location>
  </taglib>

</web-app>
```

Step 1. As you already know from Chapter 2, the first step in writing a Struts application is to add the `ActionServlet` entry in *web.xml* and also map the servlet to the url-pattern **.do*. This is shown in Listing 3.1. You already know the meaning of the initialization parameter named *config*. Here we will introduce two more initialization parameters. They are *debug* and *detail.*

The *debug* initialization parameter lets you set the level of detail in the debug log. A lower number means lesser details and a higher number implies detailed logging. It is absolutely essential that you use this logging feature especially in the beginning and also while setting up Struts application for the first time. The debug messages give you enough insight to resolve any configuration related issues. Use them to their fullest capability. In Listing 3.1, we have set the value of debug to 3.

The *detail* initialization parameter lets you set the level of detail in the digester log. Digester is the component that parses the Struts Config file and loads them into Java objects. Some of the errors can be traced by looking at the log created by the Digester as it parses the XML file.

Later in this chapter, you will also use two of the Struts Tag libraries to construct the JSP. Hence the relevant tag library definition files – *struts-html.tld* and *struts-bean.tld* are also declared in *web.xml.*

Another setting of interest in *web.xml* is the `<welcome-file-list>`. Typically you would want to type http://localhost:8080/App1 in the browser URL bar and go to *index.jsp* automatically. This goal is achieved by declaring *index.jsp* as one of the welcome files.

Step 2. Select a blank template for struts-config.xml and add the following

Listing 3.2 struts-config.xml with all entries for App1

```
<?xml version="1.0" encoding="ISO-8859-1" ?>
<!DOCTYPE struts-config PUBLIC
"-//Apache Software Foundation//DTD Struts Configuration 1.1//EN"
"http://jakarta.apache.org/struts/dtds/struts-config_1_1.dtd">
<struts-config>
  <form-beans>
    <form-bean  name="CustomerForm"
                type="mybank.app1.CustomerForm"/>
  </form-beans>

  <global-forwards>
    <forward name="mainpage"  path="index.jsp"  />
  </global-forwards>

  <action-mappings>
    <action   path="/submitCustomerForm"
              type="mybank.app1.CustomerAction"
              name="CustomerForm"
              scope="request"
              validate="true"
              input="CustomerDetails.jsp">
      <forward name="success"  path="Success.jsp"  />
      <forward name="failure"  path="Failure.jsp"  />
    </action>
  </action-mappings>

  <controller
processorClass="org.apache.struts.action.RequestProcessor"/>

  <message-resources parameter="mybank.app1.App1Messages"/>

</struts-config>
```

Step 2a. Declare the controller element in Struts Config file. The `<controller>` element tells the Struts framework to use `org.apache.struts.action.RequestProcessor` for this application. For a simple Struts application like App1, this RequestProcessor will suffice. You will use specialized sub classes of `RequestProcessor` as controllers later in this book. The struts-config.xml is shown in Listing 3.2

```
<controller processorClass=
            "org.apache.struts.action.RequestProcessor" />
```

Step 2b. Create a properties file under `mybank.app1` java package and name it as *App1Messages.properties*. You will later add key value pairs into this file. Instead of hard coding field names in the JSP, you will use key names from this file to access them. In this way, the actual name can be changed outside the JSP. For now, add the following entry into the Struts Config file.

```
<message-resources parameter="mybank.app1.App1Messages"/>
```

This is the instruction to the Struts controller to use the *App1Message.properties* file as the Message Resource Bundle.

*Step 2c.*Define the form bean by adding a form-bean entry in the form-beans section.

```
<form-bean  name="CustomerForm"
            type="mybank.app1.CustomerForm"/>
```

Step 2d. Define an ActionMapping by adding the following to the action-mappings

```
<action   path="/submitCustomerForm"
          type="mybank.app1.CustomerAction"
          name="CustomerForm"
          scope="request"
          validate="true"
          input="CustomerDetails.jsp">
</action>
```

Step 2e. Add the local forwards to the ActionMapping

```
<forward name="success"  path="Success.jsp"  />
<forward name="failure"  path="Failure.jsp"  />
```

At this point, the struts-config.xml looks as shown in Listing 3.3. All entries in bold are added for App1.

Step 3. Create the Form-bean by extending `ActionForm` in `org.apache.struts.action` package. Listing 3.3 shows the Form bean. For every field in the HTML Form, there is an instance variable with getter and setter methods in the Form bean. The Struts controller populates the HTML Form by calling the getter methods on the Form bean. When the user submits the HTML Form, the Struts controller populates the Form bean with data from HTML Form by calling setter method on the Form bean instance.

Step 4. Next, create the Action bean by extending the org.apache.struts.action.Action class. Let us call it CustomerAction. Every class that extends Action implements the execute() method. As you saw earlier in Chapter 2, the RequestProcessor calls the execute() method after populating and validating the ActionForm. In this method you typically implement logic to access middle-tier and return the next page to be displayed to the user. Listing 3.4 shows the execute() method in CustomerAction. In this method, an operation is performed to check is the Cancel button was pressed. If so, the "*mainpage*" (Global Forward for *index.jsp*) is shown to the user. The isCancelled() method is defined in the parent Action class. If the operation requested is not Cancel, then the normal flow commences and the user sees *Success.jsp*.

Listing 3.3 CustomerForm – Form Bean for App1

```
public class CustomerForm extends ActionForm {
   private String firstName;
   private String lastName;

   public CustomerForm() {
       firstName = "";
       lastName = "";
   }

   public String getFirstName() {
       return firstName;
   }

   public void setFirstName(String s) {
       this.firstName = s;
   }

   public String getLastName() {
       return lastName;
   }

   public void setLastName(String s) {
       this.lastName = s;
   }
}
```

Step 5. Create the JSP using Struts html and bean tags.

All Struts html tags including the FormTag are defined in *struts-html.tld*. These tags generate appropriate html at runtime. The TLD file *struts-html.tld* and *struts-*

bean.tld are declared at the top of JSP and associated with logical names "*html*" and "*bean*" respectively. The JSP then uses the tags with the prefix of "*html:*" and "*bean:*" instead of the actual tag class name. Listing 3.5 shows the *CustomerDetails.jsp*. Let us start from the top of this Listing.

Listing 3.4 CustomerAction – Action Bean for App1

```
public class CustomerAction extends Action {
  public ActionForward execute(ActionMapping mapping,
               ActionForm form, HttpServletRequest request,
               HttpServletResponse response) throws Exception
  {
     if (isCancelled(request)) {
       System.out.println(Cancel Operation Performed");
       return mapping.findForward("mainpage");
     }

     CustomerForm custForm = (CustomerForm) form;
     String firstName = custForm.getFirstName();
     String lastName = custForm.getLastName();
     System.out.println("Customer First name is " + firstName);
     System.out.println("Customer Last name is " + lastName);

     ActionForward forward = mapping.findForward("success");
     return forward;
  }
}
```

`<html:html>`: Under normal circumstances, this JSP tag just generates opening and closing html tags for the page i.e. `<html>` and `</html>`. However the real advantage of this tag is when the browser has to render the HTML based on the locale. For instance, when the user's locale is set to Russia, the tag generates `<html lang="ru">` instead of the plain old `<html>`, so that the browser can attempt to render the Russian characters (if any) in the best possible manner. Setting `<html:html locale="true">` tells Struts to look for the locale specific resource bundle (More on this later).

`<html:base>`: As you might be already aware of, one of the best practices in authoring pages is to use relative URLs instead of absolute ones. In order to use relative URLs in HTML, you need to declare the page context root with the declaration `<base href="…">` tag. All URLs (not starting with "/") are assumed to be relative to the *base href*. This is exactly what the `<html:base/>` tag generates.

Listing 3.5 CustomerDetails.jsp

```
<%@ page contentType="text/html;charset=UTF-8" language="java" %>
<%@ taglib uri="/WEB-INF/struts-html.tld" prefix="html" %>
<%@ taglib uri="/WEB-INF/struts-bean.tld" prefix="bean" %>

<html:html>
  <head>
    <html:base/>
  </head>

  <body>
    <html:errors/>
    <html:form action="/submitCustomerForm">
      <bean:message key="prompt.customer.firstname"/>:
      <html:text property="firstName" size="16" maxlength="16"/>
      <BR>
      <bean:message key="prompt.customer.lastname"/>:
      <html:text property="lastName" size="16" maxlength="16"/>
      <BR>
      <html:submit>
        <bean:message key="button.save"/>
      </html:submit>
       
      <html:cancel>
        <bean:message key="button.cancel"/>
      </html:cancel>
    </html:form>
  </body>
</html:html>
```

`<html:form>`: The `FormTag` represented by `<html:form>` generates the HTML representation of the Form as follows:

```
<form name=.." action=".." method="GET">)
```

It has one mandatory attribute – *action*. The *action* attribute represents the *ActionMapping* for this form. For instance, the *action* attribute in Listing 3.5 is */submitCustomerForm*. Note that the `FormTag` converts this into a HTML equivalent as follows:

```
<form name="CustomerForm" action="/App1/submitCustomerForm.do">
```

The corresponding *ActionMapping* in Struts Config file is associated with *CustomerForm*. Before displaying the page to the user, the `FormTag` searches the request scope for an attribute named *CustomerForm*. In this case, it does not find one and hence it instantiates a new one. All attributes are initialized to zero length string in the constructor. The embedded tags use the attributes of the CustomerForm in the request scope to display their respective values.

<html:text>: The <html:text> tag generates the HTML representation for the text box. It has one mandatory attribute named *property*. The value of this XML attribute is the name of the JavaBeans property from the Form bean that is being represented. For instance, the <html:text property="firstname"/> represents the JavaBeans property firstName from the CustomerForm. The <html:text> tag will get the value of the JavaBeans property as indicated by the property attribute. Since the CustomerForm was newly instantiated, all its fields have a value of zero length string. Hence the <html:text property="firstName" /> generates a html textbox tag of <input type="text" name="firstName" value="" />. Listing 3.6 shows the generated HTML.

<html:submit>: This tag generates the HTML representation for the Submit button as <input type="submit" value="Save Me">.

<html:cancel>: This tag generates the HTML representation for the Cancel button. This must have started a though process in your mind now. Why do I need a <html:cancel> when I already have <html:submit>? Well, this is because of the special meaning of Cancel in everyday form processing. Pressing a Cancel button also results in Form submission. You already know that when validate is set to true, the form submission results in a validation. However it is absurd to validate the form when form processing is cancelled. Struts addresses this problem by assigning a unique name to the Cancel button itself. Accordingly, a JSP tag <html:cancel>Cancel Me</html:cancel> will generate equivalent HTML as follows:

```
<input type="submit"
       name="org.apache.struts.taglib.html.CANCEL"
       value="Cancel Me">
```

Just before the RequestProcessor begins the Form validation, it checks if the button name was org.apache.struts.taglib.html.CANCEL. If so, it abandons the validation and proceeds further. And that's why <html:cancel> is different from <html:submit>.

<html:errors>: This tag displays the errors from the ActionForm validation method. You already looked at its working in the last chapter.

In the generated html, you might notice that the <html:errors/> tag did not translate into any meaningful HTML. When the form is displayed for the first time, the validate() method in CustomerForm hasn't been executed yet and hence there are no errors. Consequently the `<html:errors/>` tag does not output HTML response.

There is another tag used in Listing 3.5 called `<bean:message>` for which we did not provide any explanation yet. The `<bean:message>` tags in the JSP generate regular text output in the HTML (See Listing 3.6). The `<bean:message>` tag has one attribute named "*key*". This is the key to the Message Resource Bundle. Using the key, the `<bean:message>` looks up the properties file for appropriate values. Hence our next task is to add some key value pairs to the properties file created in Step 3b.

Listing 3.6 Generated HTML for CustomerDetails.jsp

```
<html lang="en">
<head>
  <base
  href="http://localhost:8080/App1/CustomerDetails.jsp" />
</head>

  <body>
    <form name="CustomerForm"
         action="/App1/submitCustomerForm.do">
        First Name:
        <input type="text" name="firstName" value="" />
        <BR>
        Last Name:
        <input type="text" name="lastName" value="" />
        <BR>
        <input type="submit" value="Save Me"/>
         
        <input type="submit"
               name="org.apache.struts.taglib.html.CANCEL"
               value="Cancel Me">
    </form>
  <body>
</html>
```

Step 6. For every `<bean:message>` tag in the JSP, add key value pairs to the Message Resource Bundle (*App1Messages.properties*) created in Step 3b. This is pretty straightforward. Listing 3.7 shows the *App1Messages.properties*. We will add more contents into this file in Step 9. But for now, this is all we have in the Message Resource Bundle.

Step 7. Now that the `CustomerForm` is displayed to the user, what if user enters wrong data and submits the form? What if the user does not enter any data? These boundary conditions have to be handled as close to the user interface as possible for reasons discussed in Chapter 2. That's why the `validate()` method is coded in every Form bean. You have seen the `validate()` method before in Chapter 2. It is repeated in Listing 3.8.

Listing 3.7 App1Messages.properties

```
prompt.customer.firstname=First Name
prompt.customer.lastname=Last Name

button.save=Save Mes
button.cancel=Cancel Me
```

According to the business requirements set for this application, first name has to exist all the time. Hence the `validate()` method checks to see if the first name is null or if the first name is all spaces. If either of this condition is met, then it is an error and according an ActionError object is created and added to the ActionErrors. Think of the ActionErrors as a container for holding individual ActionError objects. In Listing 3.8, the `ActionError` instance is created by supplying a key "`error.cust.firstname.null`" to the `ActionError` constructor. This key is used to look up the Message Resource Bundle. In the next step, the keys used for error messages are added to the Message Resource Bundle.

Listing 3.8 validate() method in CustomerForm

```
public ActionErrors validate(ActionMapping mapping,
                             HttpServletRequest request) {
    ActionErrors errors = new ActionErrors();
    if (firstName == null || firstName.trim().equals("")) {
        errors.add("firstName",
                  new ActionError("error.cust.firstname.null"));
    }
    return errors;
}
```

Step 8. In Step 7, `validate()` method was provided with the error messages identified by keys. In this step, the error message keys are added to the same old App1Messages.properties. The modified App1Messages.properties is shown in Listing 3.9. The new entry is shown in bold. Note that we have used a prefix "*error*" for the error message entries, a prefix of "*button*" for button labels and a prefix of "*prompt*" for regular HTML text. There is no hard and fast rule and it is only a matter of preference. You can name the keys anyway you want.

Step 9. In the previous steps, you created most of the artifacts needed for the Struts application. There are two more left. They are *index.jsp* and *Success.jsp*. These two JSPs are pretty simple and are shown in Listing 3.10 and Listing 3.11 respectively.

Listing 3.9 Updated App1Messages.properties

```
prompt.customer.firstname=First Name
prompt.customer.lastname=Last Name

button.save=Save Me
button.cancel=Cancel Me

error.cust.firstname.null=First Name is required
```

Here we are introducing a new tag – `<html:link>`. This generates a hyperlink in the HTML. You must be wondering why would you need another tag when `<a href="…">` might as well do the job. There are many advantages of using the `<html:link>` tag. We will explain one advantage relevant to our discussion – URL rewriting. We will look at other uses of the `<html:link>` tag in Chapter 4.

Since HTTP is stateless, J2EE web applications maintain data in a special object called `HTTPSession`. A key on the server side uniquely identifies every user's `HTTPSession`. You can think as if the Servlet container is storing all the active sessions in a big Hash Map. A per-session cookie is created when the user accesses the web application for the first time. There after the browser sends the per-session cookie to the server for every hit. The cookie serves as the key into the Servlet container's global Hash Map to retrieve the user's `HTTPSession`.

Under normal circumstances this works fine. But when the user has disabled cookies, the Servlet container uses a mechanism called URL rewriting as a work around. In URL rewriting, the Servlet container encodes the per-session cookie information into the URL itself. However the container does not do this unless you ask it to do so explicitly. You should make this provision to support users with cookie-disabled browsers since you can never anticipate the user behavior in advance. Therefore, when using the regular `<a href="…">` for the hyperlinks, you have to manually encode the URL by using the API `HttpServletResponse.encodeURL()` method to maintain the session as follows:

```
<a href="<%= response.encodeURL("CustomerDetails.jsp") %>" >
          Customer Form</a>
```

Now, that's a painful and laborious thing to do for every link in your application. In addition, you are unnecessarily introducing a scriptlet for every encoding. The good news is that the `<html:link>` does that automatically. For instance,

```
<html:link page="CustomerDetails.jsp">Customer Form</a>
```

generates a HTML as follows by rewriting the URL by including the *jsessionid*.

```
<a
href="http://localhost:7001/App1/CustomerDetails.jsp;jsessionid=1
Os1Ame91Z5XCe31648VNohduUlhA69urqOL1C2mT1EXzsQyw2Ex!-
824689399">Customer Form</a>
```

Listing 3.10 index.jsp

```
<%@ page contentType="text/html;charset=UTF-8" language="java" %>
<html:html>
  <head>
    <html:base/>
  </head>

  <body>
    <html:link page="CustomerDetails.jsp">Customer Form</a>
  </body>
</html:html>
```

Listing 3.11 Success.jsp

```
<%@ page contentType="text/html;charset=UTF-8" language="java" %>
<%@ taglib uri="/WEB-INF/struts-html.tld" prefix="html" %>

<html:html>
  <head>
    <html:base/>
  </head>

  <body>
    <h1>My First Struts Applications is a Success.</h1>
  </body>
</html:html>
```

Lights, Camera, Action!

In the previous steps, you completed all the coding that was required. Now you should compile the Java classes, create the WAR artifact and deploy onto Tomcat. Compiling the classes is a no-brainer. Just set the right classpath and invoke `javac`. The classpath should consist of the *servlet-api.jar* from Tomcat (This jar can be found in *<TOMCAT_HOME>/common/lib*, where *TOMCAT_HOME* is the Tomcat installation directory.) and all the JAR files from Struts distribution. They are found under *jakarta-struts-1.1/lib* directory. After compiling, you have to construct the WAR. Ant, Java community's de-facto build tool, can be used to perform these tasks. However we have chosen to create the WAR manually to illustrate which component goes where in the WAR. A clear understanding of the structure of Struts web applications is key to writing effective Ant scripts.

In Figure 3.2, you saw the directory structure of the Struts application. Now let us follow these steps to create the WAR that will look as shown in Figure 3.3 upon completion.

1. Create a directory called *temp* under the *App1* directory.

2. Copy all the contents of *App1/web-root* AS IS into the temp directory.

3. Create a subdirectory called classes under *temp/WEB-INF*

4. Copy the compiled classes into the directory *WEB-INF/classes*. Retain the package structure while doing this)

5. Copy the *App1Messages.properties* into the directory *WEB-INF/classes*. Copy the file according to the java package structure. See Figure 3.3 for the final structure of the WAR.

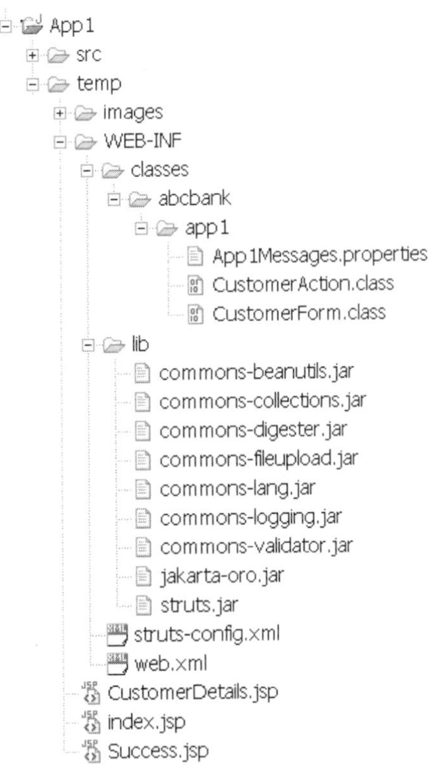

Figure 3.3 The structure of the WAR file.

6. Create a directory lib under WEB-INF and copy all the JAR files from Struts distribution into the lib folder. These JAR files are required by your web application at runtime.

7. Create a directory lib under WEB-INF and copy all the JAR files from Struts distribution into the lib folder. These JAR files are required by your web application at runtime.

8. Copy *struts-bean.tld* and *struts-html.tld* from Struts distribution into the WEB-INF directory.

9. Zip (or jar) the temp directory into a file named ***App1.war***. You WAR is ready now. Drop it into the *webapps* sub-directory in Tomcat. Start Tomcat and test it out!

Congratulations! You have successfully developed and deployed your first Struts application. However we are not done yet. Let us look at some practical issues that need to be addressed.

Handling multiple buttons in HTML Form

In the example application, we used the <html:submit> tag to submit the HTML form. Our usage of the tag was as follows:

```
<html:submit><bean:message key="button.save"/></html:submit>
```

This generated a HTML as follows.

```
<input type="submit" value="Save Me">
```

This worked okay for us since there was only one button with "real" Form submission (The other one was a Cancel button). Hence it sufficed for us to straight away process the request in CustomerAction. You will frequently face situations where there are more than one or two buttons submitting the form. You would want to execute different code based on the buttons clicked. If you are thinking, "No problem. I will have different ActionMapping (and hence different Actions) for different buttons", you are out of luck! Clicking any of the buttons in a HTML Form always submits the same Form, with the same URL. The Form submission URL is found in the action attribute of the form tag as:

```
<formname="CustomForm"action="/App1/submitCustomerForm.do"/>
```

and is unique to the Form. You have to use a variation of the <html:submit> as shown below to tackle this problem.

```
<html:submit property="step">
     <bean:message key="button.save"/>
</html:submit>
```

The above SubmitTag, has an additional attribute named *property* whose value is *step*. The meaning of the property attribute is similar to that in <html:text> - It represents a JavaBeans property in the ActionForm and generates the name of the Form input element. This tag generates a HTML as follows

```
<input type="submit" name="step" value="Save Me">
```

The generated HTML submit button has a name associated with it. You have to now add a JavaBeans property to your ActionForm whose name matches the submit button name. In other words an instance variable with a getter and setter are required. If you were to make this change in the application just developed, you have to add a variable named "step" in the CustomerForm and then add two methods getStep() and setStep(). The Struts Framework sets the value of the step by Introspection, just like it does on the other fields. In the CustomerAction, the logic corresponding to the Save Me button is executed after performing a check for the Save Me button. Listing 3.12 shows the modified `execute()` method from `CustomerAction`. The changes are shown in bold. When the Save Me button is pressed, the `custForm.getStep()` method returns a value of "Save Me" and the corresponding code block is executed.

Listing 3.12 CustomerAction modified for mutltiple button Forms

```
public class CustomerAction extends Action
{
   public ActionForward execute(ActionMapping mapping,
            ActionForm form, HttpServletRequest request,
            HttpServletResponse response) throws Exception
   {
      if (isCancelled(request)) {
         System.out.println(Cancel Operation Performed");
         return mapping.findForward("mainpage");
      }

      CustomerForm custForm = (CustomerForm) form;
      ActionForward forward = null;

      if ( "Save Me".equals(custForm.getStep()) ) {
          System.out.println("Save Me Button Clicked");
          String firstName = custForm.getFirstName();
          String lastName = custForm.getLastName();

          System.out.println("Customer First name is " +
                                            firstName);
          System.out.println("Customer Last name is " +
                                            lastName);

          forward = mapping.findForward("success");
      }

      return forward;
   }
}
```

In Struts applications, when using regular buttons, it is customary for all submit buttons to have the same name (except Cancel and Reset buttons). This is for convenience purposes. In HTML, when a form is submitted, only one of the submit buttons is pressed and hence only the value of that button is submitted. The ActionForm can thus have a single instance variable for all the submit buttons in its Form. This makes the `if-else` check in the Action class easier. Suppose that the

HTML Customer Form that we show to the users has another button with label "Spike Me". The submit button can still have the name "*step*" (same as the "Save Me" button). This means the `CustomerForm` class has a single JavaBeans property "`step`" for the submit buttons. In the `CustomerAction` you can have check if the `custForm.getStep()` is "*Save Me*" or "*Spike Me*". If each of the buttons had different names like button1, button2 etc. then the `CustomerAction` would have to perform checks as follows:

```
if ("Save Me".equals(custForm.getButton1()) {
    //  Save Me Button pressed
} else if ("Spike Me".equals(customForm.getButton2()) {
    // Spike Me button pressed
}
```

Using the HTML Button Label to distinguish the buttons works for most of the cases except when you have a internationalized Struts web application. Consider the HTML rendered for a Spanish user. By virtue of the Message Resource Bundles (`<bean:message>` tag), the Spanish user will see a label of "*Excepto Mí*" instead of "*Save Me*". However the `CustomerAction` class is still looking for the hard coded "*Save Me*". Consequently the code block meant for "*Save Me*" button never gets executed. In Chapter 4, you will see how a specialized subclass of the `Action` called `LookupDispatchAction` solves this problem.

Value replacement in Message Resource Bundle

When you constructed the web application, earlier in this chapter, you used static messages in the Resource Bundle. However consider this: You have a dozen fields in the form. The only validation rule is that all fields are required. Hence the error messages for each field differs from another only by the field name. *First name is required*, *Last name is required*, *Age is required* and so on. It would be ideal if there were a field name replacement mechanism into a fixed error message template. The good news is that it already exists. In the resource bundle file, you can define a template for the above error message as:

```
errors.required={0} is required.
```

In the `validate()` method, the `ActionError` is then constructed using one of the following overloaded constructors.

```
public ActionError(String key, Object value0);
public ActionError(String key, Object value0, Object value1)
. . .
public ActionError(String key, Object[] values);
```

The first overloaded constructor accepts the key and one replacement value. The second overloaded constructor accepts a key and two replacement values. The last constructor accepts a key and an array of objects for replacement. You can now construct an `ActionError` for the first name as follows:

```
String[] strArray = {"First name"};
ActionError err = new ActionError("errors.required" strArray);
```

This will result in an error message: `First name is required.` Beautiful isn't it! Now you can make this even better. Notice that in the above example, we hard coded the field name in the replacement value array in the process of reducing the set of error messages to a single error message template. Now, let us go one step further and get the field name from the resource bundle too. The following code shows how to do it.

```
MessageResources msgRes =
   (MessageResources) request.getAttribute(Globals.MESSAGES_KEY);
String firstName =
     msgRes.getMessage("prompt.customer.firstname");
ActionError err = new ActionError("errors.required" firstName);
```

- First, a `MessageResources` for the current module is obtained.
- Next, the display value of the first name field is obtained from the `MessageResources` (resource bundle) in the `getMessage()` method by using the key for the first name – `prompt.customer.firstName`.
- Finally, the display value of the first name field is used as a replacement parameter in the `ActionError` using the first of the overloaded constructors.

This is generally the preferred way of constructing reusable error messages when the `validate()` method is coded manually.

TIP: Using the struts-blank.war as a template

In this application we put together everything from scratch to construct the application. You can use the template so constructed for future use or you can use the ready-made template available in the Struts distribution. The ready-made template is called *struts-blank.war* is something that you can unwar and use as template for your applications. It has all the tlds and jars included in the WAR. Plus it provides the web.xml and struts-config.xml ready to be used as placeholders with default values.

Summary

In this chapter you applied all that you have learnt so far and built a Hello World Struts application. This application although simple, illustrates the basic steps in building a Struts application. In the coming chapters we will go beyond the basics and learn other features in Struts and effectively apply them to tackle real life scenarios.

Chapter 4

All about Actions

> ***In this chapter:***
>
> 1. *You will learn about all the built-in Struts Actions – ForwardAction, IncludeAction, DispatchAction, LookupDispatchAction and SwitchAction*
> 2. *You will learn about multiple sub application support in Struts and using SwitchAction to transparently navigate between them*
> 3. *You will see examples of effectively using the built-in Actions*
> 4. *You will learn of ways to prevent direct JSP access by the users*

In Chapter 2, you understood the basics of the Struts framework. In Chapter 3, you applied those basics to build a simple web application using Struts and got a clear picture of the basics. In this chapter we take you beyond the basics as you explore Struts Controller components that are interesting and timesaving that prepare you to handle realistic scenarios.

Action classes are where your presentation logic resides. In Chapter 2, you saw how to write your own Action. Struts 1.1 provides some types of Action out-of-the-box, so you don't have to build them from the scratch. The Actions provided by Struts are `ForwardAction`, `IncludeAction`, `DispatchAction`, `LookupDispatchAction` and `SwitchAction`. All these classes are defined in `org.apache.struts.actions` package. These built-in actions are very helpful to address some problems faced in day to day programming. Understanding them is the key to using them effectively. All of these the Actions are frequently used, except for `IncludeAction`.

ForwardAction

`ForwardAction` is the one of the most frequently used built-in Action classes. The primary reason behind this is that `ForwardAction` allows you to adhere to MVC paradigm when designing JSP navigation. Most of the times you will perform some processing when you navigate from one page to another. In Struts, this processing is encapsulated in the `Action` instances. There are times however when all you want to do is navigate from one page to another without performing any processing. You would be tempted to add a hyperlink on the first page for direct navigation to the second. Watch out! In Model 2 paradigm, a straight JSP invocation from another JSP is discouraged, although not prohibited. For instance, suppose you want to go from *PageA.jsp* to *PageB.jsp* in your Struts application. The easy way of achieving this is to add a hyperlink in *PageA.jsp* as follows:

```
<a href="PageB.jsp">Go to Page B</a>
```

or even better, as follows:

```
<html:link page="/PageB.jsp">Go to Page B</html:link>
```

This is what we did in Chapter 3 when navigating from *index.jsp* to the *CustomerDetails.jsp*. However this violates the MVC spirit by directly accessing the JSP. In Model 2 applications, it is the responsibility of the Controller to select and dispatch to the next view. In Struts, `ActionServlet` and `Action` classes together form the controller. They are supposed to select and dispatch to the next view. Moreover the `ActionServlet` is responsible for intercepting your request and providing appropriate attributes such as Message Resource Bundles. If you bypass this step, then the behavior of the Struts tags may become unpredictable.

MVC compliant usage of LinkTag

Struts provides a built-in Action class called `ForwardAction` to address this issue. With `ForwardAction`, the Struts Controller is still in the loop while navigating from PageA to PageB. There are two steps involved in using the `ForwardAction`. They are:

- First, declare the PageA hyperlink that takes you to PageB as follows:

```
<html:link page="/gotoPageB.do">Go to Page B</html:link>
```

- Next, add an ActionMapping in the Struts Config file as follows:

```
<action path="/gotoPageB"
        parameter="/PageB.jsp"
        type=org.apache.struts.ForwardAction" />
```

The *PageA.jsp* hyperlink now points to "*/gotoPageB.do*" instead of "*PageB.jsp*". This ensures that the controller is still in the loop. The three attributes shown above are mandatory in a `ForwardAction`. The *type* attribute is always `org.apache.struts.ForwardAction` instead of a custom Action of yours. The *path* attribute identifies the URL path, as any other *ActionMapping*. The *parameter* attribute in the above definition is the URL for the next JSP.

In the above ActionMapping you might have noticed there is no ActionForm. The Struts Config file DTD specifies that the Form bean is optional in an ActionMapping. Logically speaking ActionForm makes sense only where is data to be collected from the HTML request. In situations like this where there is no HTML data involved in the navigation, there is no need for ActionForm.

Using LinkTag's action attribute

The `LinkTag` (`<html:link>`) has several variations. It can be used in a variety of ways in conjunction with `ForwardAction`. You just saw one usage of the `LinkTag`. A second way of using the this tag is as follows:

- First, declare the PageA hyperlink that takes you to PageB as follows:

```
<html:link action="gotoPageB">Go to Page B</html:link>
```

- Next, add the ActionMapping for `/gotoPageB` in the Struts Config file same way as before:

```
<action path="/gotoPageB"
        parameter="/PageB.jsp"
        type=org.apache.struts.ForwardAction" />
```

When you use the *action* attribute instead of the *page* attribute in `<html:link>`, you need not specify the "*.do*" explicitly.

Using LinkTag's forward attribute

There is yet another way to use `<html:link>`. In this approach you use the *forward* attribute of the `<html:link>` tag instead of the action. There are two steps involved in this approach.

- First, declare the PageA hyperlink that takes you to PageB as follows:

```
<html:link forward="pageBForward">Go to Page B</html:link>
```

- Add a Global Forward for "*pageBForward*" as follows in the global-forwards section:

```
<global-forwards>
   <forward name="pageBForward" path="/PageB.jsp" />
</global-forwards>
```

When used in this manner, the `<html:link>` gets transformed into the following HTML Link.

```
<a href="App1/PageB.jsp">Go to Page B</a>
```

Oops, that doesn't seem right. The HTML Link is now displaying the actual JSP name directly in the browser. Ideally you would love to hide the JSP name from the user. And with a slight twist you can! First, define an ActionMapping as follows:

```
<action path="/gotoPageB"
        parameter="/PageB.jsp"
```

```
                    type=org.apache.struts.ForwardAction" />
```

Next, modify the global forward itself to point to the above ActionMapping.

```
<global-forwards>
      <forward name="pageBForward" path="/gotoPageB.do" />
</global-forwards>
```

When used in this manner, the <html:link> gets transformed into the following HTML Link.

```
<a href="App1/gotoPageB.do">Go to Page B</a>
```

There you go! The generated HTML is not displaying the JSP name anymore. From a design perspective this seems to be the best way of using the <html:link> tag since the link is completely decoupled from the associated ActionMapping, thanks to the global-forward.

The <html:link> points to the global-forward and the global-forward points to the ForwardAction. The extra level of indirection, although looks confusing in the beginning, is a good design decision due to the following reason:

As is true with any application, requirements change and it might just become necessary to do some processing during the navigation from PageA to PageB. A conversion from ForwardAction to a custom Action will be easier to manage with the extra level of indirection.

Using ForwardAction for Integration

In general, the ForwardAction's *parameter* attribute specifies the resource to be forwarded to. It can be the physical page like *PageB.jsp* or it can be a URL pattern handled by another controller, maybe somewhere outside Struts. For instance, consider the following ForwardAction.

```
<action path="/gotoPageB"
        parameter="/xoom/AppB"
        type=org.apache.struts.ForwardAction" />
```

In the snippet above, the value of the *parameter* is not a physical page. It is a logical resource that might be mapped to another Servlet totally outside the control of Struts. Yet from PageA's perspective, you are still dealing with a Struts URL. This is the second use of ForwardAction. You can integrate Struts applications transparently with already existing non-Struts applications.

NOTE: Even with the ForwardAction, you cannot prevent a nosy user from accessing the JSP directly. See the section *Protecting JSPs from direct access* for techniques to protect your JSPs from direct access.

ForwardAction Hands-on

In the last chapter, we modeled the navigation from *index.jsp* to *CustomerDetails.jsp* with a direct link. Let us correct the mistake we made by applying the knowledge we have gained so far. Think of *index.jsp* as PageA and *CustomerDetails.jsp* as PageB. The <html:link> in *index.jsp* will look as follows:

```
<html:link forward="CustomerDetailsPage">Customer Form</a>
```

The following Global Forward and ForwardAction are added to the Struts Config file.

```
<global-forwards>
  ..
  <forward name="CustomerDetailsPage"
           path="/gotoCustomerDetails.do"  />
</global-forwards>

<action-mappings>
   ..
   <action path="/gotoCustomerDetails"
           parameter="/CustomerDetails.jsp"
           type=org.apache.struts.actions.ForwardAction" />
</action-mappings>
```

And now, we have an application that strictly adheres to MVC. What a relief!

Protecting JSPs from direct access

According to the Model 2 paradigm, the view is always served by the controller and should not be requested explicitly from any other view. In reality a JSP can always navigate to another JSP when the JSPs are placed anywhere in a WAR other than the WEB-INF directory (or its sub-directories). Similarly a user can type in the name of the JSP in the URL bar and invoke the JSP. The web application specification does not disallow such access. Actually this makes sense. The specification should not prevent anybody from coding using the Model 1 paradigm. Consequently your JSPs are exposed to the external world for nosy users to cause unnecessary problems, for hackers to exploit any vulnerability in the system. If you are wondering what the problem is with allowing direct access to JSPs, well, here are some.

A nosy user might attempt to guess the JSP name by the operation performed in that page or request parameters or worse – if the page author used html comment tag for SCM and code comments instead of the JSP comments. Armed with this information, the user attempts to access the JSPs directly. A JSP as you know is a view and it displays information based on model objects stored in one of the four scopes – page, request, session or application, the first three being the most common. These objects are created by the back end presentation and business logic and made available for the JSP to act upon. When the JSP is accessed out of context or out of order, the required model objects may not exist in the appropriate scope and consequently almost always leads to the exceptional situations in the JSP code.

It is not common to perform null checks in every bit of code in the JSP tags, scriptlets and other helper classes. These checks are generally limited to interfaces and boundaries between modules and not later on. For instance, in a typical Model 2 scenario, when the model object cannot be created for some reason, the controller instead takes alternate route and displays an alternate view corresponding to the null model object. This assumption of model objects being not null in the main path of the presentation logic and view highly simplifies the coding. In fact when the system is accessed as intended, everything works smoothly. However whenever somebody tries to access the views out of order, all hell breaks lose. Every view starts throwing `NullPointerExceptions`, `IllegalArgumentExceptions` and other unchecked and checked exceptions depending on how the JSP page and its tags and scriptlets are authored. This is exactly what a nosy user is trying out.
The implications are even more serious when a malicious user tries to find weak points in the design to bring the system down to its knees. The first thing that might occur is to put checks for nulls and unintended access in the system. Invariably, this is nothing but a collection of if-else blocks in every part of the JSP page making it messy and buggy to maintain.

Two prominent alternatives exist. Let us look the easiest one first. As we glossed over earlier, the servlet specification explicitly states that contents located in the WEB-INF and its sub-directories are protected from outside access. Let us take a simple example to illustrate this. All contents located in a WAR belong to the same protection domain. A protection domain is a set of entities known (or assumed) to trust each other. Consequently any resource within a WAR can access resources located under WEB-INF directory without restrictions. JSP is also a resource and thus any class within the same WAR can forward to a JSP under WEB-INF. (This part is not explicitly stated in the specification) However when the request originates outside the container, it does not belong to the protection domain (at least not until it is authenticated) and hence cannot access the protected resource under WEB-INF. Thus putting all JSPs under the WEB-INF directly or as sub-directories if needed is the easiest and also the best way of protecting direct access to JSPs. What if the hyperlink in one of your page wants to really just forward to another JSP? Is that disallowed as well? Yeah! You cannot have different rules in your system right? However there is a way around.

Consider the case when a hyperlink in page A needs to forward request to page B. Instead of directly forwarding to page B, which is disallowed, you can put the following entry in the struts-config.xml

```
<action name="/gotoPageB"
        parameter="WEB-INF/pageB.jsp"
        type=org.apache.struts.ForwardAction" />
```

On the pageA, the hyperlink can point to "pageB.do" is suffix mapping is used or some other path is path mapping is used. Either ways, the ActionMapping shown above is picked up and as its type indicates, the action is just a `ForwardAction`, which as the name suggest is a forward. However since the forward is occurring from within the container, (in the protection domain) it is allowed.

A question might be popping up in your mind. The technique just highlighted is the easiest and also supposedly the best. Why do I need anything lesser than best? The answer is not all containers support the behavior just mentioned. As we stated earlier, since the specification is clear about not letting direct access to resources under WEB-INF, all J2EE compliant application servers implement it. However, the second part is not stated in the specification and consequently it is the vendor's prerogative to implement it or not. Certain providers do (For e.g. Tomcat) and others don't (For e.g. WebLogic). Hence we have to have an alternate mechanism for the less fortunate ones. This one is not difficult either. Instead of putting the JSPs underneath WEB-INF, they can stay wherever they are. The following entries are added to the *web.xml.*

```
<security-constraint>
  <web-resource-collection>
    <web-resource-name>Deny Direct Access</web-resource-name>
    <description>
      Deny direct access to JSPs by associating
      them with denied role
    </description>
    <url-pattern>*.jsp</url-pattern>
  </web-resource-collection>
  <auth-constraint>
    <role-name>Denied</role-name>
  </auth-constraint>
</security-constraint>

<security-role>
   <role-name>Denied</role-name>
</security-role>
```

First, all the url patterns ending with suffix ".jsp" are associated with a Role named "Denied". Any user who wants to access the JSP pages directly should be in that role. We further ensure that no user of the system is in that Role. Role and user association is done depending on your implementation of authentication and authorization. For instance, if you are using LDAP as the user persistence mechanism, then the users, their passwords and Roles are stored in LDAP. If you ensure nobody gets the Denied role, then you have effectively prevented everyone from directly accessing the JSPs. You will still have to have the `ForwardAction` as shown earlier in this section if you have situation when page A needs to just navigate to page B. The internal forwards to other JSPs using `RequestDispatcher` are okay because the container does not intercept and cross check internal forwards even though the url-pattern matches the ones in *web.xml.*

NOTE: The default `pagePattern` and `forwardPattern` values for `<controller>` element in *struts-config.xml* are `$M$P`, where `$M` is replaced with the module prefix and and the `$P` is replaced with the path attribute of the selected forward. If you place your JSP files under *WEB-INF* for access protection, you have to set the `pagePattern` and `forwardPattern` attributes of the `<controller>` element in the *struts-config.xml* to `/WEB-INF/$M$P` to tell Struts to construct the paths correctly.

IncludeAction

`IncludeAction` is much like `ForwardAction` except that the resulting resource is included in the HTTP response instead of being forwarded to. It is rarely used. Its only significant use is to integrate legacy applications with Struts transparently. Consider a web site that aggregates information from disparate sources – some of which are non-Struts. The JSP for such a web site consists of `<jsp:include>`s to include different resources. One of such `<jsp:include>` that might be as follows:

```
<jsp:include page="/xoom/LegacyServletA" />
```

It is very clear from the value of the *page* attribute that it is a non-Struts resource. Wouldn't it be better to have a `<jsp:include>` that pretends as if the resource exists in the current Struts application? It would be ideal if the page include looked as follows:

```
<jsp:include page="/App1/legacyA.do" />
```

The */legacyA.do* cannot be a `ForwardAction` because it would perform a HTTP Forward to the above resource instead of including the resource in the HTTP response. Since the HTTP Response OutputStream closes (The J2EE jargon for this is the response has been committed) after HTTP Forward, the servlet container cannot process the rest of the JSP and include its response in the OutputStream. Consequently it throws a `IllegalStateException` with a message that "*Response is already committed*". `IncludeAction` addresses this problem. Instead of forwarding to the specified resource, it includes the resource in the current response. Consequently the output of the LegacyServletA is displayed in the same HTML as that of the Struts application. You have to add the following ActionMapping in the Struts Config file:

```
<action path="/legacyA"
        parameter="/xoom/LegacyServletA"
        type=org.apache.struts.IncludeAction" />
```

The *parameter* attribute indicates the actual resource that has to be included in the response.

As mentioned earlier, the use of `IncludeAction` is limited to including responses from existing Servlet in the current page. This requires the use of `<jsp:include>` in the page. If you web application is aggregating response from legacy servlet applications, portlets seems to be the way to go. Portlet API – JSR 168 has been finalized and it is matter of time before you can develop standardized portals aggregating contents from disparate web applications. Tiles framework is the way to go if you are on a short-term project that wants to aggregate information now (From different applications or may be from various Actions in the same Struts application). Tiles provides a robust alternative to the primitive `<jsp:include>`. Chapter 8 provides an in-depth coverage of Tiles in conjunction with Struts.

DispatchAction

`DispatchAction` is another useful built-in Struts Action. However you cannot use it as is. You will have to extend it to provide your own implementation. An example will make things clear. Consider an online credit card application. Customers fill the credit card application online. The bank personnel get a List screen as shown in Figure 4.1 and they can act in one of four ways - Approve, Reject or Add Comment. Consequently there are three images each being a `<html:link>`.

One way of dealing with this situation is to create three different Actions – `ApproveAction`, `RejectAction` and `AddCommentAction`. This is a valid approach, although not elegant since there might be duplication of code across the Actions since they are related. `DispatchAction` is the answer to this problem. With `DispatchAction`, you can combine all three Actions into one.

The `DispatchAction` provides the implementation for the `execute()` method, but still is declared as abstract class. You start by sub-classing `DispatchAction`. Let us assume that `CreditAppAction`, a sub-class of `DispatchAction` is used to implement the above-mentioned presentation logic. It has four methods – `reject()`, `approve()` and `addComment()`. The `CreditAppAction` class definition is shown in Listing 4.1.

You might be wondering why all the three methods take the same four arguments – `ActionMapping`, `ActionForm`, `HttpServletRequest`, `HttpServletResponse`. Don't worry, you will find the answer soon.

For a moment, look at the four URLs submitted when the bank staff perform the three actions as mentioned before. They would look something like this.

- http://localhost:8080/bank/screen-credit-app.do?**step=reject**&id=2
- http://localhost:8080/ bank/screen-credit-app.do?**step=approve**&id=2
- http://localhost:8080/bank/screen-credit-app.do?**step=addComment**&id=2

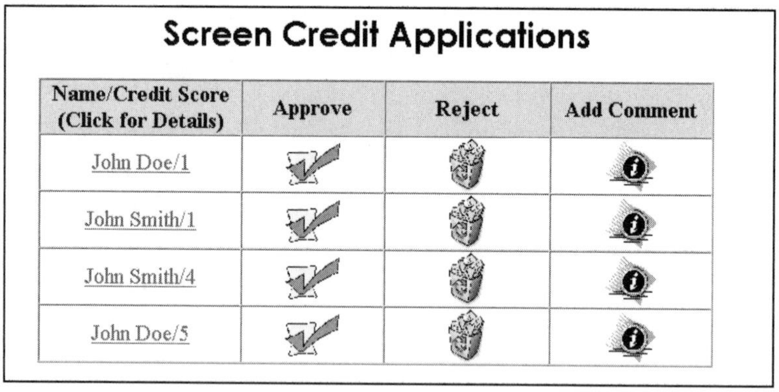

Screen Credit Applications

Name/Credit Score (Click for Details)	Approve	Reject	Add Comment
John Doe/1			
John Smith/1			
John Smith/4			
John Doe/5			

Figure 4.1 Screen Credit Applications page as seen by the bank staff.

An interesting thing to notice is that the value of the HTTP request parameter named *step* is same as the four method names in `CreditAppAction`. This is no coincidence. `DispatchAction` (the parent class of `CreditAppAction`) uses the value of the HTTP request parameter *step* to determine which method in `CreditAppAction` has to be invoked. In the `execute()` method, `DispatchAction` uses reflection to invoke the appropriate method in `CreditAppAction`. For this reason, the arguments on all the three methods in `CreditAppAction` are fixed and have to be – `ActionMapping`, `ActionForm`, `HttpServletRequest`, and `HttpServletResponse` in that order. Otherwise the method invocation by Reflection fails.

Okay, so part of the puzzle is solved. But how does `DispatchAction` know to look for the HTTP request parameter specifically named *step* in the URL? The simple answer is that it doesn't. You will have to tell it explicitly. And this is done in the ActionMapping for */screen-credit-app.do*. The ActionMapping for the URL path "*/screen-credit-app.do*" is declared in *struts-config.xml* as shown in Listing 4.2.

The section highlighted in bold is what makes this Action different from the rest. The type is declared as `mybank.example.list.CreditAppAction` – you already knew that. Now, let us look at the second attribute in bold. This attribute, named ***parameter*** has the value "*step*". Notice that one of the HTTP request parameter in the four URLs is also named "*step*". Now, it is all coming together. `DispatchAction` knows what parameter to look for in the incoming URL request through this attribute named *parameter* in *struts-config.xml.* From the value of *parameter* attribute, it knows the method to be invoked on the subclass. Since the arguments and their order in these methods is fixed by DispatchAction, the method invocation by reflection at runtime is successful. If for any reason, the arguments on these methods are different; the method invocation fails at runtime.

Listing 4.1 Example DispatchAction

```
public class CreditAppAction extends DispatchAction {
  public ActionForward reject(ActionMapping mapping,
              ActionForm form, HttpServletRequest request,
              HttpServletResponse response) throws Exception
  {
      String id = request.getParameter("id");
      // Logic to reject the application with the above id
      ... ... ...
      mapping.findForward("reject-success");
  }

  public ActionForward approve(ActionMapping mapping,
              ActionForm form, HttpServletRequest request,
              HttpServletResponse response) throws Exception
  {
      String id = request.getParameter("id");
      // Logic to approve the application with the above id
      ... ... ...
      mapping.findForward("approve-success");
  }

  public ActionForward addComment(ActionMapping mapping,
              ActionForm form, HttpServletRequest request,
              HttpServletResponse response) throws Exception
  {
      String id = request.getParameter("id");
      // Logic to view application details for the above id
      ... ... ...
      mapping.findForward("viewDetails");
  }
   ...
  ...
}
```

DispatchAction can be confusing in the beginning. But don't worry. Follow these steps to setup the DispatchAction and familiarize yourself with the steps.

1. Create a subclass of DispatchAction.

2. Identify the related actions and create a method for each of the logical actions. Verify that the methods have the fixed method signature shown earlier.
3. Identify the request parameter that will uniquely identify all actions.
4. Define an ActionMapping for this subclass of `DispatchAction` and assign the previously identified request parameter as the value of the *parameter* attribute.
5. Set your JSP so that the previously identified request parameter (Step 3) takes on `DispatchAction` subclass method names as its values.

Listing 4.2 ActionMapping for the DispatchAction

```
<action path="/screen-credit-app"
  input="/ListCreditApplications.jsp"
  type="mybank.example.list.CreditAppAction"
  parameter="step"
  scope="request"
  validate="false">
      <forward name="reject-success"
               path="RejectAppSuccess.jsp"
               redirect="true"/>
  ..
 </action>
```

Design Tip: Use `DispatchAction` when a set of actions is closely related and separating them into multiple Actions would result in duplication of code or usage of external helper classes to refactor the duplicated code. In the above example `DispatchAction` was used handle hyperlinks. `DispatchAction` is a good choice when there are form submissions using the regular buttons (not the image buttons). Just name all the buttons same. For instance,

```
<html:submit property="step>Update</html:submit>
<html:submit property="step>Delete</html:submit>
```

and so on. Image buttons is a different ball game. Image button usage for form submission and `DispatchAction` are exclusive. You have to choose one. See Chapter 6 on Struts tags for details on Image buttons.

In the above example we used the `DispatchAction` and used methods that has ActionForm as one of its arguments. As you learnt in the last chapter, an ActionForm always existed in conjunction with the Action. Earlier in this chapter, we dealt with `ForwardAction` and we neither developed our Action or ActionForm. In that context we stated that having an ActionForm was optional. That holds true even if the Action is a custom coded one like the `CreditAppAction`. If the ActionMapping does not specify a form bean, then the

ActionForm argument has a null value. In the Listing 4.1, all the four methods got a null ActionForm. But that did not matter since the HTTP request parameters were used directly in the Action. You can have a Form bean if there are a lot of HTTP parameters (and perhaps also require validation). The HTTP parameters can then be accessed through the Form bean.

LookupDispatchAction

In Chapter 3 you were introduced to a Localization problem with the Action class when the form has multiple buttons. Using `LookupDispatchAction` is one way of addressing the problem when regular buttons are used. Chapter 6 presents another alternative that works irrespective of whether an Image or a grey button is used to submit the Form. One has to choose the most appropriate solution under the given circumstances.

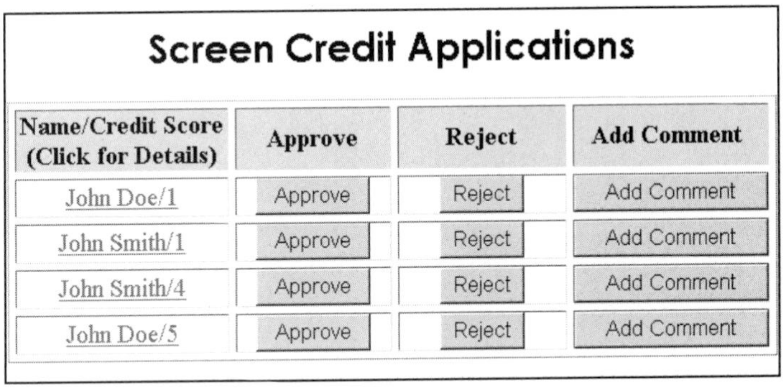

Screen Credit Applications

Name/Credit Score (Click for Details)	Approve	Reject	Add Comment
John Doe/1	Approve	Reject	Add Comment
John Smith/1	Approve	Reject	Add Comment
John Smith/4	Approve	Reject	Add Comment
John Doe/5	Approve	Reject	Add Comment

Figure 4.2 Modified Screen Credit Applications page as seen by the bank staff.

`LookupDispatchAction` is a subclass of `DispatchAction` as its name suggests. We will use a slightly modified example to illustrate the use of `LookupDispatchAction`. We will still use the list of credit applications as before, but with one twist. Each row in the list is a HTML Form and the images are now replaced with grey buttons to submit the Form. Figure 4.2 shows the modified application list as seen by the bank personnel.

A `LookupDispatchAction` for this example is created by following these steps.

1. Create a subclass of `LookupDispatchAction`.
2. Identify the related actions and create a method for each of the logical actions. Verify that the methods have the fixed method signature as similar to `DispatchAction` methods in Listing 4.1.
3. Identify the request parameter that will uniquely identify all actions.
4. Define an ActionMapping in *struts-config.xml* in the same way as

DispatchAction (Listing 4.2). Assign the previously identified request parameter as the value of the parameter attribute in the ActionMapping. All the steps up until this point are the same as what you did before with DispatchAction. From here on, they will differ.

Listing 4.3 Example LookupDispatchAction

```
public class CreditAppAction extends LookupDispatchAction
{
    public ActionForward reject(ActionMapping mapping,
                                ActionForm form,
                                HttpServletRequest request,
                                HttpServletResponse response)
                                throws Exception
    {
        ... ... ...
    }

    //Other methods go here

    public Map getKeyMethodMap()
    {
        Map map = new HashMap();
        map.put("button.approve", "approve");
        map.put("button.reject", "reject");
        map.put("button.comment", "addComment");
    }
}
```

5. Implement a method named getKeyMethodMap() in the subclass of the LookupDispatchAction. The method returns a java.util.Map. The keys used in the Map should be also used as keys in Message Resource Bundle. The values of the keys in the Resource Bundle should be the method names from the step 2 above. If the CreditAppAction from the bank example were to be implemented as a LookupDispatchAction it would look like Listing 4.3.

6. Next, create the buttons in the JSP by using <bean:message> for their names. This is very important. If you hardcode the button names you will not get benefit of the LookupDispatchAction. For instance, the JSP snippet for Approve and Add Comment button are:

```
<html:submit property="step">
    <bean:message key="button.approve"/>
</html:submit>
```

```
<html:submit property="step">
    <bean:message key="button.comment"/>
</html:submit>
```

The <bean:message> keys point to the messages in the Resource Bundle.

```
button.approve=Approve
button.reject=Reject
button.comment=Add Comment
```

In summary, for every form submission, LookupDispatchAction does the reverse lookup on the resource bundle to get the key and then gets the method whose name is associated with the key into the Resource Bundle (from getKeyMethodmap()). That was quite a bit of work just to execute the method. DispatchAction was much easier!

But the implications of LookupDispatchAction are significant. The method name in the Action is not driven by its name in the front end, but by the Locale independent key into the resource bundle. Since the key is always the same, the LookupDispatchAction shields your application from the side effects of I18N.

Configuring multiple application modules

So far we have covered several important built-in Actions with examples. There is one more feature that is very important and useful addition in 1.1 – Multiple Application module support. In Struts1.0 (and earlier), a single config file was supported. This file, normally called *struts-config.xml,* was specified in *web.xml* as an initialization parameter for the ActionServlet as follows:

```
<servlet>
  <servlet-name>mybank</servlet-name>
  <servlet-class>org.apache.struts.action.ActionServlet
  </servlet-class>
  <init-param>
    <param-name>config</param-name>
    <param-value>/WEB-INF/struts-config.xml</param-value>
  </init-param>
</servlet>
```

The single configuration file is bottleneck in large projects as all developers had to contend to modify this resource. In addition managing a monolithic file is painful and error prone. With Struts1.1 this problem has been resolved by the addition of multiple sub application support better known as application modules. You can now have multiple configuration files, one for each module or logical group of forms. The configuration files are specified in web.xml file using multiple <init-param> - initialization parameters as shown in Listing 4.4.

Listing 4.4 web.xml setting for Multiple Application module Support

```
<servlet>
   <servlet-name>mybank</servlet-name>
   <servlet-class>org.apache.struts.action.ActionServlet
   </servlet-class>
   <init-param>
     <param-name>config</param-name>
     <param-value>/WEB-INF/struts-config.xml</param-value>
   </init-param>
   <init-param>
     <param-name>config/module1</param-name>
     <param-value>
          /WEB-INF/struts-module1-config.xml
   </param-value>
   </init-param>
</servlet>
```

The newly added application module is shown in bold. The default application module based on *struts-config.xml* can still continue to exist. The new module is defined by adding an initialization parameter *config/module1*. In fact any init-param prefixed with "*config/*" is interpreted as configuration for a separate module. Its corresponding value – */WEB-INF/struts-module1-config.xml* is the struts configuration file containing Form bean definitions and ActionMappings for the module module1. If the URLs in the default *struts-config.xml* were accessed as http://localhost:8080/App1/start.do, and the corresponding ActionMapping were moved to *struts-module1-config.xml* then the URL would be accessed as http://localhost:8080/App1/module1/start.do where *App1* is the web application context. Notice that the application URL contains the module name after the web application context as if it is a sub directory name.

Even though a application module has a separate struts configuration file and a sub-directory like url pattern while accessing through the browser, the physical organization need not necessarily be the same although that is generally the route taken since the application module was after all created for logical division (driven by functional requirements) and there are less headaches if the physical organization matches the logical division as much as possible.

The benefits of application modules are immediately obvious. You can now split your monolithic struts application into logical modules thus making maintenance easier. It will cause less contention during development time as developers working on different modules get to work on their own struts configuration files. Each Struts Configuration file and hence each application module can choose its own `RequestProcessor`, `MessageResources` and `PlugIn`. You can now choose to implement one or more modules with Tiles. If you find this convenient and useful then you can migrate your application to Tiles or JSF or plug in any other Struts extensions for one module at a time.

Here is a tip: Generally web applications are organized so that navigation occurs from generic to specific. For instance, you start from the initial welcome page for the web application and then navigate to a specific module. You can organize you struts modules so that the initial welcome page and other top-level pages are defined in the default application module (*struts-config.xml*). The pages correspond to individual use cases are defined in different application modules (*struts-config-xxx.xml*). You can then navigate from the default application module to the use case specific module.

That brings up the question: How do you move between application modules? It is quite simple actually. Struts 1.1 provides a specialized Action called `SwitchAction`. We will illustrate its usage with an example.

Consider a Struts banking application with a default module (with top level pages) and another module named *loanModule*. The JSPs of the loan module are present in a directory called *loanModule* and its action mappings are defined in *struts-config-loan.xml*.

- The top-level page defined in the default application module provides hyperlink to navigate to the loan module as shown below. This hyperlink indicates points to a global-forward named `goto-loanModule` in the default *struts-config.xml*.

```
<html:link forward="goto-loanModule">
     Go to Loan Module
</html:link>
```

- Add the action mapping for `SwitchAction` to the default *struts-config.xml* as follows:

```
<action path="/switch"
        type="org.apache.struts.actions.SwitchAction"/>
```

- Now, add a global-forward named `goto-loanModule` to the default *struts-config.xml* as follows:

```
<forward name="goto-loanModule"
path="/switch.do?page=/listloans.do&amp;prefix=/loanModule" />
```

This global-forward turn points to an action mapping called `switch.do` and also adds two request parameters. The `switch.do` is the ActionMapping for the `SwitchAction`. The two request parameters – `prefix` and `page` stand for the module and the action mapping within that module. In this case, the module is *loanModule* (identified by the *struts-config-loan.xml*) and the `listloans.do` stands for an action mapping within the *struts-config-loan.xml* – the Struts Config file for Loan module.

- In the *struts-config-loan.xml*, add the action mapping for `listloans.do` as follows:

```
<action     path="/listloans"
            type="mybank.app1.ListLoanAction">
</action>
```

The `ListLoanAction` is a normal Struts Action that decides the next resource to forwards in its `execute()` method. If you don't have additional processing to do, you can use a `ForwardAction` too.

If you want to go from the Loan module to the default module, repeat the same process, by setting the `prefix` attribute to a zero length string.

Roll your own Base Action and Form

You have looked at different types of Actions offered by Struts. Now, let us look at some recommended practices in using Action. When it comes to using Actions, the brute force approach is to extend the actions directly from the `org.apache.struts.action.Action`. But a careful look at your web application will certainly reveal behavior that needs to be centralized. Sooner or later you will discover functionality common to all the actions. While it is impossible to predict the exact purposes of why you might need the base Action, here are some samples:

- You might like to perform logging in Action classes for debugging purposes or otherwise to track the user behavior or for security audit purposes.
- You might want to retrieve the user's profile from application specific database to check if the user has access to your application and act appropriately.

Whatever the purpose, there is always something done always in web applications warranting a parent Action class. Start with a common parent Action class. Let us call it `MybankBaseAction`. Depending on the complexities of the web application, you can further create child classes for specific purposes. For instance, an Action subclass for dealing with form submissions and another for dealing with hyperlink-based navigation is a logical choice if the Action classes handling hyperlink don't need an ActionForm. You might want to filter out some words typed in the form fields.

In conjunction with the base Action, you can also roll a base Form extending the `org.apache.struts.action.ActionForm`. Let us call this class

MybankBaseForm. The base form fits well into the base action strategy. In chapter 2, we introduced the term *View Data Transfer Object* to refer an ActionForm. This isn't without a reason. Data Transfer Object is a Core J2EE pattern name. It is typically used between tiers to exchange data. The ActionForm serves similar purpose in a Struts application and you use to its very best. Typical uses of a base form would be:

- Add attributes to the base form that are needed frequently in the web application. Consider a case when every Action in your web application needs to reference an attribute in the request or session. Instead of adding the code to access this attribute as request.getAttribute("attribName") everywhere, you can set this as an ActionForm attribute and access it in a type-safe manner in the application.
- Retrieving the user's profile from application specific database and then set it as a form attribute on every call to MybankBaseAction's execute() method.

Listing 4.5 shows the MybankBaseAction using the MybankBaseForm. It implemented the execute() method and adds audit logging for entry and exit points. Further down the line, it retrieves the application specific profile for the user. This is helpful if you have a portal with a single sign-on and the user rights and profiles differ from one application to another. Then it casts the ActionForm to MybankBaseForm and assigns its variables with the values of commonly accessed request and session attributes. MybankBaseAction defines three abstract methods – preprocess(), process() and postprocess(). These methods when implemented by the subclasses respectively perform pre-processing, processing and post-processing activities. Their signatures as as follows:

```
protected abstract void preprocess(ActionMapping mapping,
            MybankBaseForm form, HttpServletRequest request,
            HttpServletResponse response) throws Exception;

protected abstract ActionForward process(ActionMapping mapping,
            MybankBaseForm form, HttpServletRequest request,
            HttpServletResponse response) throws Exception;

protected abstract void postprocess(ActionMapping mapping,
            MybankBaseForm form, HttpServletRequest request,
            HttpServletResponse response) throws Exception;
```

Pre-processing activities involve validating the form (Validations requiring access to backend resources to are typically performed in the Action instead of ActionForm, where the validations are limited to trivial checking and inter-depdendent fields), checking for duplicate form submissions (In the next section you will look at the facilities in Struts to handle duplicate form submissions. In Chapter 10 we will develop the generalized strategy for duplicate form handling – not just repeating *synchronizer token* in the Action classes.), checking if the action (page) was invoked in the right order (if a strict wizard like behavior is desired) etc.

Processing activities are the meat of the application and do not need any more explanation. Validation errors can be discovered in this stage too.

Post-processing activities may involve setting the sync token (for checking duplicate form submission), cleaning up unnecessary objects from request and session scopes and so on. The bottom line is that all applications have recurring tasks that need to be refactored into the parent class and hence a base Form and Action are a must for every serious application. In Chapter we will add a lot of functionality into the base Action giving you that many reasons to create the base Action.

Listing 4.5 The Base Action class

```
public class MybankBaseAction extends Action {
   public ActionForward execute(ActionMapping mapping,
               ActionForm form, HttpServletRequest request,
               HttpServletResponse response) throws Exception
   {
      // Add centralized logging here (Entry point audit)

      // Check here if the user has rights to this application
      // or retrieve app specific profile for the user

      MybankBaseForm myForm = (MybankBaseForm) form;
      // Set common MybankBaseForm variables using request &
      // session attributes for type-safe access in subclasses.
      // For e.g. myForm.setUserProfile(
      //                request.getAttribute("profile"));

      preprocess(mapping, myForm, request, response);
      ActionForward forward =
          process(mapping, myForm, request, response);
      postprocess(mapping, myForm, request, response);

      // More code to be added later.

      // Add centralized logging here (Exit point audit)

      return forward;
   }
}
```

Handling Duplicate Form Submissions

Duplicate form submissions can occur in many ways

- Using Refresh button
- Using the browser back button to traverse back and resubmit form
- Using Browser history feature and re-submit form.
- Malicious submissions to adversely impact the server or personal gains
- Clicking more than once on a transaction that take longer than usual

Duplicate form submissions are acceptable in some cases. Such scenarios are called *idempotent transitions.* When multiple submissions of data are not critical enough to impact the behavior of the application, duplicate form submissions do not pose a threat.

They can cause a lot of grief if for instance you are buying from an online store and accidentally press refresh on the page where you are charged. If storefront is smart enough, it will recognize duplicate submissions and handle it graciously without charging you twice.

Why is the form submitted again after all, when the refresh button is pressed? The answer lies in the URL seen in the URL bar of your browser after the form submission. Consider a form as: `<form name=CustomerForm" action="/App1/submitCustomerForm.do">`. The above form is submitted with the URL `/App1/submitCustomerForm.do` and the same URL is shown in the URL bar. On the back end, Struts selects the action mapping associated with submitCustomerForm and executes the action instance. When you press refresh, the same URL is submitted and the same action instance is executed again. The easy solution to this problem is to use HTTP redirect after the form submission. Suppose that the CustomerForm submission results in showing a page called *Success.jsp*. When HTTP redirect is used, the URL in the URL bar becomes `/App1/Success.jsp` instead of `/App1/submitCustomerForm.do`. When the page refreshed, it is the *Success.jsp* that is loaded again instead of `/App1/submitCustomerForm.do`. Hence the form is not submitted again. To use the HTTP redirect feature, the forward is set as follows:

```
<forward name="success" path="/Success.jsp" redirect="true" />
```

However there is one catch. With the above setting, the actual JSP name is shown in the URL. Whenever the JSP name appears in the URL bar, it is a candidate for ForwardAction. Hence change the above forward to be as follows:

```
<forward name="success" path="/GotoSuccess.do" redirect="true" />
```

where *GotoSuccess.do* is another action mapping using ForwardAction as follows:

```
<action path="/GotoSuccess"
        type="org.apache.struts.actions.ForwardAction"
        parameter="/Success.jsp"
        validate="false" />
```

Now, you have now addressed the duplicate submission due to accidental refreshing by the customer. It does not prevent you from intentionally going back in the browser history and submitting the form again. Malicious users might attempt this if the form submissions benefit them or adversely impact the server. Struts provides you with the next level of defense: Synchronizer Token.

The `Action` class has a method called `saveToken()` whose logic is as follows:

```
HttpSession session = request.getSession();
String token = generateToken(request);
if (token != null) {
  session.setAttribute(Globals.TRANSACTION_TOKEN_KEY, token);
}
```

The method generates a random token using session id, current time and a MessageDigest and stores in the session with the key Globals.TRANSACTION_TOKEN_KEY. The value of this field is `org.apache.struts.taglib.html.TOKEN`.

The Action class that renders the form invokes the `saveToken()` method to create a session attribute with the above name. In the JSP, the token is used as a hidden field in the form as follows:

```
<html:hidden name="org.apache.struts.taglib.html.TOKEN" />
```

The `<html:hidden>` tag looks for a bean named `org.apache.struts.taglib.html.TOKEN` in different scopes and renders its value as the `value` attribute of the `<input>` element.

When the client submits the form, the hidden field is also submitted (It is not set as a property on the ActionForm, since it does not belong there.). In the Action that handles the form submission (which most likely is different from the Action that rendered the form), compare the token in the form submission with the token in the session by using the `isTokenValid()` method. The method compares the two tokens and returns a true if both are same. Be sure to pass `reset="true"` in the `isTokenValid()` method to clear the token from session after comparison. If the two tokens are equal, the form was submitted for the first time. However, if the two tokens do not match or if there is no token in the session, then it is a duplicate submission and handle it in the manner acceptable to your users.

Although the above approach is good, it requires you as a application developer to add the token checking method pair – `saveToken()` and `isTokenValid()` in methods rendering and submitting the sensitive forms respectively. Since the two tasks are generally performed by two different Actions, you have to identify the pairs and add them manually. In chapter 10, we will look at an approach to declaratively turn on the synchronizer token.

You can use the same approach for sensitive hyperlink navigations. Just set the tranaction attribute in `<html:link>` to true and use the same logic in the Action classes to track the duplicate hyperlink navigations.

The `reset` argument of the `isTokenValid()` is useful for multi-page form scenario. Consider a form that spans across multiple pages. The form is submitted every time the user traverses from one page to another. You definitely want to validate token on every page submission. However you also want to allow the user to traverse back and forth using the browser back button until the point of final submission. If the token is reset on every page submission, the possibility of back and forth traversal using the browser button is ruled out. The solution is not disabling back button (using JavaScript hacks) but to handle the token intelligently. This is where the `reset` argument is useful. The token is initially set before showing the first page of the form. The `reset` argument is false for all the `isTokenValid()` invocations except in the Action for the last page. The last page uses a true value for the `reset` argument and hence the token is reset in the `isTokenValid()` method. From this point onwards you cannot use back button to traverse to the earlier form pages and successfully submit the form.

What goes into Action (and what doesn't)

Don't even think twice – Action classes should contain only the presentation logic. If it is business logic it does not belong here. What qualifies as presentation logic? The following do – analyzing request parameters and creating data transfer objects (for server side processing), invoking business logic (preferably through business delegates), creating view-models – the model JavaBeans for the JSPs, selecting the next view and converting exceptions into appropriate action errors. That's probably it.

The common mistake while coding the Action is stuffing the `execute()` with a lot of things that don't belong there. By the time it is noticed, the `execute()` method has intermingled request handling and business logic beyond the point of separation without considerable effort. The separation is tough because, when there is no architectural separation, the `HttpServletRequest` and `HttpSession` attributes will be used all over the place and hence the code cannot be moved enmasse to the server side to "*extract a class*". The first resolution you have to make for a cleaner and better design is to avoid this temptation.

A preferred way of splitting the code in Action's `execute()` method (or rather `MybankBaseAction`'s `process()` method is by layering. The functionality in `process()` method can be divided into three distinctive steps.

1. User Action Identification
2. Transfer Object Assembly
3. Business Logic invocation using Business Delegates

The `postprocess()` method is suitable for forwarding the user to the chosen view based on the output from business tier. Let us start looking in detail at the above three steps in `process()`.

User Action Identification: The first step in `process()` is to check what action the user performed. You don't have to do this if DispatchAction or LookupDispatchAction is used. The framework itself calls the appropriate method.

```
if (user pressed save button) {
        //Do something
} else if (user pressed delete button) {
        //Do something else
}
```

Transfer Object Assembly: The next step is creating serializable data transfer objects (DTO) that are independent of the HttpServletRequest and HttpServletResponse (and the entire javax.servlet.http package). This involves copying the ActionForm attributes into a regular serializable JavaBeans. The formal term used to describe this copying process is Transfer Object Assembly. The class that assembles the transfer object is called Transfer Object Assembler. Every tier uses object assemblers when transferring objects across the tier boundary. In general, the object assemblers used to send data from business tier to presentation tier have some intelligence. However the object assemblers used to send data from presentation tier to business tier are straightforward. They are monotonous and dumb (It better be dumb. Otherwise you are coding business logic here). You can take advantage of their straightforward nature and easily develop a framework using Java Reflection API to perform the object assembly. The framework thus developed takes the ActionForm-to-DTO mapping information in a XML file and creates the DTOs.

To make life a bit easier, you can offload some of the conversions to the `BeanUtils` class in Commons BeanUtils. This jar is packaged along with Struts. You can use the `BeanUtils.copyProperties(dest, orig)` method to copy the properties with same names between the form bean and the DTO. It also does the required data type conversions in the process.

Business Logic Invocation: The DTOs thus created are transferred to the business tier as arguments while invoking the busiess logic methods. Consider how a Loan Session EJB containing the business logic for loan management is invoked using the standard Service Locator pattern. Service Locator is a core J2EE pattern that is used widely to locate the business service – in this case used to locate the EJB.

```
LoanMgmt loanmgmt = (LoanMgmt)
            ServiceLocator.getInstance().lookup("LoanMgmtEJB");
```

The above method call can throw `RemoteException`, `CreateException`. If the same business service is implemented using CORBA, a different Exception might be thrown. At times you will certainly have a lethal combination of EJB and mainframe serving as the business tier. Whatever be the case, you should isolate the web tier from these dependencies that are a direct result of the choice of implementation for the business logic tier. This is exactly where the ***Business Delegate*** comes in.

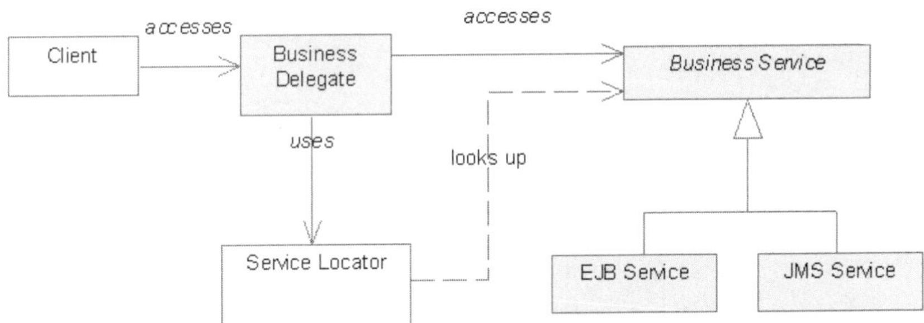

Figure 4.3 Business Delegate.

The *Business Delegate* is another Core J2EE Pattern and decouples the web tier from dependencies on the choice of business logic implementation. Typically business delegate is a class with implementation for all the business methods. Figure 4.3 shows the Business Delegate class. The client invokes the methods on business delegate. The delegate, true to its name delegates the client calls to the actual implementation. It uses the ServiceLocator to lookup the Service, invoke methods on it and convert the implementation exceptions into application exceptions thus reducing coupling.

When to use Action chaining (and when not to)

The process of forwarding to another action mapping from an action is called Action Mapping. Let's say that the `execute()` method from an Action forwards to an ActionForward called `pageB`. Assume that the forward is as follows:

```
<forward name="pageB" path="/pageBAction.do" />
```

The forward itself points to another action mapping called `pageBAction`. Accordingly the Action instance associated with `pageBAction` is invoked. This can continue until an actual JSP is shown to the user.

There are scenarios where the action chaining is a good idea. Consider the example used earlier in the chapter: A page shows a list of loans with option to delete loans one at a time. After deletion, the same loan list is shown again. If the user is forwarded directly to the List JSP after deletion, then the task of creating the loan list is left to the JSP. That is a bad design. Action chaining saves the day here. In the Action for the delete, just forward to the *listLoan.do* after a successful deletion. The Action corresponding to *listLoan.do* then creates the List of Loans to display.

Using the action mapping of self as the `input` attribute is a preferred than using a JSP name. This is a special case of action chaining and comes handy when a lot or preprocessing is needed to show a page, irrespective of whether page is shown for the first time in the normal way or because of validation errors.

Then there are scenarios where action chaining is a bad idea. If the chaining is used for linking several units of business logic one after the other, it is better to do this in the business tier. If this is one of your goals, then use a session ejb method as a façade to hide the execution of fine-grained business logic snippets as one unit instead of chaining actions. Use the Transfer Object Assembly from the lsat section to create a DTO from the form bean and pass it to the business tier. Also, avoid having more than two actions in the chain. If you are having more than two actions in the chain, chances are that you are trying to do business logic by chaining Actions. A strict no-no. Nada.

Actions for complex transitions

Perfectly reusable Actions are not a reality yet. Suppose that you have a common page accessed from two different pages and what the page shows where the page goes next depends on where you came from. You can never create totally reusable Actions and chain them in this scenario.

Wiring the handlers

If the web application you are designing is entirely of the format "where you came from drives what to do and where to go next", then consider using a different approach. Split the current request handling and presenting next page into two different handler classes. Write atomic piece of "do"s as Commands for each. In a separate XML, wire them up together as you would like. The Action class serves very little purpose here other than to figure out which handlers are wired together. In fact a single Action for the whole application suffices. All that this Action does is to look up in the XML for commands to be executed in a pipeline. Similarly if your web application provides personalization features, then you have to create atomic handlers and wire them together dynamically.

State aware Forms

Consider a scenario when you can enter a page from N different places and exit in N different ways. Figure 4.4 shows the scenario. There is a common page. It can be accessed from Page1 and Page2. After executing the common action in common page, the user is forwarded to Page3 and Page4 respectively on success. On pressing Cancel, Page1 and Page2 are shown respectively.

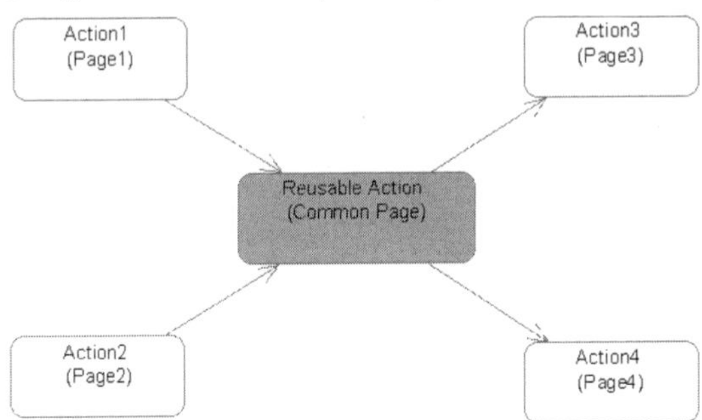

Figure 4.4 Complex Page transition example.

An easy way to achieve this is to track where the user came from in session and then accordingly act in the common action. This however makes the common action less reusable. If a lot of your pages behave in this manner you should consider developing a framework to abstract the complexities of the transition. A simple approach is illustrated here. Start with an interface with two methods as shown below:

```
public interface StateAware {
  public String getPreviousState()
  public String getNextState()
}
```

The ActionForms involved in the complex transitions implement this interface. Consider that ActionForm1 is associated with Page1. The ActionForm1 implements the StateAware interface. The getPreviousState() returns the forward for Page1 and the getNextState() returns the forward for Page3. The Common Action now becomes really reusable.

```
public class CommonAction extends Action {
   public ActionForward execute(ActionMapping mapping,
              ActionForm form, HttpServletRequest request,
              HttpServletResponse response) throws Exception {
       StateAware sw = (StateAware) form;
       if (isCancelled(request)) {
         return mapping.findForward(sw.getpreviousState());
       }
       //do common action here

       //success
       return mapping.findForward(sw.getNextState());
   }
}
```

Refer to http://www.livinglogic.de/Struts/ for more about Struts based workflow approach to solve similar problems.

For multi page forms, use multiple Action classes; one Action per page submission. Multi-page forms generally have buttons with same names: Prev, Next etc. This will result in confusion when forwarding to appropriate page if a single Action class is used to handle buttons with the same names in multiple pages.

Managing struts-config.xml

When the development begins, the struts-config.xml is always small and manageable. But as time passes and features are added, the file continues to grow to become a monster. Splitting the application into modules definitely helps, but modules can be relatively large too. There are better ways to mange the *struts-config.xml* than simply editing by hand or even an XML editor. Some of the popular tools to manage *struts-config.xml* are described below.

Struts-GUI

Struts-GUI is a Visio Stencil from Alien Factory (http://www.alienfactory.co.uk/strutsgui/). It lets you visually edit the *struts config.xml* as a Visio diagram and generate the xml file from it. One of the biggest challenges in maintaining the *struts-config.xml* is understanding the flow and tracking down what is going on. With Struts-GUI, you can follow the visually trace the actions, their forwards and the web pages they lead to. You can even trace action chaining. You can add documentation in the Visio diagram reducing the maintenance hurdle even further. Struts-GUI is a commercial tool.

Struts Console

Struts Console is a Swing based editor to manage the struts-config.xml from James Holmes (http://www.jamesholmes.com/struts/console/). It is not visually driven as Struts GUI, but very intuitive. It has tree like navigation to traverse the individual elements. It is much more flexible than Struts GUI in that it can be used to maintain customized *struts-config.xml* (More about Struts customization in Chapter 10). Wizards and drop downs are provided to add inidividual elements, thus eliminating the chances of typo.

XDoclet

XDoclet based management of struts-config.xml is a entirely different concept. The two tools cited earlier are based on maintaining the *struts-config.xml*, while in XDoclet approach, there is no struts-config.xml at all! All the requisite information linked to the form-bean, action and action-mapping are specified in the Action and Form classes using special XDoclet tags. During build time the struts-config.xml is generated. XDoclet is project on sourceforge that started off with auto-generating home interface, remote interface, *ejb-jar.xml* from special tags in the EJB implementation class. It was a good idea with EJBs since the EJB implementation class would drive everything else - home, remote and the *ejb-jar.xml*. With *struts-config.xml*, none of the individual classes drive the flow in entirety. Everything works always in relation to another. You always want to track what is going on, how various pieces interact together and how the flow works. Providing this information via piecemeal approach in different files using XDoclet tags defeats the purpose. Hence our advice is not to use the XDoclet approach for auto-generating *struts-config.xml*.

Guidelines for Struts Application Development

Struts application development in enterprise applications requires desicipline. We are not referring to any particular methodology; just some guidelines for Struts based application development for enterprise applications. In this section a step-by-step approach for Struts application development cycle is provided.

1. First design your flow at a usecase level on a whiteboard. A JAD session with

business expert, page author and developer is recommended. JAD stands for Joint Application development. Judging by its name, you might think that this technique only applies to developing software, but that's not the case. The JAD technique can be applied to a wide variety of areas where consensus is needed.

2. Decide how many forms are involved in the flow. Which comes when and so on. This will tell you which form should be in request and session scope. (If possible, try to maintain as many forms in request scope).
3. Forms in a web application have aspects related to it – Creating and populating a form and setting in the right scope before display and handling the submitted form. Decide when each of this would happen.
4. The JAD session will give following inputs:
   - Page author knows which form to create and navigation using DynaActionForm (Refer to Chapter 5 for more on DynaActionForm) and navigation using `ForwardAction` with `<html:link>`
   - Application developer knows what inputs are availble for the business logic invocation methods (Session EJB methods)
5. Application developer designs the business logic for each page (not the Action class) and unit tests them and page author develops and formats the pages. Both tasks can occur in parallel.
6. Application developer creates Form and Action using the DynaActionForm and updates the *struts-config.xml* and invokes the already tested business logic from Action classes.
7. Page author and developer integrate the pieces and unit test them with StrutsTestCase (http://strutstestcase.sourceforge.net/).

Summary

Make the best use of the built-in Actions. Review the systems you build and see how you can use `ForwardAction` to stick to MVC, how to use `DispatchAction` and `LookupDispatchAction` to simplify things and perhaps even internationalize your application. Split your application into modules and create separate struts config files. Smaller files are easier to comprehend and manage. Doing so will benefit you in the long run.

Chapter 5

Form Validation

> ***In this chapter:***
>
> 1. *You will learn how to use Commons Validator with Struts via ValidatorForm and ValidatorActionForm*
> 2. *You will learn about DynaActionForm and DynaActionValidatorForm*

Validation is a beast that needs to be addressed at various levels using different strategies for different complexity levels in the validation itself.

1. It is commonly accepted principle that the user input validation should happen as close to the presentation tier as possible. If there are only a bunch of HTML forms with trivial checks and the validation is limited to the UI, you can afford to implement validations using JavaScript.
2. Getting too close with JavaScript is one extreme and is not pragmatic in everyday projects. On the other hand, postponing the validation until it manifests as a business logic exception, runtime exception or a database exception is unacceptable too. Another option is to programmatically validate the HTML Form data using helper classes in the web tier or code the validation right in the `validate()` method of the ActionForm itself – which is what we did in Chapter 3.
3. The third option is to externalize the validation into a XML file that confirms to the Commons Validator syntax and integrate it into Struts. This approach works very well for trivial checks, which is a case in approximately 50% of the projects. Examples of trivial checks are: Null Checks - Checking if a field is null, Number Check – checking if the field value is numeric or not, Range Check – checking if a numeric values lies within a range. These validations depend just on the fields being validated and nothing else.

Validator is a part of the Jakarta Commons project and depends on the following Commons Projects - *BeanUtils*, *Logging*, *Collections*, *Digester* and also on Jakarta ORO library. All of these are shipped with the Struts 1.1. You can find them in the lib directory of the Struts distribution.

Struts is bundled with Commons Validator 1.0. Commons Validator 1.1.1 has support for validating interdependent fields. It can be downloaded from the Jakarta Commons website and used instead of the validator bundled with Struts.

Using Commons Validator with Struts

The interoperation of Commons Validator and Struts is like a jigsaw puzzle with several pieces. It is not possible to explain one piece in entirety and move on to the next since they are all interconnected. Hence our approach is to explain part of a puzzle before moving on to the next. And then several half-baked pieces are joined together. You might have read through this section twice to get a clear picture.

The twin XML files

In Struts, the XML based validations are located in two files – *validation-rules.xml* and *validation.xml*. The *validation-rules.xml* file contains the global set of rules that are ready to use (Henceforth referred to as global rules file). It is shipped along with the Struts distribution in the lib directory. The second file – *validation.xml* is application specific. It associates the rules from the global rules file with individual fields of your ActionForm. Suppose there is a generic rule named `required` in the global rules file that checks if a field is empty. You can use this rule to check if any field is empty including the `firstName` field in the `CustomerForm` by adding the following declaration in *validation.xml*:

```
<form name="CustomerForm">
    <field property="firstName" depends="required">
    ..
    ..
    </field>
    <field .. ..
    ..
    </field>
   ..
</form>
```

The above xml contains a XML block with a `<form>` element, which stands for an ActionForm named `CustomerForm`. All the rules associations for the `CustomerForm` fields exist inside this `<form>` block. One such validation – the validation for the `firstName` field is also shown in a `<field>` element. The `<field>` has an attribute named depends that lists the set of rules (comma separated) on which the field is dependent upon. In other words, the *validation.xml* is just an association of the actual rules with the application specific forms. The actual rules are defined in the *validation-rules.xml.*

validation-rules.xml – The global rules file

For a while, let us go back to *validation-rules.xml* – the global rules file where all the rules are actually defined. Listing 5.1 shows a sample file. Each `<validator>` element defines one validation rule. The Listing shows a required rule validator. The required rule validator uses a class called `org.apache.struts.validator.FieldChecks`. Where did this come from? Well, that requires some background too.

Listing 5.1 Required rule in validation-rules.xml

```
<form-validation>
  <global>
    <validator name="required"
            classname="org.apache.struts.validator.FieldChecks"
            method="validateRequired"
            methodParams="java.lang.Object,
                org.apache.commons.validator.ValidatorAction,
                org.apache.commons.validator.Field,
                org.apache.struts.action.ActionErrors,
                javax.servlet.http.HttpServletRequest"
            msg="errors.required">
    </validator>
    <validator name="…">
       … …
       … …
    </validator>
    <!- More validators defined here -->
  </global>
</form-validation>
```

The basic validator class in Commons Validator is `org.apache.commons.validator.GenericValidator`. It contains atomic and fine-grained validation routines such as `isBlankOrNull()`, `isFloat()`, `isInRange()` etc. Struts provides the `FieldChecks` that uses the `GenericValidator` but has coarse grained methods such as `validateRequired()`, `validateDate()`, `validateCreditCard()` etc. Each of these methods accept four arguments of type

```
java.lang.Object,
org.apache.commons.validator.ValidatorAction,
org.apache.commons.validator.Field,
```

ActionErrors and HttpServletRequest
in that order. Notice that the same arguments are listed under the methodParams attribute in Listing 5.1.

NOTE: The FieldChecks couples the ActionForm validations to the Struts framework by adding dependency on Struts specific classes in the XML, but makes it easy to use the Commons Validator with Struts.

With this background info, the required validator in Listing 5.1 translates into plain English as: "The rule named "*required*" is defined in method validateRequired within a class named FieldChecks that accepts the above listed four arguments in that order. On error, an error message identified by the key errors.required is displayed. The errors.required is a key to the Resource Bundle". Quite a mouthful indeed!

The next step is to add the message for errors.required to the Resource Bundle. The key-value pair added is: errors.required={0} is required. By default, the rules in global rules file use the following keys for the error messages - errors.required, errors.minlength, errors.maxlength, errors.date and so on. To use different error keys, make appropriate changes in *validation-rules.xml.*

A rule in the global rules file can itself depend on another rule. For example, consider the minlength rule. It checks if a field is less than a specified length. However it doesn't make sense to check the length of an empty field is less than a specified length. In other words, minlength rule depends on required rule. If the required rule fails, the minlength rule is not executed. This depends relationship among rules is shown below.

```
<validator name="minlength"
    classname="org.apache.struts.validator.FieldChecks"
    method="validateMinLength"
    methodParams="java.lang.Object,
      org.apache.commons.validator.ValidatorAction,
      org.apache.commons.validator.Field,
      org.apache.struts.action.ActionErrors,
      javax.servlet.http.HttpServletRequest"
      depends="required"
      msg="errors.minlength">
</validator>
```

validation.xml – The application specific rules file

Now, let us get back to the *validation.xml.* A sample is shown in Listing 5.2. The xml consists of a <formset> block with multiple <form> blocks, one for each form.

Listing 5.2 Application specific validations for CustomerForm

```
<form-validation>
  <formset>
    <form name="CustomerForm">
      <field property="firstName"
             depends="required,minlength ">
        <arg0 key="customerform.firstname"/>
        <arg1 name="len" key="1" resource="false"/>
      </field>
    </form>
  </formset>
</form-validation>
```

In Listing 5.2, the topmost xml block is `<form-validation>`. It contains a single `<formset>` element, which in turn can contain a collection of `<form>`s. Each `<form>` corresponds to the Struts Form. The `<form>` contains a set of `<field>`s to be validated. The `firstName` field depends on two rules – `required` and `minLength`. The `required` and `minLength` are defined in the *validation-rules.xml.*

Then comes the `arg0` and `arg1`. The `<field>` element accepts up to four args – `arg0`, `arg1`, `arg2` and `arg3`. These *argN*s are the keys for replacement values in `ActionError`. Sure Sounds confusing. Here is an example to make things clear. Assume that the `required` rule has failed. An `ActionError` with key `errors.required` needs to be created. The error message for this key is defined in the resource bundle as "`{0} is required`". This message needs a literal value to replace `{0}`. That replacement value itself is obtained by first looking up the resource bundle with key attribute of `<arg0>` element. In Listing 5.2, the key attribute of `<arg0>` is `customer.firstname`. The key is used to lookup the resource bundle and obtain the replacement value. Suppose that the resource bundle defines these messages.

```
customer.firstname=First Name
errors.required={0} is required
```

Then, the replacement value for `{0}` is *First Name*. This value is used to replace `{0}` and the resulting error message is *First Name is required.* Notice that the Resource bundle is looked up twice – once using the `arg0` key and then during the rendering of the `ActionError` itself.

You might be wondering why `arg1` is needed. The answer is when the `minlength` rule fails; it looks for an error message with a predefined key called `errors.minlength`. The `errors.minlength` requires two replacement values – `arg0` and `arg1`. `arg0` was also used by the `errors.required` key. The `errors.minlength` needs `arg1` in addition to `arg0`. I can hear you are saying – "All that is fine. But how will I know what predefined error keys should be added to the resource bundle". It is simple actually. Just open the *validation-rules.xml* and you will find all the error message keys are provided. They are:

```
errors.required={0} is required.
errors.minlength={0} can not be less than {1} characters.
errors.maxlength={0} can not be greater than {1} characters.
errors.invalid={0} is invalid.
errors.byte={0} must be a byte.
errors.short={0} must be a short.
errors.integer={0} must be an integer.
errors.long={0} must be a long.
errors.float={0} must be a float.
errors.double={0} must be a double.
errors.date={0} is not a date.
errors.range={0} is not in the range {1} through {2}.
errors.creditcard={0} is an invalid credit card number.
errors.email={0} is an invalid e-mail address.
```

As you can see, every error message key needs `arg0`. The `errors.minlength`, `errors.maxlength` and `errors.range` need `arg1`. In addition, the `errors.range` also needs `arg2`.

In Listing 5.2, the `arg1` has an attribute called `resource` and it set to `false`. The `resource="false"` implies that there is no need to lookup the message resource bundle for `arg1` (as was done with `arg0` key – `customerform.firstname`).

More validation.xml features

Let us investigate some more interesting validator features. Listing 5.3 shows the same `CustomerForm` validation rules with some additions and modifications. Those are highlighted in bold.

The first addition is the `<global>` block to `<form-validation>`. The `<global>` can hold as many `<constant>`s. A `<constant>` is much like a Java constant. Declare it once and use wherever needed. In this case, a constant called `nameMask` is declared and a regular expression `^[A-Za-z]*$` is assigned to it. This regular expression is interpreted as: "The field can have any number of characters as long as each of them is between A-Z and a-z". This constant is used to define the `mask` rule for `CustomerForm` in two steps as follows:

1. First, a variable `<var>` called `mask` is created and the value of `nameMask` is assigned to it. This is done by setting the `<var-value>` to be `${nameMask}`. [Any variable within the `${` and `}` blocks is evaluated. You will find the same convention in JSTL too.] The `<var>` scope is limited to the `<field>` where it

is declared.

2. Next, a rule called `mask` is added to the `CustomerForm`'s **depends** attribute. The `mask` rule is defined in the *validation-rules.xml*. It checks if the current field value confirms to the regular expression in a predefined variable called `mask` (This is the reason why we created a variable called `mask` in the `firstName` `<field>` and assigned it the `nameMask` value. Doing so, lets us reuse the `nameMask` expression for all the forms in *validation.xml* if necessary and at the same time satisfy the constraint imposed by the `mask` rule that the regular expression is always available in a `<var>` called `mask`.

Listing 5.3 Application specific validations for CustomerForm

```
<form-validation>
  <global>
    <constant>
      <constant-name>nameMask</constant-name>
      <constant-value>^[A-Za-z]*$</constant-value>
    </constant>
  </global>
  <formset>
    <form name="CustomerForm">
      <field property="firstName"
             depends="required,minlength,mask">
        <arg0 key="customerform.firstname"/>
        <arg1 name="len"  key="${var:minlen}"
                          resource="false"/>
         <var>
           <var-name>minlen</var-name>
           <var-value>1</var-value>
         </var>
         <var>
           <var-name>mask</var-name>
           <var-value>${nameMask}</var-value>
         </var>
      </field>
    </form>
  </formset>
</form-validation>
```

The second new feature in Listing 5.3 is the use of variable for `arg1`. `arg1` as you know, represents the minimum length of the first name. In Listing 5.2, the `arg1` key was hard coded. A bit of flexibility is added this time round by declaring it as a field scoped variable and then accessing it through the shell syntax `${..}`.

Using the ValidationForm

There is one last piece pending in the puzzle. How does the validation failure become `ActionError` and get displayed to the user? We will answer it right away. Struts has a class called `ValidatorForm` in `org.apache.struts.validator` package. This is a subclass of `ActionForm` and implements the `validate()` method. The `validate()` method invokes the Commons Validator, executes the rules using the two xml files and generates `ActionErrors` using the Message Resources defined in the *struts-config.xml*. All you have to do is extend your form from `ValidatorForm` and write your rules in XML. The framework does the rest. More details on the validator are covered later in this chapter. For now, let us see how the Validator is configured.

Configuring the Validator

Starting from 1.1, Struts provides a facility to integrate third party utilities seamlessly through what is called as a *PlugIn*. A *PlugIn* is simply a configuration wrapper for a module-specific resource or service that needs to be notified about application startup and application shutdown events (through the methods `init` and `destroy`). A *PlugIn* is a class that implements `org.apache.struts.action.PlugIn` interface. This interface defines two methods:

```
public void init(ActionServlet servlet, ModuleConfig config)
public void destroy()
```

You can respectively implement logic to initialize and destroy custom objects in these methods. PlugIns are configured in the *struts-config.xml* file, without the need to subclass `ActionServlet` simply to perform application lifecycle activities. For instance the following XML snippet (from the *struts-config.xml*) configures the validator plugin:

```
<plug-in className="org.apache.struts.validator.ValidatorPlugIn">
  <set-property property="pathnames"
                value="/WEB-INF/validator-rules.xml,
                       /WEB-INF/validation.xml"/>
</plug-in>
```

The `ValidatorPlugIn` is a class that implements the `PlugIn` interface. It has an attribute called `pathnames`. The two input rule XML file names are specified using this attribute. As you know already, Struts reads the *struts-config.xml* file during initialization – during which it also reads the Validator plugin and accordingly initializes it. Consequently the rules are loaded and available to the `ValidatorForm` class when the time comes to execute the `validate()` method.

Steps to use Commons Validator in Struts

Now, let us summarize the steps involved in using Commons Validator with Struts. They are:

1. Create the application specific ActionForm by extending the ValidatorForm
2. Add the corresponding <form> element with <field> sub-element for every form field that needs validation.
3. List the rules to execute in the <field>'s depends attribute.
4. For every rule, add the error message with predefined name to the message bundle.
5. For every rule, supply the argNs either as inline keys or keys to the resource bundle.
6. If the rules in validation-rules.xml do not meet your needs, add new rules and follow the steps above for the new rules. Be sure to have the classes executing the rules are available in the appropriate class path.

DynaActionForm – The Dynamic ActionForm

Struts 1.0 mandated that every HTML form in the JSPs have an associated ActionForm. Struts 1.1 changed all that with the introduction of `DynaActionForm` – dynamic ActionForm as the name suggests. `DynaActionForm` is defined in the *struts-config.xml* as a form-bean. A sample `DynaActionForm` is shown in Listing 5.4.

Listing 5.4 Sample DynaActionForm

```
<form-bean  name="CustomerForm"
            type="org.apache.struts.action.DynaActionForm">

    <form-property name="firstName" type="java.lang.String "/>
    <form-property  name="lastName" type="java.lang.String
                                              initial="Doe"/>
</form-bean>
```

There are two major differences between a regular `ActionForm` and a `DynaActionForm`.

1. For a `DynaActionForm`, the type attribute of the form-bean is always `org.apache.struts.action.DynaActionForm`.
2. A regular ActionForm is developed in Java and declared in the *struts-config.xml*. The JavaBeans properties of a regular ActionForm are created by first defining

the instance variable and then adding a getter and setter for that instance variable. A DynaActionForm has no associated Java class. Its JavaBeans properties are created by adding the `<form-property>` tag in Struts Config file (and also declaring its Java type). In Listing 5.4, CustomerForm is declared as a DynaActionForm with two JavaBeans properties – firstName and lastName. The *type* attribute of the `<form-property>` is the fully qualified Java class name for that JavaBeans property; it cannot be a primitive. For instance `int` is not allowed. Instead you should use `java.lang.Integer`. You can also initialize the *form-property*, so that the html form shows up with an initial value.

Listing 5.5 CustomerAction – Action Bean for App1

```
public class CustomerAction extends Action {
    public ActionForward execute(ActionMapping mapping,
                                 ActionForm form,
                                 HttpServletRequest request,
                                 HttpServletResponse response)
                                 throws Exception
    {
        if (isCancelled(request)) {
           System.out.println(Cancel Operation Performed");
           return mapping.findForward("mainpage");
        }

        DynaActionForm custForm = (DynaActionForm) form;
        String firstName = (String) custForm.get("firstName");
        String lastName = (String) custForm.get("lastName");
        System.out.println("Customer First name is " +
                                        firstName);
        System.out.println("Customer Last name is " +
                                        lastName);
        ActionForward forward = mapping.findForward("success");
        return forward;
    }
}
```

How about an example of using DynaActionForm? Remember, the Hello World application from Chapter 3. Well, now let us rewrite that example using DynaActionForm. You will be surprised how easy it is.

The first step obviously is to develop the DynaActionForm itself. Listing 5.4 is the DynaActionForm version of the `CustomerForm` from Chapter 3. The

`<form-property>` tags are the equivalent of the JavaBeans properties of the ActionForm.

What about the `validate()` method? In Chapter 3, you were able to code the `validate()` method since you had the `CustomerForm` as a Java class. What about the DynaActionForm? With DynaActionForm, unfortunately this is not possible. Don't be disappointed. You can use the `DynaValidatorForm` (a subclass of `DynaActionForm`) in concert with Validator Plugin. We will cover this topic in the next section.

Rearranging the `execute()` method in `CustomerAction` is the second and the final step in ActionForm to DynaActionForm conversion. Listing 5.5 shows the `CustomerAction`. Compare this with the `CustomerAction` in Chapter 3 (Listing 3.5). Instead of using compile time checked getters and setters, the JavaBeans properties in `DynaActionForm` as accessed just like `HashMap`.

One thing is obvious. The `DynaActionForm` is quick and easy. It is very convenient for rapid prototyping. Imagine a Struts 1.0 world where an ActionForm was absolutely needed to prototype an HTML form in JSP using Struts custom tags. Thing were good until the separation of concern came into picture. In real life projects, different people play different roles. Application developers have the responsibility of developing Java code and page authors would exclusively prototype the page and its navigation using JSP markup tags. Since the Java code being developed is constantly changing, the developer does local builds on his machine. Similarly the page author would certainly like to add or remove fields from the prototype during the page design. Since the HTML forms map to ActionForms, the above scenario implies one of two things.

1. The page author constantly pesters the Java application developer to modify the ActionForm.
2. The page author develops the ActionForm all by himself.

While the former hampers the developer productivity, the latter leads to overlap of responsibilities and headaches. Both options are not ideal. Struts 1.1 has solved this problem by introducing `DynaActionForm`. Although originally designed for developer's ease of use, it has been serving the purpose of role separation in a project very well. One can envision an ideal project development as follows.

A page author can be isolated from the Java application development by having a application server environment available for page design. He develops the JSPs as JSPs using the Struts (and other) custom tags, not just HTML prototypes. He also creates `DynaActionForms` using XML instead of relying on the application developer to create the Java `ActionForms`. In other words, the page author is isolated from the nitty-gritty's of the build, deploy and all that chaos accompanying it – at least in the prototype phase.

The page author designs the page Navigation as plain forwards instead of Form submissions; In other words he uses `<html:link>` to prototype navigation instead of `<html:submit>`s. In case you are wondering why anybody would go this route, here is the answer: In Struts framework, the presentation logic resides in the Action classes. It is highly unlikely that the presentation logic (Action) for the ActionForm will be ready even before the prototype is ready. Hence the page author uses the `<html:link>` and `ForwardAction` to model the navigation. Once the prototype is approved, the application developer works on the presentation logic by developing the Action classes. When doing so, the application developer creates equivalent ActionForms for the existing DynaActionForms, one form at a time. The application developer also replaces the forwards in the JSP with form submissions and adds the glue code in Action classes to handle the form submissions.

Okay, so DynaActionForms are great, why replace them with ActionForms anyway? In my opinion, DynaActionForms are good only in the prototyping stage. Once past that stage, it is always better to have strongly typed ActionForms. Here are some more downsides of using DynaActionForms

1. The DynaActionForm bloats up the Struts config file with the xml based definition. This gets annoying as the Struts Config file grow larger.
2. The DynaActionForm is not strongly typed as the ActionForm. This means there is no compile time checking for the form fields. Detecting them at runtime is painful and makes you go through redeployment.
3. ActionForm can be cleanly organized in packages as against the flat organization in the Struts Config file.
4. ActionForm were designed to act as a Firewall between HTTP and the Action classes, i.e. isolate and encapsulate the HTTP request parameters from direct use in Actions. With DynaActionForm, the property access is no different than using request.getParameter("..").
5. DynaActionForm construction at runtime requires a lot of Java Reflection machinery that can be expensive.
6. Time savings from DynaActionForm is insignificant. It doesn't take long for today's IDEs to generate getters and setters for the ActionForm attributes. (Let us say that you made a silly typo in accessing the DynaActionForm properties in the Action instance. It takes less time to generate the getters and setters in the IDE than fixing your Action code and redeploying your web application)

That said, DynaActionForms have an important role to play in the project lifecycle as described earlier, which they do best and let us limit them to just that. Use them with caution, only when you absolutely need them.

DynaValidatorForm

An application specific form can take advantage of XML based validation by virtue of sub classing the ValidatorForm. The XML based dynamic forms can also avail this feature by specifying the type of the form to be DynaValidatorForm as follows:

```
<form-bean  name="CustomerForm"
            type="org.apache.struts.validator.DynaValidatorForm">

    <form-property name="firstName" type="java.lang.String "/>
    <form-property  name="lastName" type="java.lang.String
                                         initial="Doe"/>

</form-bean>
```

DynaValidatorForm is actually a subclass of DynaActionForm. It implements the validate() method much like the ValidatorForm and invokes the Commons Validator. DynaValidatorForm brings the capability of writing XML based validation rules for dynamic forms too.

Validating multi-page forms

When large amount of data is collected from the user, it is customary to split the form into multiple pages. The pages follow a wizard like fashion. However the ActionForm would still exists as a single Java class. Moreover at any point, the data validation should be limited to only those pages that have been submitted. Fortunately, this feature is already built into the Validator. However it requires some setup from your side. There are two alternatives – the first uses a single action mapping and the second uses multiple action mappings. The *struts-validator.war* provided with the Struts distribution adopts the first approach, while we recommend the latter.

Both approaches require the use of an optional hidden variable called `page`. Consider an html form split into two JSPs – *PageA.jsp* and *PageB.jsp*. Since both JSPs will have the hidden variable mentioned earlier, it is sent as a request parameter from both form submissions. The hidden variable is assigned the value of 1 in PageA and 2 in PageB. The `ValidatorForm` already has a JavaBeans property named page of type `int`. All validation for any field on a page less than or equal to the current page is performed on the server side. This will of course require that each rule defined for the field in the *validation.xml* should have a page attribute as follows:

```
<form name="CustomerForm">
  <field property="firstName" page="1"
         depends="required">
    <arg0 key="customerform.firstname"/>
```

```
    </field>
    <field property="fieldX" page="2"
           depends="required">
      <arg0 key="customerform.fieldX"/>
    </field>
  </form>
```

With this background, we will first explain the single action mapping approach. The html forms in both pages have the same action - `<html:form action="/submitForm">`.

In the struts config file, set validate=false for the `/submitForm` action mapping and add forwards for each of the pages as follows:

```
<action  path="/submitForm"
         type="mybank.example.CustomerAction"
         name="CustomerForm"
         scope="request"
         validate="false">
  <forward name="success"  path="/Success.jsp"/>
  <forward name="cancel"  path="/Cancelled.jsp"/>
  <forward name="input1"   path="/PageA.jsp"/>
  <forward name="input2"   path="/PageB.jsp"/>
</action>
```

Since validate is set to false, the `execute()` method in Action gets control immediately after the `RequestProcessor` populates the form. You have to now explicitly call the `form.validate()` in the `execute()` method (Since the `CustomerForm` extends from `ValidatorForm`, the `validate()` is already implemented). After that you have to forward to the appropriate page depending on the current page and whether there are ActionErrors in the current page. For instance, if PageA is submitted and there are no ActionErrors, then PageB is displayed to the user. However if there were ActionErrors in PageA, then it is displayed back to the user. The code is shown below.

```
public ActionForward execute(.. ..) throws Exception {
  CustomerForm info = (CustomerForm)form;

  // Was this transaction cancelled?
  if (isCancelled(request)) {
    // Add code here to remove Form Bean from appropriate scope
    return (mapping.findForward("cancel"));
  }

  ActionErrors errors = info.validate(mapping, request);
```

```
  if (errors != null && errors.isEmpty()) {
    if (info.getPage() == 1)
            return mapping.findForward("input2");
    if (info.getPage() == 2){
      //Data collection completed. Invoke Business Logic here
      return mapping.findForward("success");
    }
  } else {
    saveErrors(request, errors);
    return mapping.findForward("input" + info.getPage());
  }
}
```

This approach is counter-intuitive. After all, `validate()` method was supposed to be invoked automatically by the framework, not manually in the `execute()` method. The second approach eliminates the need to manually invoke the `validate()`. In this method, the two forms in two pages have different actions as follows:

Page A Form submission - `<html:form action="/submitPageA">`
Page B Form submission - `<html:form action="/submitPageB">`

Two action mappings are added to the Struts Config file for the above form submissions. Note that both of the action mappings use the same Action class. Moreover there is no need to set `validate=false`. The action mapping for PageA form submission is as follows:

```
<action  path="/submitPageA"
         type="mybank.example.CustomerAction"
         name="CustomerForm"
         scope="request"
         validate="true"
         input="/PageA.jsp">
   <forward name="success"  path="/PageB.jsp"/>
   <forward name="cancel"  path="/Cancelled.jsp"/>
</action>
```

Similarly, the action mapping for PageB form submission is as follows:

```
<action  path="/submitPageB"
         type="mybank.example.CustomerAction"
         name="CustomerForm"
         scope="request"
         validate="true"
         input="/PageB.jsp">
```

```
  <forward name="success"  path="/Success.jsp"/>
  <forward name="cancel"  path="/Cancelled.jsp"/>
</action>
```

Both action mappings define an input value. When the form is validated by the RequestProcessor and there are errors, the `mapping.getInput()` page is shown to the user. Similarly the `mapping.findForward("success")` page is shown when there are no ActionErrors. Any business logic invocation happens only after the PageB data is collected. The code below shows the `execute()` method.

```
public ActionForward execute(.. ..) throws Exception {
  CustomerForm info = (CustomerForm)form;

  // Was this transaction cancelled?
  if (isCancelled(request)) {
    // Add code here to remove Form Bean from appropriate scope
    return (mapping.findForward("cancel"));
  }

  if (info.getPage() == 2) {
    //Data collection completed. Invoke Business Logic here
  }
  return mapping.findForward("success");
}
```

With the second approach, the `execute()` method in Action is simplified. While you may not see much difference between the two `execute()` methods shown earlier, it will be much pronounced as the number of pages increase and the last thing you want is page navigation logic intermingled with business logic invocation.

Validating form hierarchy

There are still two more validation related Form classes – `ValidatorActionForm` and `DynaValidatorActionForm`. A class diagram will resolve some of the confusion arising out of plethora of Form classes. Figure 5.1 shows the relationship between these classes. `ActionForm` and `DynaActionForm` reside at the top of the figure as the root class for two branches. `ValidatorForm` and `DynaValidatorForm` are their immediate siblings. Each of them has a subclass – `ValidatorActionForm` and `DynaValidatorActionForm`. The last two classes deserve some explanation. Suppose that you have a Form and want to reuse it in various scenarios. Each scenario has its own validation. However with the

XML based validation, a set of rules are associated with the form name, not where it is invoked from. Both the `ValidatorActionForm` and `DynaValidatorActionForm` match the action mapping instead of the form name. The name attribute is used to match the action mapping and thus multiple rules can be defined for the same form based on the action mapping.

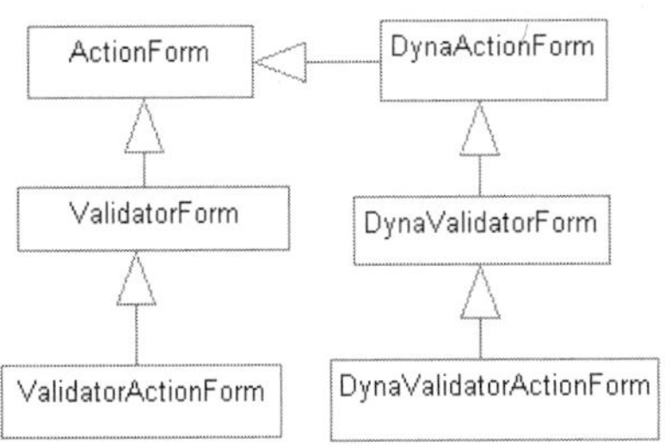

Figure 5.1 Relationship hierarchy among Validating Forms.

Summary

In this chapter, you learnt about using Commons Validator with Struts – this is probably the approach you will adopt in your project too. You also understood the importance of DynaActionForm and its role in projects. You also learnt the best approach to handle validation in multi page forms.

Chapter 6

Struts Tag Libraries

In this chapter:

1. *You will learn about frequently used Html, Bean and Logic tags*
2. *We will customize these Html tags – base, text, checkbox, errors & image*
3. *You will learn about JSTL and Expression Language*
4. *You will understand how to use Struts-EL Tags and which of the Struts tags should be replaced with JSTL and Struts-EL*
5. *You will see how various Struts tags, their derivatives and other related tags can work together to create multi-page lists and editable lists.*

Custom Tags were introduced in JSP 1.1 specification. They are elegant replacement for the scriptlets. Without the custom tags, the "*edge of the system*" where the decisions in presentation logic based on middle tier models would be exposed to the JSP page author as Java scriptlets. While not only causing confusions and headaches to the page author, scriptlets also required the involvement of the Java developer in the page authoring. Custom Tags changed all that. The application developer now provides the custom tags written as a Java class with a pre-defined structure and hierarchy. The page author independently designs the pages and decides on the contents using the custom tags and their formatting using general HTML and CSS.

Struts ships with these Tag libraries – Html, Bean, Logic, Template, Nested, Tiles. We will deal with the first three tag libraries in this chapter. The TLD file for each of these libraries is included in the Struts distribution. For instance, the Html Tags are defined in *struts-html.tld*. The Bean tags are defined in *struts-bean.tld* and so on. These tags are like any other custom tags. You have to include the TLD declarations in the web.xml and also the JSP. For e.g., you have to add the following lines in the *web.xml* to use the Html Tag library:

```
<taglib>
    <taglib-uri>/WEB-INF/struts-html.tld</taglib-uri>
    <taglib-location>/WEB-INF/struts-html.tld</taglib-
location>
</taglib>
```

and the following line in the JSP:

```
<%@ taglib uri="/WEB-INF/struts-html.tld" prefix="html" %>
```

Excellent documentation is available with the Struts distribution for each of the custom tags and their attributes. It will be merely a repetition of going over each of those attributes and tags here. Instead we will gloss over the categories and characteristics of the Struts Tags and more importantly cover tags that need to be customized for use in serious applications.

> Here is how to access the tag documentation in Struts distribution:
> Deploy the *struts-documentation.war* from Struts *webapps* in Tomcat. Use the URL http://localhost:8080/struts-documentation/ to access the documentation in the browser. Click on the link named "*Learning*" on the left hand side. Click on "*User and Developer Guides*" on the resulting page. The page that you see at this point is loaded with information and links including links for Struts tag documentation. The direct link for Struts HTML Tag documentation is: http://localhost:8080/struts-documentation/userGuide/dev_html.html. The direct link for Struts Bean Tag documentation is: http://localhost:8080/struts-documentation/userGuide/dev_bean.html.

Struts HTML Tags

Struts HTML tags are useful for generating HTML markup. The Struts HTML tag library defines tags for generating HTML forms, textboxes, check boxes, drop downs, radio buttons, submit buttons and so on. You have already used some of these in Chapter 3. We will look at other important html tags not covered there.

Modifying the Base Tag

This tag renders the `<base href=…">` html tag pointing to the absolute location of the JSP containing the tag as follows:

```
<base href="http://localhost:8080/App1/abc/CustomerDetail.jsp"/>
```

This can be problematic at times. Assume that the JSP itself is present somewhere down in a hierarchy of directories. Also the images directory will be generally at the top level in a web application (See the WAR structure in Figure 3.3). Since the base href is referring to the absolute location of the JSP, the URL for the images might look like "*../../images/banner.jsp*". Three reasons why this is not a good idea:

1. Referring to a same image with different URLs depending on from which JSP it is called is error prone and creates a lot of confusion.
2. If the JSP is moved from one folder to another (which is not uncommon), every URL in the page should be inspected and changed if needed. Not a great idea.

3. Even though the Servlet specification encourages the idea of bundling the images JavaScript and other static resource along with the WAR, it is not a good idea in practice. It is a norm to deploy the static resources separately so that the web server serves these documents instead of the servlet container.
4. When using frameworks such as Tiles (Chapter 8), there is no concept of a single JSP. There is a single layout that aggregates the JSPs

The solution is to modify the Base Tag itself so that the output is:

```
<base href="http://localhost:8080/App1" />
```

Listing 6.1 MybankBaseTag – Customized BaseTag

```
public class MybankBaseTag extends BaseTag {

   public int doStartTag() throws JspException {
      HttpServletRequest request =
            (HttpServletRequest) pageContext.getRequest();
      String baseTag = renderBaseElement(
        request.getScheme(), request.getServerName(),
        request.getServerPort(),request.getContextPath());

      JspWriter out = pageContext.getOut();
      try {
         out.write(baseTag);
      } catch (IOException e) {
         pageContext.setAttribute(Globals.EXCEPTION_KEY, e,
                   PageContext.REQUEST_SCOPE);
         throw new JspException(e.toString());
      }
      return EVAL_BODY_INCLUDE;
   }
..
}
```

Now, the URL of the image is always a constant no matter which JSP it is used in. Another advantage of this arrangement is that a directory named App1 can be created on the web server to contain the static resources and the images with no impact on the image URLs. With this background let us get started on modifying the `BaseTag`.

Consider a URL http://localhost:8080/App1/cust/CustomerDetail.jsp. This is generated as the output of the `BaseTag`. It can be dissected into:

`request.getScheme()` (*http://*),
`request.getServerName()` (*localhost*),

`request.getServerPort()` (*8080*) and
`request.getRequestURI()` (*App1/customer/CustomerDetails.jsp*).

The desired output for the `BaseTag` is http://localhost:8080/App1. This can be dissected into

`request.getScheme()` (*http://*),
`request.getServerName()` (*localhost*),
`request.getServerPort()` (*8080*) and
`request.getContextPath()` (*App1*).

There you go! This is what we want to output from our version of `BaseTag`. Let us call this `MyBaseTag`. Listing 6.1 shows `doStartTag()` method from `MyBaseTag`.

Form Tag

Another Tag that deserves extra attention is the `FormTag`. You have learnt about the working of this tag in Chapter 2 and used it in Chapter 3. At that point, we looked at only one attribute of this tag – the `action` attribute.

It also has a set of attributes based on JavaScript events. For instance, the `onreset` and `onsubmit` attributes do exactly what their JavaScript equivalents do; they invoke the corresponding JavaScript event handler functions. The JavaScript event based attributes is not limited to just the `FormTag`. In fact all the tags in HTML Tag library have similar features.

Another attribute of interest is the `enctype`. Normally you don't have to set the `enctype`. When you are uploading files however, the value of `enctype` should be set to `multipart/form-data`. More details await you in the section on `FileTag`.

FileTag

`FileTag` lets you select file to upload from the HTML page. When you are uploading files, the value of `enctype` (on the `FormTag`) should be set to `multipart/form-data`. The `FileTag` in its simplest format, generates an output of `<input type="file" name="xyz" value"abc" />`. This results in the rendering of a text field for entering the file name and a Browse button as shown in the figure below.

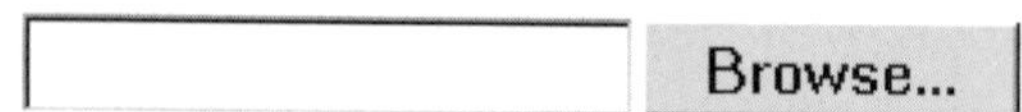

On clicking the browse button a file selection dialog box appears. The selected file is uploaded when the form is submitted. In the JSP, the `FileTag` is used as `<html:file property="uploadFile"/>`. The `uploadFile` is a JavaBeans property in the ActionForm. Struts mandates the type of this property to be `org.apache.struts.upload.FormFile`. `FormFile` is an interface with methods to get the `InputStream` for the uploaded file. For more details refer to the example web application named *struts-upload.war* in the *webapps* directory of wherever you installed Struts.

Smart Checkbox – The state aware checkbox

Consider a HTML form containing a checkbox in a JSP as follows:

```
<html:form action="/submitCustomerForm">
    <html:text property="firstName" />
    <html:checkbox property="agree" />
    <html:submit>Submit</html:submit>
</html:form>
```

In addition to the usual text field, it has a checkbox that Customer checks to indicate he agrees with the terms and conditions. Assume that the associated ActionForm has `validate()` method checking if the `firstName` is not null. If the first name is not present, then the user gets the same page back with the error displayed. The user can then submit the form again by correcting the errors. Further assume that the associated ActionForm is stored in session scope. Now starts the fun.

1. First, submit the form by checking the checkbox but leaving the `firstName` blank. The form submission request looks like this:

   ```
   http://localhost:8080/App1/submitCustomer.do?
                                   firstName=""&agree="true"
   ```

   The ActionForm is created in the session with blank `firstName` and `agree` attribute set to true (Checkbox is mapped to Boolean attributes in ActionForm).
2. Since the `firstName` is blank, the user gets the same page back. Now fill in the `firstName` but uncheck the `agree` checkbox. The form submission request looks like this:

   ```
   http://localhost:8080/App1/submitCustomer.do?firstName="John"
   ```

   Note that the agree request parameter is missing. This is nothing unusual. According to the HTTP specification, if a checkbox is unchecked, then it is not submitted as request parameter. However since the ActionForm is stored in the Session scope, we have landed in a problem. In our case, Struts retrieves the ActionForm from Session and sets the `firstName` to "*John*". Now the ActionForm has the `firstName=John` and `agree=true`, although you intended to set the `agree` to be false.

The Smart Checkbox we are about to present is the solution to this problem. This solution uses JavaScript and it works as expected only if your target audience enables JavaScript in their browser. The solution is as follows:

- Define the ActionForm as usual with the Boolean property for checkbox.

- Define a new class SmartCheckboxTag by extending the CheckboxTag in org.apache.struts.taglib.html package and override the doStartTag(). In the doStartTag(), do the following:
  - Render a checkbox with name "agreeProxy", where agree is the name of the boolean property in ActionForm.
  - Render a hidden field with the name agree.
  - Define an inline JavaScript within the <script> block as follows. Substitute appropriate values into [property] and [formName].

```
<script>
   function handle" + [property] + "Click(obj) {
     if ( obj.checked == true) {
        document.form.[formName]."
                + [property] + ".value = 'true';
     } else {
        document.form.[formName]."
                + [property] + ".value = 'false';
     }
  }
</script>
```

  - Invoke the above JavaScript function for the onclick event of the checkbox.

The crux of this solution is to invoke a JavaScript function on clicking (check or uncheck) the checkbox to appropriately set the value of a hidden field. The hidden field is then mapped to the actual property in ActionForm. If you can ensure that your target audience has JavaScript enabled, this solution works like a charm!

Many might classify this solution as a hack, but the truth is there is no elegant solution for this problem. Where applicable and feasible you can adopt this solution. If you are unsure about your target audience or deploying the application into the public domain, never use this solution. It is impossible to predict the environment and behavior of an Internet user.

Using CSS with Struts HTML Tags

Cascading Style Sheets (CSS) is the mechanism used by page authors to centralize and control the appearance of a HTML page. Some of the uses of CSS are:

- Text formatting, indentation and fonts
- Add background color to text, links and other HTML tags
- Setting table characteristics such as styled borders, widths and cell spacing.

CSS allows the page author to make changes to formatting information in one location and those changes immediately reflect on all pages using that stylesheet thus resulting in application with consistent appearance with the least amount of work – in other words a highly maintainable application.

The developers of Struts tags had this in mind and thus most of the HTML tags support the usage of stylesheet in the form of styleClass and style attributes. The styleClass refers to the CSS stylesheet class to be applied to the HTML element and the style attribute refers to the inline CSS styles in the HTML page. You can use either but styleClass is most frequently used.

Enhancing the error display with customized TextTag

You already know how to validate an ActionForm and display the error messages to the user. This approach works great so long as the forms are small enough and the resulting error display fits into the viewable area without scrolling. If the forms are larger, it is a hassle for the user to scroll down and check for the messages. We address this usability challenge with an error indicator next to the field as shown in the figure below. In addition to the quick visual impact, the error indicator can also provide more information such as displaying a popup box with errors for that field in a JavaScript enabled browser thus enriching the user experience.

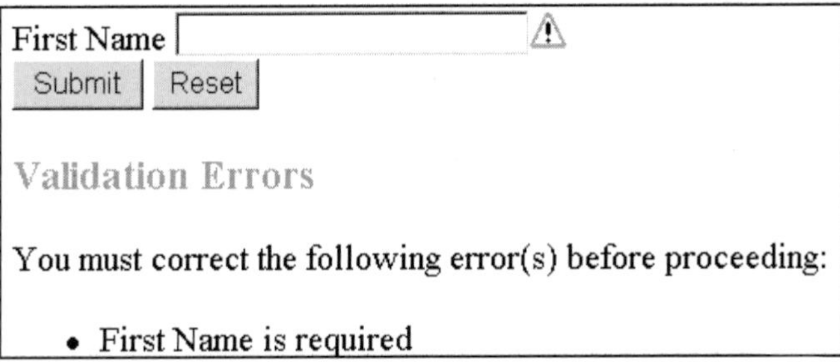

There are many ways to implement this. One simple way is to extend the `TextTag` class and override the `doStartTag()` method. The `doStartTag()` from the Struts `TextTag` generates the `<input type="text" name=".." >`. The subclass of the Struts `TextTag` has to then add an image next to it when there is `ActionError`(s) associated with the input field. Listing 6.2 shows the implementation with the above approach. The new tag called `MyTextTag` is used in the JSP as follows:

```
<mytags:mytext property="…." errorImageKey="img.error.alert" />
```

The `errorImageKey` is the key to get the name of the error image from the resource bundle. In the `doStartTag()` method, a check is performed if the text field has any associated errors. If there are no errors, no extra processing is done. However if there are errors, the `errorImageKey` is used to retrieve the image source and a `<img src="…" >` markup is constructed alongside the text tag.

There are other ways of implementing this feature. One of them is to develop a separate custom tag to generate the error indicator.

Listing 6.2 TextTag with built-in error indicator

```
public class MyTextTag extends TextTag {
    private String errorImageKey;

    public int doStartTag() throws JspException {
        int returnValue = super.doStartTag();

        ActionErrors errors = RequestUtils.getActionErrors(
                                  pageContext, this.property);

        if ((errors != null) && ! errors.isEmpty()) {
            String imageSrc = RequestUtils.message(pageContext,
                                          getBundle(),
                                          getLocale(),
                                          this.errorImageKey);
            if (imageSrc != null) {
                StringBuffer imageResults = new StringBuffer();
                imageResults.append("<img src=\"");
                imageResults.append(imageSrc);
                imageResults.append("\"");

                // Print the image to the output writer
                ResponseUtils.write(pageContext,
                                 imageResults.toString());
            }
        }
        return returnValue;
    }
        ...
        ...
    public void release() {
        super.release();
        errorImageKey = null;
    }
}
```

Further customizations can also be performed to pop up Java Script alerts to show the error, if needed. This requires communication between Java and

JavaScript. Sounds complex right. It is easier than you think! You can achieve this in three steps. All you need is a basic understanding of JavaScript.

First, create a JavaScript function as shown in Listing 6.3. This function simply creates a JavaScript data structure and adds individual ActionError to a JavaScript object called `errorMessageArray`. An array is created for every for form field to hold multiple error messages.

Listing 6.3 JavaScript function to add ActionError into a Java! cript data structure

```
function addActionError(window, formFieldName, errorMessage) {
    if (! window.errorMessageArray)  {
        window.errorMessageArray = new Object();
    }
    var value = window.errorMessageArray[formFieldName];

    if ( typeof(value) == "undefined") {
      window.errorMessageArray[field] = new Array();
      window.errorMessageArray[formFieldName][0] = errorMessage
;
    }
    else {
      var length =
        window.errorMessageArray[formFieldName].length;
       window.errorMessageArray[formFieldName][length] =
                                                errorMessage;
    }
}
```

Second, create your own Errors tag by extending the `ErrorsTag` from Struts. This JavaScript function is invoked repetitively from the `ErrorsTag`'s `doStartTag()` method for every `ActionError` in `ActionErrors`. Listing 6.4 shows the `doStartTag()` method for the `MyErrorsTag`. As usual the method first invokes the `super.doStartTag()` to write the ActionErrors as locale specific error messages to the output stream. It then invokes the JavaScript function `addActionError()` inline with the rest of HTML for every `ActionError`. The JavaScript invocation is made inline by using `<script>` and `</script>` demarcations. At the end of this method, every `ActionError` associated with the form fields is added to the JavaScript data structure (`errorMessageArray`). Any JavaScript code in the page can now access the data structure to do whatever it likes.

Listing 6.4 MyErrorsTag invoking the JavaScript functions

```
public class MyErrorsTag extends ErrorTag {
  public int doStartTag() throws JspException {
    int returnValue = super.doStartTag();

    //Retrieve the ActionErrors
    ActionErrors errors = RequestUtils.getActionErrors(
                         pageContext, Globals.ERROR_KEY);
    StringBuffer results = new StringBuffer();
    results.append("<script>");

    //Retrieve all the form field names having ActionError
    Iterator properties = errors.properties();
    String formFieldName = null;

    while (properties.hasNext()) {
      formFieldName = (String) properties.next();
      if (formFieldName.equals(ActionMessages.GLOBAL_MESSAGE))
      continue;

      //Retrieve all ActionError per form field
      Iterator reports = errors.get(formFieldName);
      String message = null;
      while (reports.hasNext()) {
        ActionError report = (ActionError) reports.next();
        message = RequestUtils.message(pageContext, bundle,
                     locale, report.getKey(),
report.getValues());

        //Invoke the JavaScript function for every ActionError
        results.append("addActionError(window,\"" +
                             formFieldName + "\",\"" +
                             message + "\");\n");
      }
    }
    results.append("</script>");
    ResponseUtils.write(pageContext, results.toString());
    return returnValue;
  }
      ...
    ...
}
```

Finally the error messages in the JavaScript data structure (added by `MyErrorsTag`) have to be displayed when clicking on the error indicator. This can be done with a simple JavaScript function as shown in Listing 6.5. The `displayAlert()` function iterates over the error messages for the given form field. This function has to be invoked on the `onclick` JavaScript event of the error indicator image.

Listing 6.5 JavaScript function to display alert with ActionError messages

```
function displayAlert(window, formFieldName) {
  var length = window.errorMessageArray[formFieldName].length;
  var aggregateErrMsg = "";
  for(var i = 0;  i < length; i++) {
    aggregateErrMsg = aggregateErrMsg +
            window.errorMessageArray[formFieldName][i];
  }
  alert(aggregateErrMsg);
}
```

The recommended way to use ImgTag

The `ImgTag` is used to render a HTML `<img>` element such as follows:

```
<img src="images/main.gif" alt="The Main Image"/>
```

If you are wondering why you need a Struts tag for such a simple HTML tag, consider this. Sometimes, the images actually spell out the actual English word. Users worldwide access your application. You want to localize the images displayed to them. You also want the alt text on your images to be internationalized. How do you do this without adding the big and ugly if-else block in your JSPs? The answer is to use the `ImgTag`. With `ImgTag`, the actual image (`src`) and the alternate text (`alt`) can be picked from the Message Resources. You can easily setup different Resource Bundles for different Locales and there you have it. Your images are internationalized without any extra effort. Even if you are not internationalizing the effort is well worth it. JSPs can remain untouched when the image is changed. The usage of the `ImgTag` is as follows:

```
<html:img srcKey="image.main" altKey="image.main.alttext" />
```

There are many more attributes in `ImgTag` and you can find them in the Struts documentation.

Using Images for Form submissions

All along, you have submitted HTML forms with the grey lackluster buttons. Life requires a bit more color and these days most of the web sites use images for Form submission. The images add aesthetic feeling to the page well. Struts provides <html:image> tag for Image based Form submission. Although the ImageTag belongs to the HTML Tag library, it requires an in-depth treatment and deserves a section by itself. Let us look at the ImageTag and how it fits into the scheme of things. Consider an HtmlTag used in a JSP as follows:

```
<html:image src="images/createButton.gif"
            property="createButton" />
```

This gets translated to:

```
<input type="image"    name="createButton"
       src="images/createButton.gif" />.
```

When the Form is submitted by clicking on the image, the name is added to the X and Y coordinates and sent to the server. In this case, two request parameters createButton.x and createButton.y are sent. Suppose that the HTML form has two or more images each with a different name. How do you capture this information in the ActionForm and convey it to the Action? The answer to this is ImageButtonBean in org.apache.struts.util package.

The ImageButtonBean has five methods – getX(), setX(), getY(), setY() and isSelected(). All you have to do is add JavaBeans property of type ImageButtonBean to the ActionForm (Listing 6.6). For instance, if the JSP has image buttons named and createButton and updateButton, you have to add two ImageButtonBean properties to the ActionForm with the same name. When the createButton image is clicked, two request parameters createButton.x and createButton.y are sent to the server. Struts interprets the dot separated names as nested JavaBeans properties. For example, the property reference:

```
<.. property="address.city"/>
```

is translated into

```
getAddress().getCity()
```

while getting the property. The setters are called for setting the property as follows:

```
getAddress().setCity()
```

For createButton.x and createButton.y, Struts invokes getCreateButton() on the ActionForm and then setX() and setY() on createButton. Since createButton is an ImageButtonBean, its x and y are set to non-null values, when the button is clicked. The `isSelected()` method returns true if at least one of `x` or `y` is non-null.

Listing 6.6 CustomerForm using ImageButtonBean

```
public class CustomerForm extends ActionForm {
   private String firstName;
   ..
   ..
   private ImageButtonBean createButton;
   private ImageButtonBean updateButton;

   public CustomerForm() {
       firstName = "";
       lastName = "";
       createButton = new ImageButtonBean();
       updateButton = new ImageButtonBean();
   }

   ...
   ...
   public ImageButtonBean getCreateButton() {
       return createButton;
   }

   public void setCreateButton(ImageButtonBean imgButton) {
       this.createButton = imgButton;
   }

   public ImageButtonBean getUpdateButton() {
       return updateButton;
   }

   public void setUpdateButton(ImageButtonBean imgButton) {
       this.updateButton = imgButton;
   }
}
```

Listing 6.6 shows the ActionForm with `createButton` and `updateButton`. It is pretty straightforward. In the Action instance, you can find which of the buttons is pressed by using the `isSelected()` method as follows:

```
public ActionForward execute(ActionMapping mapping,
                ActionForm form, HttpServletRequest request,
                HttpServletResponse response) throws Exception
```

```
{
  CustomerForm custForm = (CustomerForm) form;
  if (custForm.getCreateButton().isSelected()) {
    System.out.prinitln("Create Image Button is pressed");
  } else if (custForm.getUpdateButton().isSelected()) {
    System.out.prinitln("Update Image Button is pressed");
  }
}
```

Compare this with the Action using grey buttons. It would look like: `custForm.getCreateButton().equals("Create")`. Obviously, changing the grey button to image button on the JSP is not gone unnoticed in the Action. The Action class has changed accordingly. The ActionForm has changed too. Previously a String held on to the submit button's name. Now an `ImageButtonBean` has taken its place. You might be wondering if it is possible to eliminate this coupling between the Action and the JSP? The good news is that this can be achieved quite easily. Listing 6.7 shows `HtmlButton` that extends the `ImageButtonBean`, but overrides the `isSelected()` method. `ImageButtonBean` has basically taken care of handling the image button in `isSelected()` method. The extra functionality in `HtmlButton` takes care of grey button submission. The attribute called `name` is the name of the grey button submitting the form. The `isSelected()` method now checks if the `name` is not null in addition to invoking the `super.isSelected()`. Now you can use the `HtmlButton` for whatever mode of JSP submission – grey button or image button. The `ActionForm` will use `HtmlButton` in both cases and never change when the JSP changes. Neither does the Action change. Decoupling Nirvana indeed!
The Image button in JSP will look like:

```
<html:image property="createButton"
            src="images/createButton.gif" />
```

If grey button were used in the JSP, it would look like:

```
<html:submit property="createButton.name">
   <bean:message key="button.create.name" />
<html:submit>
```

Notice that the grey button is called "`createButton.name`". The dot separated naming is essential to maintain the ActionForm and Action unchanged. Moreover, the suffix of the property – "`.name`" is fixed since the `HtmlButton` has the JavaBeans property called `name` (Listing 6.7).

Large projects need a simple and systematic way of handling Form submissions and deciding on the back end. Minor innovations like `HtmlButton` go a long way in making your application cleaner and better.

The alt text and the image source for `ImageTag` can also be externalized into the Message Resource Bundle much like the `ImgTag`. As it turns out the names of the attribute for externalizing these are also the same. `<html:image>` has `srcKey` to externalize the name of the image `src` and `altKey` to externalize the alternate text (`alt`). In Chapter 10, we will develop a DispatchAction-like capability for `HtmlButton` by exploiting the Struts customization facility.

Listing 6.7 HtmlButton

```
public class HtmlButton extends ImageButtonBean {
  private String name;

  public String getName() {
    return name;
  }

  public void setName(String aName) {
    this.name = aName;
  }

  public boolean isSelected() {
    boolean returnValue = super.isSelected();
    if (returnValue == false) {
      returnValue = (name != null && name.trim().length() > 0);
    }
    return returnValue;
  }
}
```

In Chapter 4, you looked at the goodies offered by `DispatchAction` and `LookDispatchAction`. In particular with `LookupDispatchAction`, you were able to assign methods in Action instance based on the button names in a locale independent manner. The only pre-requisite was that, all the form submission buttons have the same name. With the `HtmlButton` (or `ImageButtonBean` for that matter), we started with different names for different buttons from the outset. For this reason, `DispatchAction` and `LookupDispatchAction` cannot be used in conjunction with image based form submissions. They can be however used with html links using images.

ImageButton and JavaScript

`ImageButton` is all cool and dandy as long as you don't have to execute JavaScript and support multiple browser versions. Microsoft Internet Explorer 4 (and above) and Netscape 6 (and above) provide support for JavaScript event handlers in the `<input type="image">`. If the JavaScript execution is critical to the application logic, you might want to switch between the image buttons and grey buttons depending on the browser version. This is another instance where `HtmlButton` saves the say. Irrespective of whether the front end uses Image button or grey button, the presentation logic in the ActionForm and Action doesn't change.

Struts Bean Tags

Struts Bean tag library contains tags to access JavaBeans and resource bundles among others. Two frequently used tags are MessageTag (bean:message) and WriteTag (bean:write).

Message Tag and Multiple Resource Bundles

You have already used the message Tag for accessing externalized messages in resource bundles using locale independent keys. In this section, we will go further and investigate the applicability of multiple resource bundles. When the application is small, a single resource bundle suffices. When the application gets larger, the single properties file gets cluttered much like a single struts-config.xml getting cluttered.

> It is advisable to have multiple resource bundles based on the message category from the outset. This saves the pain involved in splitting the single bundle into pieces and updating all the resources accessing it.

The first step in using multiple resource bundles is to declare them in the struts-config.xml first. The semantic for declaring multiple resource bundle is as follows:

```
<message-resources parameter="mybank.example.DefaultMsgResource"
                   null="false"/>
<message-resources parameter="mybank.example.AltMsgResource"
                   null="false" key="bundle.alt" />
<message-resources parameter="mybank.example.ErrorMsgResource"
                   null="false" key="bundle.error" />
```

The above snippet declares three resource bundles identified by a key. The default resource bundle does not have a key. As the key suggests, the *AltMsgResource* contains alternate messages and the *ErrorMsgResource* contains error messages. The message tag accesses the default resource bundle as follows:

```
<bean:message key="msg.key" />
```

The key specified in the `<bean:message>` tag is the key used in the properties file to identify the message.

The non-default resource bundles are accessed by specifying the bundle key as declared in struts-config.xml (key="bundle.alt", key="bundle.error" etc.). For instance, a message tag accesses a message in *AltMsgResource* as follows:

```
<bean:message key="msg.key" bundle="bundle.alt" />
```

Similarly a errors tag access the messages in the non-default bundle by using the bundle attribute as follows:

```
<html:errors bundle="bundle.error" />
```

You can also specify alternate bundles to the following tags in HTML Tag library – messages, image, img and option.

Write Tag

Write Tag is another frequently used tag. The usage of this tag is as follows:

```
<bean:write name="customer" property="firstName" />
```

It accesses the bean named *customer* in the page, request, session and application scopes in that order (unless a scope attribute is specified) and then retrieves the property named *firstName* and renders it to the current JspWriter. If format attribute is specified, the value is formatted accordingly. The format can be externalized to the resource bundle by using the formatKey attribute instead. Alternate resource bundle can also be specified. This is handy when the display format is locale specific.

Going further, <c:out> and other JSTL formatting tags are preferred over write tag for formatting and output.

Struts Logic Tags

The frequently used tags in the Logic tag library are for logical comparison between values and for iteration over collection. The important logical comparison tags are: equal, notEqual, greaterEqual, greaterThan, lessEqual and lessThan. The following are the important attributes are common to these tags.

- value – The constant value against which comparison is made.
- name – The name of the bean in one of the 4 scopes
- property – The property of the bean that is compred with the value.

A sample usage of the tags is as follows:

```
<logic:equal name="customer" property="firstName" value="John">
   //do whatever when the customer first name is John
</logic:equal>
```

The above tag searches for a bean named customer in the 4 scopes and checks if its `firstName` property is equal to John. You can also specify the scope to restrict the search scope by using the scope attribute on these tags.

Another tag attribute is `parameter`. You have to specify only one: `parameter` or (`name` and `property`). As the name suggests, the `parameter` attribute looks for the specified request parameter and compares it with the `value` attribute. In the example below, the request parameter named `firstName` is compared with a value of *John*.

```
<logic:equal parameter="firstName" value="John">
   //do whatever when the request parameter firstName
   //is equal to John
</logic:equal>
```

There are more comparison tags of interest: `empty`, `notEmpty`, `present` and `notPresent`. These tags do not compare against a given value, but check if an entity (bean property or request parameter) is empty or present respectively. Hence they don't need the `value` attribute. The following snippet checks if a request parameter named *firstName* is present.

```
<logic:present parameter="firstName" >
//do whatever when the request parameter firstName is present
//(Irrespective of its value)
</logic:equal>
```

Nested Logic Tags

Consider how you would write the following logical condition using Logic tags:

```
if (customer.firstName == "John" && customer.lastName == "Doe"
    && customer.age == 28)
{
   do something.....
}
```

This can be done by nesting the `logic:equal` tags as follows:

```
<logic:equal name="customer" property="firstName" value="John">
   <logic:equal name="customer" property="lastName" value="Doe">
      <logic:equal name="customer" property="age" value="28">
         //do something….
```

```
        </logic:equal>
    </logic:equal>
</logic:equal>
```

Nesting of `<logic:xxx>` tags always results in logical ANDing. There is no convenient way to do an "OR" test however; that's where the expression language in JSTL comes in handy (introduced in next section). With JSTL, the above AND condition can be written as follows:

```
<c:if test='${customer.firstName == "John" &&
              customer.lastName == "Doe" && customer.age == 28}'>
      //do something ...
</c:if>
```

Writing the OR condition is also no different

```
<c:if test='${customer.firstName == "John" ||
              customer.lastName == "Doe" || customer.age == 28}'>
      //do something ...
</c:if>
```

The `c` in the `c:if` stands for JSTL's core tag library TLD. There are other tag libraries in JSTL such as formatting. Refer to the section "**A crash course on JSTL**" for details.

Iterate Tag

The iterate tag is used to iterate over a collection (or a bean containing collection) in any of the four scopes (page, request, session and application) and execute the body content for every element in the collection. For instance, the following tag iterates over the collection named customers.

```
<logic:iterate name="customers">
   //execute for every element in the collection
</logic:iterate>
```

Another alternative is to use a bean and iterate over its collection property. The following tag accesses the company bean from one of the scope and then invokes `getCustomers()` on it to retrieves a collection and iterate over it.

```
<logic:iterate name="company" name="customers">
   //execute for every element in the collection in company bean
</logic:iterate>
```

Most of the times a collection is iterated over to display the contents of that collection, perhaps in the table format. This requires the individual element of the collection is exposed as a scripting variable to the inner tags and scriptlets. This is done using the id attribute as follows:

```
<logic:iterate id="customer" name="company" name="customers">
   //for every element in the collection in company bean
</logic:iterate>
```

NOTE: The JSTL tag `<c:forEach>` performs similar functionality. It is recommended that you switch to these new tags where applicable.

A crash course on JSTL

JSTL stands for JSP Standard Template Library. It is one of the new specifications from Sun for standardizing common tags. Due to the lack of standard tags for most of the common tasks such as iterating over a collection and displaying it as a table, custom tags from different vendors have sprung up (including Struts Logic tags), thus presenting a formidable learning curve for the developers every time a new vendor is chosen. JSTL has standardized the set of tags. This standardization lets you learn a single tag and use it across the board. Table 6.1 shows the JSTL tag categories. Core and Formatting tags are most relevant to the discussion on Struts.

Table 6.1 JSTL Libraries

Library	Description
Core	Contains Core tags for if/then, output, iterating collections,
Formatting	Contains I18N and formatting tags. Localizing text, Setting Resource Bundles, Formatting and parsing number, currency, date
SQL	Database Access tags
XML	Tags for XML Parsing and Transforming with Xpath

JSTL also introduced a new expression language (called EL henceforth) as an alternative for using full-blown JSP expressions. For e.g. consider the following scriptlet. It checks for the "user" in page, request, session and application scopes and if it is not null, prints out the roles of that user.

```
<%
    User user = (User) (pageContext.findAttribute("user");
    if (user != null) {
        Role[] roles = user.getRoles();
%>
<ul>
        <% for (int i=0;i<roles.length;i++) { %>
           <li>Role Name is <%= roles[i].getName() %></li>
        <% }%>
```

```
    <% }%>
</ul>
```

This can be easily written using JSTL and EL as follows:

```
<ul>
<c:forEach items="${user.roles}" var="role">
    <li><c:out value=${role.name}/></li>
</c:forEach>
</ul>
```

Any value to be evaluated in a JSTL tag lies in `${` and `}` blocks. EL defines several implicit objects much like JSP defines its implicit objects. Table 6.2 gives a complete list of implicit objects. If the name of the variable in the `${` and `}` block does not match one of the implicit objects, then EL searches the page, request, session application scopes in that order for the variable name specified. In the above code snippet, "user" is the name of an attribute in one of these scopes. Once the `<c:forEach>` tag gets the value, it iterates over the specified collection. In this case it iterates over the array of roles and provides a *scripting variable* called `role` (`var="role"`) for the embedded tags. The `<c:out>` tag access the name property of the Role object (obtained from the `role` scripting variable) and renders it. The `c` in the `<c:out>` represents the Core JSTL tag library.

Table 6.2 Implicit objects in EL

Category	Identifier	Description
JSP	pageContext	PageContext for the current page
Scope	pageScope	Map holding page scoped attributes
	requestScope	Map holding request scoped attributes
	sessionScope	Map holding session scoped attributes
	ApplicationScope	Map holding application scoped attributes
Request Parameters	Param	Map holding request parameter names
	ParamValues	Map holding request parameter values as arrays
Request headers	Header	Map holding header names
	HeaderValues	Map holding header values
Cookies	Cookie	Map holding cookies by name
Initialization Parameters	InitParams	Map holding web application context initialization parameters by name

NOTE: JSTL 1.0 works with JSP 1.2 containers only, such as Tomcat 4.x. JSTL 1.1 works only with JSP 2.0 containers such as Tomcat 5.x. With JSP 1.2, the expression language can be used only within JSTL tags. JSP 2.0 specification defines a portable expression language. With JSP 2.0, the expression language will become part of the specification and can be used even outside the JSTL.

You have already seen an example of using JSTL Core library earlier in conjunction with EL. Now, let us look at an example of formatting library tags. Consider the case when you want to display the currency 12.37 in the user's Locale. You can use the `formatNumber` tag for this purpose. In the following example the currency is formatted and displayed in a variable called "money". For the U.S. Locale, money will contain the value "$12.37".

```
<fmt:formatNumber value="12.367" type="currency" var="money"/>
```

This is somewhat similar to the <bean:write> tag in terms of formatting the currency. Similarly there is a JSTL equivalent for <bean:message> tag.

```
<fmt:message key="firstName">
```

In JSTL, the Resource Bundle for the above tag can be specified in a number of ways. Unless specified otherwise, JSTL looks for a servlet context parameter named `javax.servlet.jsp.jstl.fmt.localizationContext` and uses its value as the bundle name. You can also use the tag `<fmt:setBundle baseName="mybank.MyMessages">` in JSP and the rest of the JSP uses the specified bundle. You can scope a bundle by wrapping other tags with `<fmt:bundle>` tag as follows:

```
<fmt:bundle baseName="mybank.MySecondMessages">
   <fmt:message key="firstName">
   <fmt:message key="lastName">
</fmt:bundle>
```

In the above snippet, all the inner tags use `mybank.MySecondMessages` as their resource bundle. The resource bundle lookup is similar to Struts. In the above scenario for instance, the servlet container looks for `MySecondMessages.properties` in *WEB-INF/classes/mybank* and then in the system classpath.

> ***Design Tip***
> Since, Struts allows you to specify resource bundles on a tag basis, it seems easier (and logical) to use separate bundles per category. For instance, all the errors can reside in one bundle and all the messages of one type can reside in one bundle and so on.
> JSTL on the other hand seems to encourage the practice of using resource bundle per module. This is evident from the way you specify the bundles at a JSP level, scope it and so on. It is easier this way to use a resource bundle for a set of JSPs belonging to one module.

JSTL Binaries – Who's who

If you download JSTL Reference Implementation from Sun, it has two important jar files – *jstl.jar* and *standard.jar*. The former contains the classes from javax.servlet.jsp.jstl package and the latter contains Sun's JSTL Reference Implementation.

From a perspective of this book, we will be using Struts-EL, the JSTL compliant port of Struts tags. Struts-EL is shipped with Struts 1.1 release as a contributed library and can be found under the *contrib* folder. Struts-EL uses the same *jstl.jar* containing javax.servlet.jsp.jstl package – it is the vendor independent JSTL standard. However it uses the implementation from Jakarta TagLibs as the underlying expression evaluation engine (This implementation is also named *standard.jar* and found under *Struts-EL/lib*). If you explode the *standard.jar*, you will find classes belonging to org.apache.taglibs package.

Struts-EL

As you might know already, Struts-EL is a port of Struts tags to JSTL. This provides a migration path for the existing Struts applications to the expression language syntax in a non-intrusive manner. Normal Struts tags rely on runtime scriptlet expressions to evaluate dynamic attribute values. For example, the key of the bean:message below is dependent on some business logic.

```
<bean:message key="<%= stringVar %>" />
```

This assumes that stringVar exists as a JSP scripting variable. This tag can be rewritten with the Struts-EL version of the message tag as follows:

```
<bean-el:message key="${stringVar}" />
```

Although, not much exciting is going on in the above tag, it shows how easy it is to port the existing Struts tags to Struts-EL. The real power of Struts-EL comes to the fore especially when the scriptlet deciding the attribute value starts becoming complex.

Not all tags from Struts are ported to Struts-EL. In areas where there is already a JSTL tag available, porting of the Struts tags will only cause redundancy. Hence those Struts tags are not ported. For e.g., the bean:write tag can be implemented with the c:out JSTL tag. Similarly most of the logic tags (such as equal, notEqual, lessThan etc.) are not ported since the JSTL tag c:if can take any expression and evaluate it (with the test="${....}" option). You have already seen how a logic:equal tag can be replaced with c:if in the earlier section on Nested Logic Tags.

Struts-EL hands-on

Enough theory. Let's get down to business and use some Struts-EL tags to get the feel. Here is the step-by-step process to do so.

- You will need new jar files to use the Struts-EL in your application. Copy the following jars from the Struts *contrib* folder into the *WEB-INF/lib* folder of the web application – *jstl.jar*, *standard.jar* (remember to use the Jakarta Taglibs version, not the Sun reference implementation jar), *struts-el.jar*. These jars are needed in addition to the already existing jars from regular Struts.
- From the *Struts-EL/lib* folder copy the following tlds to the WEB-INF of your web application – *c.tld*, *struts-bean-el.tld*, *struts-html-el.tld* and *struts-logic-el.tld*.
- Add the `<taglib>` declaration for all the new tlds in *web.xml* as follows:

```
<taglib>
  <taglib-uri>/WEB-INF/struts-bean-el</taglib-uri>
  <taglib-location>/WEB-INF/struts-bean-el.tld</taglib-location>
</taglib>

<taglib>
  <taglib-uri>/WEB-INF/struts-html-el</taglib-uri>
  <taglib-location>/WEB-INF/struts-html-el.tld</taglib-location>
</taglib>

<taglib>
  <taglib-uri>/WEB-INF/struts-logic-el</taglib-uri>
  <taglib-location>/WEB-INF/struts-logic-el.tld</taglib-location>
</taglib>

<taglib>
  <taglib-uri>/WEB-INF/c</taglib-uri>
  <taglib-location>/WEB-INF/c.tld</taglib-location>
</taglib>
```

- In the JSPs, add the declaration for these TLDs as follows:

```
<%@ taglib uri="/WEB-INF/struts-bean-el" prefix="bean-el" %>
<%@ taglib uri="/WEB-INF/struts-html-el" prefix="html-el" %>
<%@ taglib uri="/WEB-INF/struts-logic-el" prefix="logic-el" %>
<%@ taglib uri="/WEB-INF/c" prefix="c" %>
```

That's it! Now you are ready to use the Struts-EL tags in conjunction with JSTL tags to reap the benefits of expression language and make your applications a little bit simpler and cleaner.

Practical uses for Struts-EL

When was the last time you wrestled to use a custom tag as the attribute value of another tag and failed? Something like this:

```
<html:radio name="anotherbean"
   value="<bean:write name="mybean" property="myattrib"/>" />
```

Nesting custom tag within a tag element is illegal by taglib standards. The alternatives are no good. Thankfully now, with JSTL, you can solve this problem in a clean way. In Struts tags, JSTL can be combined only with Struts-EL and the problem can be solved as follows:

```
<html-el:radio name="anotherbean" value="${mybean.myattrib}" />
```

Beautiful isn't it! Struts-EL provides you the best of both worlds, the elegance of JSTL and the power of Struts.

List based Forms

All along you have seen how to handle regular Forms. Now let us see how to handle list-based forms. List based forms are used for editing collections of objects. Examples include weekly hours-of-operation, contacts etc. Such collections may be limited to a single page or span across multiple pages. We will deal with a collection limited to single page first. Techniques for dealing with multi page lists are illustrated later.

Indexed struts-html tags are used to display editable collections of objects. Consider a HTML form used to collect information about the weekly hours of operation for a company and send the data back to an Action as shown in Figure 6.1. The brute force approach is to create 7 pair of text fields to collect the opening and closing time for each day of the week. An elegant approach is to use indexed `<html:...>` tags.

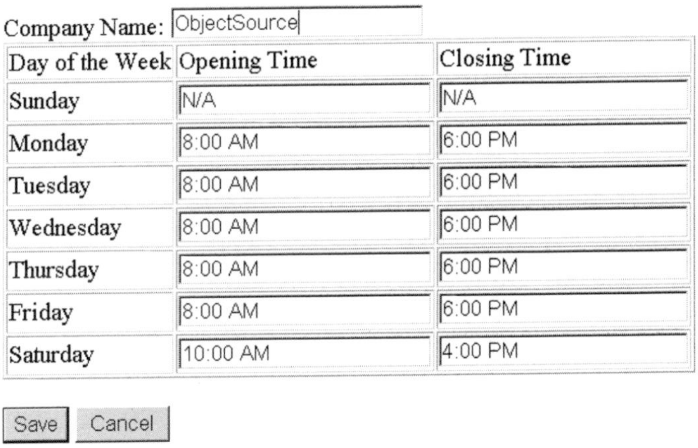

Company Name: ObjectSource

Day of the Week	Opening Time	Closing Time
Sunday	N/A	N/A
Monday	8:00 AM	6:00 PM
Tuesday	8:00 AM	6:00 PM
Wednesday	8:00 AM	6:00 PM
Thursday	8:00 AM	6:00 PM
Friday	8:00 AM	6:00 PM
Saturday	10:00 AM	4:00 PM

Save Cancel

Figure 6.1 Current and Future page layout for the banking application

Listing 6.8 ListForm

```
public class ListForm extends ActionForm {
   private List hourOfOperationList;

   public ListForm() {
      reset();
   }

   public void reset() {
      hourOfOperationList = new ArrayList(7);
      hourOfOperationList.add(new HourOfOperation(0));
      hourOfOperationList.add(new HourOfOperation(1));
      hourOfOperationList.add(new HourOfOperation(2));
      hourOfOperationList.add(new HourOfOperation(3));
      hourOfOperationList.add(new HourOfOperation(4));
      hourOfOperationList.add(new HourOfOperation(5));
      hourOfOperationList.add(new HourOfOperation(6));
   }

   public List getHourOfOperationList() {
      return hourOfOperationList;
   }

   public HourOfOperation getTiming(int index) {
      return (HourOfOperation) hourOfOperationList.get(index);
   }
}
```

The ActionForm for the above HTML in Figure 6.1 is shown in Listing 6.8. The `ListForm` has a `java.util.List` named `hourOfOperationList`. It is a list containing hours of operation. The `HourOfOperation` itself is a Serializable Java class with three JavaBeans properties – `day`, `openingTime` and `closingTime`. The zeroth day is a Sunday and sixth day is a Saturday. Back to the `ListForm`. The `ListForm` has a getter method for the hours of operation List, but no setter method. The `reset()` method initializes the List with exactly seven `HourOfOperation` objects. In reality, you would populate this list from database. Also there is an odd method called `getTiming()` that takes an integer index as argument and returns the corresponding `HourOfOperation` object from the List. This method replaces the setter method and is the key for the Struts framework when populating the list using form data. The details will become clear once you look at the JSP code in Listing 6.9 and the generated HTML in Listing 6.10.

Listing 6.9 JSP for the ListForm

```
<html:form action="/submitListForm">
Company Name: <html:text property="companyName" /><BR>
<table border=1 cellpadding=1>
 <tr><td>Day</td><td>Opening                    Time</td><td>Closing
Time</td></tr>
 <logic:iterate id="timing" name="ListForm"

property="hourOfOperationList">
   <tr>
     <td><bean:write name="timing" property="dayName"/></td>
     <td><html:text name="timing" property="openingTime"
                                          indexed="true"/></td>
     <td><html:text name="timing" property="closingTime"
                                          indexed="true"/></td>
   </tr>
 </logic:iterate>
</table>
 <BR>
 <html:submit>Save</html:submit>
 <html:cancel>Cancel</html:cancel>
</html:form>
```

In Listing 6.9, the JSP displays a form containing the company name and the hours of operation List. The `<logic:iterate>` is used inside the `<html:form>` tag to iterate over the `hoursOfOperationList` property in the `ListForm` bean. Each hour of operation is exposed as a scripting variable named `timing`. You may be able to relate now between the `getTiming()` method in the `ListForm` and this scripting variable. The `indexed=true` setting on each of the html tags makes the array index to be part of the text field name. For instance, the following tag

```
<html:text name="timing" property="openingTime" indexed="true"/>
```

generates the HTML as follows in the second iteration (`i=1`):

```
<input type="text" name="timing[1].openingTime" .. />
```

Notice the relation between the Struts text tag and the generated input tag. Each text field now has a unique name as the name is partly driven the array index. This magic was done `indexed="true"` setting. When the form is edited and is submitted via POST, the request parameter names are unique (`timing[0].openingTime`, `timing[1].openingTime` etc.), thanks to the array index being part of the text field names. The HTML is shown in Listing 6.10.

Listing 6.10 Generated HTML from JSP in Listing 6.9

```
<form name="ListForm" action="/mouse/submitListForm.do">
Company Name:
<input type="text" name="companyName" value="ObjectSource"><BR>
<table border=1 cellpadding=1>
 <tr><td>Day</td><td>Opening                 Time</td><td>Closing
Time</td></tr>
 <tr>
    <td>Sunday</td>
    <td><input type="text" name="timing[0].openingTime"
                                    value="N/A"></td>
    <td><input type="text" name="timing[0].closingTime"
                                    value="N/A"></td>
 </tr>
<tr>
    <td>Monday</td>
    <td><input type="text" name="timing[1].openingTime"
                                    value="8:00 AM"></td>
    <td><input type="text" name="timing[1].closingTime"
                                    value="6:00 PM"></td>
 </tr>
  .. .. ..
</table>
<BR><input type="submit" value="Save">
<input                                           type="submit"
name="org.apache.struts.taglib.html.CANCEL"
                        value="Cancel" onclick="bCancel=true;">
</html:form>
```

Upon form submission, when Struts sees the request parameter named `timing[1].openingTime`, it calls the following method:

```
listForm.getTiming(1).setOpeningTime(...)
```

and so on for every request parameter. This is exactly where the `getTiming()` method in `ListForm` comes in handy. Without it, Struts can never access the individual items in the list. Thanks to `getTiming()`, individual `HourOfOperation` are accessed and their attributes are set using the corresponding request parameters.

List based form editing is frequently a necessity in day-to-day Struts usage. The above approach is perhaps the only clean way to achieve this.

Multi-page Lists and Page Traversal frameworks

As seen in the last section, `<logic:iterate>` can be used in conjunction with indexed html tags to display and edit list forms. However read-only tabular displays are more common than editable list forms in enterprise applications. Such read-only tables span multiple pages with data ranging from ten rows to thousands. The `IterateTag` can also be used for displaying read-only data by iterating over a collection and rendering the data using `<bean:write>`. For multi-page lists, the attributes `offset` and `length` are useful. The `offset` indicates the index from where to start the iteration in the page relative to the first element (index = 0). The `length` indicates the maximum number of entries from the collection to be displayed in the page. Using these two attributes it is possible to build a multi-page list.

But the task is more daunting than you can imagine. Believe us. Multi-page list display will not be your only worry. You will be asked to provide a browsing mechanism – previous, next, first and last to traverse the collection. You will have to sort the data for the chosen column (and still do a previous, next etc.). You will be asked to group the data, aggregate and sum columns and format them. In addition you will have to make it easier to the page author to apply different display styles to the list. Before you know it, the seemingly trivial task has turned into a Frankenstein!

The plain vanilla `IterateTag` simply cannot be stretched too far. A robust framework exclusively to perform the above tasks is needed. Fortunately such frameworks are available at no charge. Why reinvent the wheel unless you have a unique and stringent requirement not satisfied by one of these frameworks? Three such frameworks are reviewed below. One is free, the other two are open source Let us examine what is available and what is missing in these frameworks and how they fit into the Struts way of building applications. The three frameworks are:

1. Pager Taglib (http://jsptags.com/tags/navigation/pager/)
2. displayTag (http://displaytag.sourceforge.net/)
3. HtmlTable (http://sourceforge.net/projects/htmltable/)

Pager Taglib

Pager Taglib covers the display aspects of list traversal very well. Provide it the minimal information such as rows per page and URL and it will control the entire paging logic. You are in complete control of the iterating logic and table display. (If using the IterateTag, offset and length attributes are not needed). Hence you can completely customize the look and feel of the table using CSS. The Pager taglib does not provide any assistance for the table display. Neither does it handle editable list forms, sorting or grouping. If all you need is an easy and elegant way to traverse list data, you should definitely consider using the Pager taglib and you will be glad you did. Below we cover a short note on how to use the Pager Taglib with Struts.

First Name	Last Name	Address	City
John5	Doe5	5 ABC Ave	City5
John6	Doe6	6 ABC Ave	City6
John7	Doe7	7 ABC Ave	City7
John8	Doe8	8 ABC Ave	City8
John9	Doe9	9 ABC Ave	City9

[<< Prev] 1 2 3 4 5 6 7 [Next >>]

Figure 6.2 Traversing the multi page list using Pager Taglib from jsptags.com

Start with an `Action` that creates the collection to iterate and put it in `HttpSession` using results as the key name. Then forward to the JSP that uses the Pager taglib. This JSP is shown in Listing 6.11. The resulting HTML is shown in Figure 6.2. The `pg:pager` tag has two important attributes – `url` and `maxPageItems`. They specify the destination URL when any of the navigation links are clicked and the number of items per page respectively. In Listing 6.11, the `url` is *traverse.do* – a simple ForwardAction that forwards to the same JSP. The JSP uses the `iterate` tag to iterate the collection. Th `pg:item` defines each displayable row. The `pg:index`, `pg:prev`, `pg:pages` and `pg:next` together display the page numbers, previous and next links. These tags even provide you the flexibility of using your own images instead of plain old hyperlinks. Using `pg:param` (not shown in the listing), additional request parameters can also be submitted with the url.

DisplayTag and HtmlTable frameworks

The pager taglib does paging through a table and nothing more. If sorting and grouping are one of your requirements, you can use one of DisplayTag or HtmlTable frameworks. Each of them has their own paging logic and should not be used in conjunction with the Pager Taglib. Covering these frameworks is beyond the scope of this book. Please check their respective web sites for documentation and user guide. Table 6.3 provides a comprehensive feature comparison between the two. DisplayTag shines in many categories but lacks the table based editing features. DisplayTag is not tied to Struts in any way. Neither does it enforce MVC. HtmlTable on the other hand mandates strict adherence to MVC. All the pagination, sort requests are handled by a pre-defined Action class (ServeTableAction) provided with the library. Further customization is needed to chain it to your own business processing before/after ServeTableAction does its job.

Listing 6.11 Using Pager taglib with Struts

```
<pg:pager url="traverse.do" maxIndexPages="10"
                                    maxPageItems="5">
 <TABLE width="100%">
  <TR>
   <TD align="center">
    <TABLE width="80%" border="1">
     <TR>
      <TH width="20%">Name</TH>
      <TH width="20%">Address</TH>
      <TH width="20%">City</TH>
     </TR>
     <logic:iterate id="row" name="results" scope="session"
                             type="mybank.app1.CustomerData">
      <pg:item>
       <TR>
        <TD><bean:write name="row" property="name"/></TD>
        <TD><bean:write name="row" property="address"/></TD>
        <TD><bean:write name="row" property="city"/></TD>
       </TR>
      </pg:item>
     </logic:iterate>
    </TABLE>
    <TABLE width="80%" border="0">
     <TR><TD> </TD></TR>
     <TR align="center">
      <TD>
       <pg:index>
        <pg:prev><a href="<%=pageUrl%>">[<< Prev]</a></pg:prev>
        <pg:pages>
          <a href="<%= pageUrl %>"><%= pageNumber %></a>
        </pg:pages>
        <pg:next><a         href="<%=          pageUrl%>">[Next
>>]</a></pg:next>
       </pg:index>
      </TD>
     </TR>
    </TABLE>
   </TD>
  </TR>
 </TABLE>
</pg:pager>
```

Table 6.3 Feature Comparison between DisplayTag and HtmlTable

Feature	DisplayTag	HtmlTable
Display Formatting	Very rich and customizable using CSS.	Limited features. Formatting is based on a back end XML file and hence not directly under page author's control.
Column Grouping	Yes	Yes
Nested Tables	Yes	No
Coding Style	The display model should be created in advance, but the formatting can be invoked from the JSP using hooks called decorators Does not require controller (such as Struts or its Action). The JSP itself can control the paging.	The display model and its formatting should be performed in advance (in a Action). The paging is tied to Struts. Needs a predefined Action called ServeTableAction. Strictly MVC based.
Paging	Customizable auto paging	Fixed style auto paging
Sorting	Yes	Yes
I18N	No. Messages can be externalized to a properties file but cannot be localized as of 1.0b2. Full support is expected soon.	Yes. Can use Struts resource bundle
Editable column	No	Yes, but form is submitted to a predefined Action. Action chaining for custom processing can be setup with minor customization.
Documentation and examples	Good	Limited
User community	Relatively high	Less

Creating the Model for iteration

In the last two sections, you looked at three options for traversing and displaying the collection. For limited amount of data, creating the collection is a no-brainer. The size of the result set is managable and you can tolerate the database returning it anoe shot. As the collection gets larger, it consumes a significant amount of memory and absolutely does not make sense to waste the precious runtime resources. Instead of maintaining the entire collection in memory, you can use the `Value List Handler` pattern (Core J2EE Patterns). Figure 6.3 shows the class diagram for Value List Handler.

`ValueListHandler` can be thought of as a façade for the underlying collection. `ValueList` - the data object collection is traversed using the `ValueListIterator`. The `Data Access Object` encapsulates the logic to access the database in the specified format – read-only EJB, direct JDBC or O/R mapper, the latter two approaches being preferred. We recommend designing the Value List Handler intelligently so that it fetches data in bulk using read-ahead (a.k.a pre-fetch) mechanism – i.e. data to serve two to three pages is retrieved and in advance if needed so that the delay in retrieval is minimized. The beauty of this pattern is that you can expose the `ValueListIterator` to the `IterateTag` and the tag will believe that it is traversing the original Iterator, while you can intelligently serve the requested rows and keep fetching in the background.

In this context it is advantageous to combine an O/R mapping framework that allows you use SQLs to search the database. Most of the O/R mapping frameworks provide caching mechanisms. Hence the overhead of object creation after retrieval is eliminated since the object in already in the cache. Moreover you can take advantage of the features provided in the RDBMS. For instance, DB2 provides a feature called ROW_NEXT.

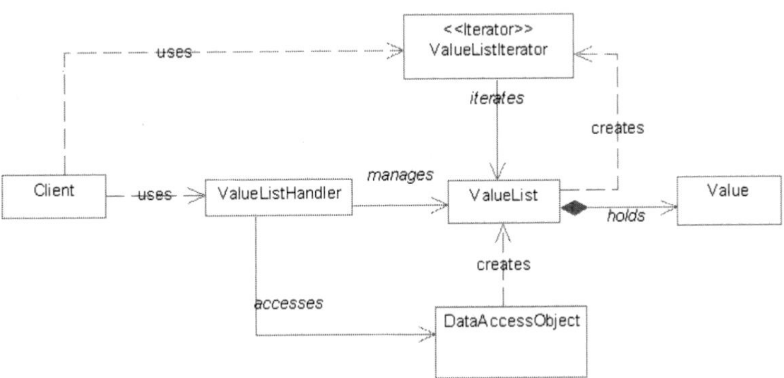

Figure 6.3 Value List Handler pattern

Suppose that the requirement is to display 10 rows per page. Here is strategy for devising a responsive system while working with large data set. When the query is first made, data for three pages (30 rows) is prefetched and maintained in the HttpSession. When the user requests the third page, the ValueListHandler realizes that the end of the cache is reached. It goes ahead and serves the third page (21-30 rows). After that it initiates an asynchronous request to fetch another 30 rows from the database (This will need a scheduling mechanism to which individual valueListHandlers submit their pre-fetch requests). When the next 30 rows are retrieved, it caches them along with the original 30 rows. Hence a cache of 60 rows is maintained per user. (This is to prevent a "cache-fault" if the user decides to go to previous page while on third page). Depdending on the size of the displayed objects, you have to choose an optimal cache within the Value List Handler. If the objects are 1K each, 60 objects means 60K of memory consumed by the corresponding HttpSession. This is absolutely not recommended. A rule of thumb is that HttpSession size should not exceed 20K per user. [Another reason to make the display objects only as big as needed and no bigger. Overcome the tendency to reuse bloated value objects and data transfer objects from elsewhere.]

Coming back to the database features for large result sets. The following SQL can be used to fetch the first 30 rows:

```
SELECT FIRST_NAME, LAST_NAME, ADDRESS
  FROM CUSTOMER, … …
WHERE … … …
ORDER BY FIRST_NAME
FETCH FIRST 30 ROWS ONLY
OPTIMIZED FOR READ ONLY
```

When the user reaches the third page, the ValueListHandler makes a prefetch request for the next 30 rows (Rows 31 to 60). The following SQL can be used to fetch them:

```
SELECT * FROM
(
  SELECT FIRST_NAME, LAST_NAME, ADDRESS
    FROM CUSTOMER, … …
  WHERE … … …
  ORDER BY FIRST_NAME
)
AS CUST_TEMP WHERE
  ROW_NEXT BETWEEN 31 AND 60
  OPTIMIZED FOR READ ONLY
```

This SQL consists of two parts. The inner SQL is exactly the same as the SQL issued earlier and can be thought to be fetching the data into a temporary table. The ROW_NEXT in the outer SQL identifies the exact rows to be returned from the retrieved result set. The values 31 and 60 can be substituted dynamically. The propreitory SQL no doubt impacts the portability, but almost every database used in the enterprise today has this feature. The Java code still is portable.

Summary

In this chapter you got an overview of Struts tags and more importantly learnt to customize these tags for your projects. In addition you looked at JSTL and Struts-EL. Hopefully this chapter has prepared you to use Struts tags better.

Chapter 7

Struts and Tiles

In this chapter:

You will learn to use Tiles with Struts for web page design using Layouts

What is Tiles

Consider a banking application whose current web page layout has a header, body and footer as shown by the first layout in Figure 7.1. The management recently decided that all pages in the application should confirm to the corporate look and feel as shown in the second layout in Figure 7.1. The new layout has a header, footer, a varying body and a navigation sidebar.

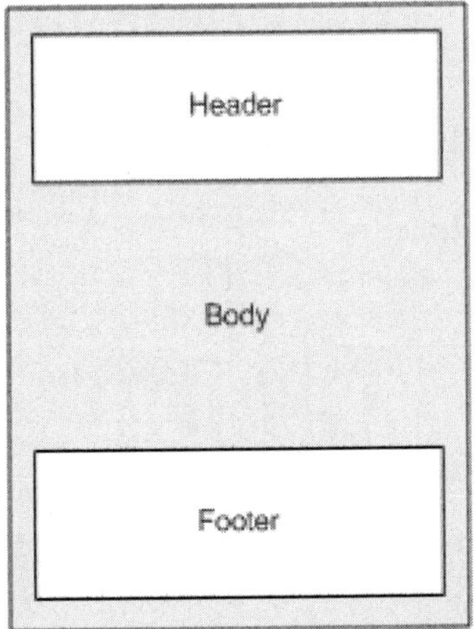

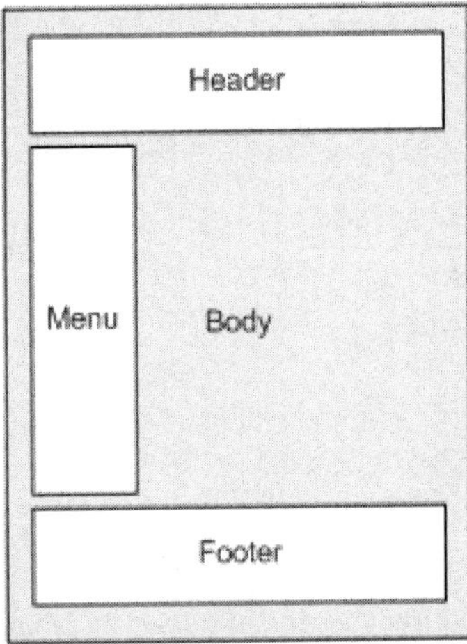

Figure 7.1 Current and Future page layout for the banking application

When the application was first designed, the development team had two alternatives.

- Use "JSP based" approach. In this approach each JSP page is coded separately. Although the header and footer are common to every page, the common JSP markup for header and footer was added into each JSP by direct copy and paste.

This quick and dirty solution is unacceptable even for the smallest of the web applications and poses a maintenance hurdle. Anytime the header and footer changes, it has to be manually applied to every page. Further, any changes to the page layout will have to be made in every page.

- Use `<jsp:include>` approach. This approach is better than the previous one since it avoids repetition of common markup. The common markup related to header and footer is moved into JSPs of their own. The header and footer JSPs are added to the main JSP by using the standard `<jsp:include>` directive. Whenever header or footer changes, it affects only one or two files. However, if at any point in time, the layout of the pages itself changes (as it has happened for the banking application now), every JSP page with this structure has to be updated accordingly.

The team chose the second option at the time of development. However the new management directive is now posing a challenge. It is a tedious task to change every page of the system and there are chances that the current system might break in the process. Had they had Tiles framework at their disposal at the time of development, this change would have been a breeze!

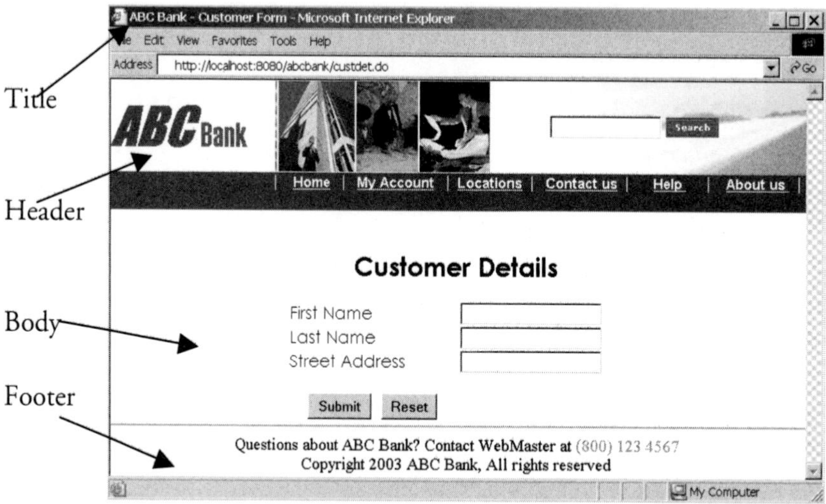

Figure 7.2 Current Customer Details Page for My Bank

Figure 7.2 shows a sample HTML page from the banking application. Listing 7.1 shows the (simplified) JSP for that page. The JSP contains the `<jsp:include>` for the common header and footer, but has the entire layout written in terms of html `table` with various `tr` and `td`. All JSPs in the application also might have the same layout copied over and over. This is "copy and paste technology" taken to the next dimension and exactly where Tiles comes into picture.

Listing 7.1 CustomerDetail JSP using <jsp:include>

```
<%@ taglib uri="/WEB-INF/struts-html.tld" prefix="html" %>
<html:html locale="true">
<head>
  <html:base/>
  <title><bean:message key="title.customerform"/></title>
</head>
<body>
<TABLE border="0" width="100%" cellspacing="5">
  <tr><td><jsp:include page="/common/header.jsp"/></td></tr>
  <tr>
    <td>
      <html:form action="/submitCustomerForm">
      <table>
        <tr>
          <td>
            <bean:message key="prompt.customer.firstname"/>
          </td>
          <td><html:input property="firstName"/></td>
        <tr>
        <tr>
          <td>
            <bean:message key="prompt.customer.lastname"/>
          </td>
          <td><html:input property="lastName"/></td>
        <tr>
        <tr>
          <td><html:submit>Save Me</html:submit></td>
          <td><html:cancel>Cancel</html:cancel></td>
        <tr>
      </table>
    </td>
  </tr>
  <tr><td><hr></td></tr>
  <tr><td><jsp:include page="/common/footer.jsp"/></td></tr>
</TABLE>
</body>
</html:html>
```

The basic principle behind Tiles is to refactor the common layout out of the individual JSPs to a higher level and then reuse it across JSPs.

If the management wants a new look and feel, so be it; you can change the common layout JSP and the whole web application has the new look and feel! Redundancy is out and Reuse is in. In OO parlance this is similar to refactoring common functions from a set of classes into their parent class.

In Tiles, layouts represent the structure of the entire page. Layout is simply a JSP. Think of it as a template with placeholders (or slots). You can place other JSPs in these slots declaratively. For instance, you can create a layout with slots for header, body and footer. In a separate XML file (called XML tile definition file), you specify what JSPs go into these slots. At runtime, Tiles framework composes the aggregate page by using the layout JSP and filling its slots with individual JSPs.

In essence, Tiles is a document assembly framework that builds on the "include" feature provided by the JSP specification for assembling presentation pages from component parts. Each part (also called a tile, which is also a JSP) can be reused as often as needed throughout the application. This reduces the amount of markup that needs to be maintained and makes it easier to change the look and feel of a website. Tiles framework uses a custom tag library to implement the templates.

Comparing this approach with `<jsp:include>` will help you to understand the Tiles better. In the `<jsp:include>` approach, all included JSPs (header, footer etc.) become part of the core JSP before being rendered. In Tiles, all the JSPs – header, footer and the core become part of the Layout JSP before being rendered. The outermost JSP rendered to the user is always the same; it is the layout JSP. This approach reduces redundancy of HTML and makes maximum reuse of formatting logic. The entire chapter deals with using Tiles for effective design in conjunction with Struts. In the next section, you will see how the banking application can be converted into a Tiles oriented design.

Your first Tiles application

In this section, you will learn how to assemble a Tiles application. We will start with the *CustomerDetails.jsp* in Listing 7.1 and change it to use Tiles. The Customer Details page is first shown to the user. When the submit button in the Customer Form is pressed, a Success page is shown. Note that we are not referring to "*.jsp*" files any more. Instead they are being referred to as "pages". There is a reason for this. Strictly speaking, the only JSP file that the user gets every time is the Layout JSP – the aggregate page. Hence the several incarnations of *Layout.jsp* that the user sees are distinguished by their core contents – Customer Details information, Success information and so on.

Step 1: Creating the Layout

To start with, let us concentrate on Tiles enabling the Customer Details Page. The first step is to create the Layout JSP with placeholders for header, footer, body and anything else you want by using Tiles `insert` tags. The `insert` tag is defined in *struts-tiles.tld*, the TLD file that is part of Struts distribution. The Layout JSP factors out most of the formatting markups. Typical things performed in a layout are:

- Defining the outer structure of the page with html tables with defined widths.
- Creating placeholders for pages relative to one another in the overall presentation scheme.

The first tag used in the listing above is `getAsString`. This tag retrieves the title as a string. The `insert` tags are used to insert different JSPs into the *SiteLayout.jsp*. For example the header of the page is inserted as: `<tiles:insert attribute="header" />`. The layout we have used is simple. In reality however, nested tables with bells and whistles are used for professional looking pages. Although required, they result in indentation and hence error prone and visually displeasing. With the layout taking care of these two things, the individual pages don't have to deal it. That makes the design of included page simpler and cleaner.

Listing 7.2 SiteLayout.jsp – The layout used by Tiles in the ba king app

```
<%@ taglib uri="/WEB-INF/struts-tiles.tld" prefix="tiles" %>
<html:html locale="true">
<head>
  <html:base/>
  <title><tiles:getAsString name="title"/></title>
</head>
<body>
<TABLE border="0" width="100%" cellspacing="5">
  <tr><td><tiles:insert attribute="header"/></td></tr>
  <tr><td><tiles:insert attribute="body"/></td></tr>
  <tr><td><hr></td></tr>
  <tr><td><tiles:insert attribute="footer"/></td></tr>
</TABLE>
</body>
</html:html>
```

Step 2: Creating the XML Tile definition file

The *SiteLayout.jsp* created in the previous step uses the `insert` tag to insert the individual JSPs. The `insert` tags however do not specify the JSPs directly. They contain an attribute named attribute. The value of attribute is the reference to the actual JSP. The actual JSP name is specified in a XML based file called tiles definition. A sample definition is shown below.

```
<definition name="/customer.page" path="/Sitelayout.jsp">
  <put name="title" value="My Bank - Customer Form"/>
  <put name="header" value="/common/header.jsp" />
  <put name="footer" value="/common/footer.jsp" />
  <put name="body"   value="/CustomerDetail.jsp" />
</definition>
```

The Tiles definition shown above defines the JSPs that go into each of the insert tag placeholders in the *SiteLayout.jsp* for the Customer Details page and identify it them a unique name. Note that the name of each put in the definition is same as the value of attribute in the insert tag. Similarly a XML definition for the Success page is added as follows:

```
<definition name="/success.page" path="/Sitelayout.jsp">
  <put name="title" value="MyBank - Success"/>
  <put name="header" value="/common/header.jsp" />
  <put name="footer" value="/common/footer.jsp" />
  <put name="body"   value="/Success.jsp" />
</definition>
```

Compare the above definition for the Customer Details Page definition shown earlier. You will see that only the title and body differ between the two. The header and footer remain the same. Tiles allows you to factor out these common elements in the definition and create a base definition. Individual definitions can then extend from the base definition, much like concrete classes extend from an abstract base class. Factoring out, the common elements of the two page definitions results in a base definition as:

```
<definition name="base.definition" path="/Sitelayout.jsp">
  <put name="title" value="MyBank"/>
  <put name="header" value="/common/header.jsp" />
  <put name="footer" value="/common/footer.jsp" />
  <put name="body"   value="" />
</definition>
```

The individual definitions are created by extending the above definition. Accordingly, the new definitions for Customer Detail and Success pages are as follows:

```
<definition name="/customer.page" extends="base.definition">
  <put name="title" value="MyBank - Customer Form"/>
  <put name="body"   value="/CustomerDetails.jsp" />
</definition>

<definition name="/success.page" extends="base.definition">
  <put name="title" value="MyBank - Success"/>
  <put name="body"   value="/Success.jsp" />
</definition>
```

Each of the definition extends from the `base.definition` and overrides the settings for title and body. They will however reuse the header and footer settings from the `base.definition`. Notice that we have left the `body` section blank in the base definition but provided a default `title`. Individual page definitions must provide the `body` JSP. If `title` is not provided, then the default `title` from the base definition is used.

The definitions thus created are stored in a file called *tiles-defs.xml*. Generally this file is placed under WEB-INF and is loaded at Struts startup. The file contains the definitions for each aggregate page (combination of several jsps) accessed by the user.

Step 3: Modifying the forwards in struts-config.xml

Suppose that you had the following action mapping in the *struts-config.xml* for the Customer form submission prior to using Tiles.

```
<action    path="/submitCustomerForm"
           type="mybank.app1.CustomerAction"
           name="CustomerForm"
           scope="request"
           validate="true"
           input="CustomerDetails.jsp">
   <forward name="success"  path="Success.jsp"   />
</action>
```

The above action mapping uses the JSP name directly. With Tiles, you have to replace the JSP name with the tiles definition name. The resulting action mapping is shown below. The changes are highlighted in bold.

```
<action    path="/submitCustomerForm"
           type="mybank.app1.CustomerAction"
           name="CustomerForm"
           scope="request"
           validate="true"
```

```
            input="customer.page">
      <forward name="success"  path="success.page"  />
   </action>
```

Step 4: Using TilesRequestProcessor

You have so far used `org.apache.struts.action.RequestProcessor` as the request processor with regular Struts pages. This request processor forwards to a specified JSP and commits the response stream. This does not work with Tiles as individual JSPs have to be included in the response stream even after the stream data is flushed and data is committed. Moreover, the regular Struts `RequestProcessor` can only interpret forwards pointing to direct physical resource such as a JSP name or another action mapping. It is unable to interpret "`/customer.page`" – a Tiles definition. Hence Tiles provides a specialized request processor called `TilesRequestProcessor` to handle this scenario. For a given Struts module, only one request processor is used. A Tiles enabled module uses the `TilesRequestProcessor`, even if the module has regular Struts pages. Since `TilesRequestProcessor` extends from the regular Struts `RequestProcessor`, it inherits all its features and can handle regular Struts pages as well. `TilesRequestProcessor` is declared in the *struts-config.xml* as follows:

```
<controller processorClass=
        "org.apache.struts.tiles.TilesRequestProcessor"/>
```

The `TilesRequestProcessor` contains the logic to process includes and forwards. It checks if the specified URI is a Tiles definition name. If so, then the definition is retrieved and included. Otherwise the original URI is included or forwarded as usual.

Step 5: Configuring the TilesPlugIn

As you know, TilesRequestProcessor needs the XML Tiles definition at runtime to interpret Tiles specific forwards. This information created in Step 2 is stored in a file called *tiles-defs.xml*. Generally this file is placed under WEB-INF. At startup this file is loaded by using the Tiles PlugIn. The `TilesPlugIn` initializes Tiles specific configuration data. The plugin is added to the *struts-config.xml* as shown below.

```
<plug-in className="org.apache.struts.tiles.TilesPlugin" >
  <set-property property="definitions-config"
                value="/WEB-INF/tiles-defs.xml" />
  <set-property property="moduleAware" value="true"/>
</plug-in>
```

The `classname` attribute refers to the plugin class that will be used. In this case `org.apache.struts.tiles.TilesPlugin` class is used.

NOTE: CSS or Cascading Style Sheets is a way to add formatting rules and layout to existing HTML tags. CSS greatly simplifies changes to page appearance by only having to make edits to the stylesheets. Tiles, as we saw in the previous section deals with the organization of different parts of the JSP page as against enhancing the look and feel of individual components. CSS deals more with enhancing individual features of the components in each tile or area of the page. Tiles and CSS are complementary and can be used together to improve the look and feel of a JSP page.

In this section, you converted the Struts based Customer page and the subsequent page to use Tiles. The complete working application can be downloaded from the website (http://www.objectsource.com).

Rules of thumb

1. Although Tiles provides several ways to construct a page, some of them don't provide much advantage over the `<jsp:include>` approach at all. The approach we have illustrated above is usually the one used most. It is in this approach the real strength of Tiles get expressed.
2. Thanks to the multiple application module support in Struts 1.1, you don't have to Tiles enable your entire application and watch it collapse. Start by breaking the application into multiple modules. Test if the modules are working as expected. Also test inter-module navigation. Then Tiles-enable the modules one at a time. This provides you a rollback mechanism, if something goes wrong.
3. Never use the Tiles definition as the URL on the browser. This will not work. Struts can forward to a Tiles definition only when the control is within the `TilesRequestProcessor`, not when an external request arrives. If you want to display an aggregate Tiles page on clicking a link, define an action mapping for the URL (You can also use a global-forward instead). Then create an action mapping for a ForwardAction and set the parameter attribute to be the Tiles definition.
4. In the application shown earlier, JSPs were used as Tiles. You can also use action mappings as page names.

```
<definition name="/customer.page" extends="base.definition">
    <put name="body"   value="/custdet.do" />
</definition>
```

Tiles and multiple modules

The application seen earlier used Tiles in a single application module. In this section you will see Tiles works across modules. Tiles provides two modes of operation: Non-module-aware and module-aware modes. They are distinguished by the setting moduleAware attribute on the Tiles PlugIn. The definition file is specified by the definitions-config attribute on the Tiles PlugIn.

In non-module-aware mode, all modules use the same tiles definition file specified in the struts-config.xml for the default module. If there is no default module, all modules use the tiles definition file specified in the struts-config.xml for the first module listed in web.xml.

In module-aware mode, each module has its own tiles definition file. A module cannot see definitions in a tiles definition file belonging to another module unless it uses that file itself.

Summary

In this chapter you saw how to use Tiles along with Struts to build a maintainable and cleaner page layout. By transitioning your Struts modules to Tiles, you will see a boost in productivity for both developers and page authors.

Chapter 8

Struts and I18N

In this chapter:

1. *You will understand the basics of I18N*
2. *You will learn the basics of Java I18N API*
3. *You will review the features in Struts for I18N*
4. *You will look how Tiles application is I18N enabled*
5. *You will understand how localized input is processed*

The Internet has no boundaries and neither should your web application. People all over the world access the net to browse web pages that are written in different languages. A user in Japan can access the web and check her Yahoo! Email in Japanese. How does Yahoo do it? Is it because the user's machine has a Japanese operating system or do web-based applications automatically adjust according to the users' region? This chapter answers these questions and shows you how to internationalize and localize your Struts web applications.

Terminology

Before diving deep into the bliss of Internationalization and Localization, coverage of some basic terminology is essential. That's what we are doing in this section.

Internationalization or I18n is the process of enabling your application to cater to users from *different* countries and supporting *different* languages. With I18n, software is made portable between languages or regions. For example, the Yahoo! Web site supports users from English, Japanese and Korean speaking countries, to name a few.

Localization or L10n on the other hand, is the process of customizing your application to support a *specific* location. When you customize your web application to a specific country say, Germany, you are localizing your application. Localization involves establishing on-line information to support a specific language or region.

A *Locale* is a term that is used to describe a certain region and possibly a language for that region. In software terms, we generally refer to applications as supporting certain *locales.* For example, a web application that supports a locale of "fr_FR" is enabling French-speaking users in France to navigate it. Similarly a locale of "en_US" indicates an application supporting English-speaking users in the US.

A *ResourceBundle* is a class that is used to hold locale specific information. In Java applications, the developer creates an instance of a `ResourceBundle` and populates it with information specific to each locale such as text messages, labels, and also objects. There will be one `ResourceBundle` object per Locale.

What can be localized?

When your application runs anywhere in the US, everyone, well almost everyone speaks English and hence, they won't have any trouble trying to figure out what your application is trying to say. Now, consider the same application being accessed by a user in a country say Japan where English is not the mainstream language. There is a good chance that the very same message might not make much sense to a Japanese user. The point in context is very simple: Present your web application to foreign users in a way they can comprehend it and navigate freely without facing any language barriers.

Great, now you know where this is leading, right? That's right, localization! In order to localize your web application, you have to identify the key areas that will have to change. There are three such key areas. From a Struts perspective, you only have to deal with the first two.

a. The visible part of your application – the User Interface. The user interface specific changes could mean changes to text, date formats, currency formats etc.

b. Glue Layer – Presentation Logic that links the UI to the business logic.

c. The invisible parts of your application – Database support for different character encoding formats and your back-end logic that processes this data.

Here is a list of the commonly localized areas in a web application. We will de dealing only with the highlighted ones in this chapter.

1. **Messages and Labels on GUI components – labels, button names**
2. **Dates and Times**
3. **Numbers and Currencies**
4. Personal titles, Phone numbers and Addresses
5. **Graphics – Images specific for every locale and cater to each region's cultural tastes.**
6. Colors – Colors play a very important role in different countries. For example, death is represented by the color white in China.
7. Sounds
8. Page layouts – that's right. Just like colors, page layouts can vary from

locale to locale based on the country's cultural preferences.

9. **Presentation Logic in Struts Action classes.**

There are other properties that you might require to be localized, but the ones mentioned are the commonly used ones. Struts provides mechanisms to address some of these, but the actual I18N and L10N capabilities lie in the Java API itself. You will see in the next section, a brief overview of the Java Internationalization API and some examples on how to update some of these fields dynamically based on Locale information.

The Java I18N and L10N API

The primary I18N and L10N Java APIs can be found in the `java.util` and `java.text` packages. This section shows some of the commonly used classes and their functions. Figure 8.1 shows the classes in the Java I18n API. If you are already familiar with the Java Internationalization API, you can skip this section and proceed to the next section.

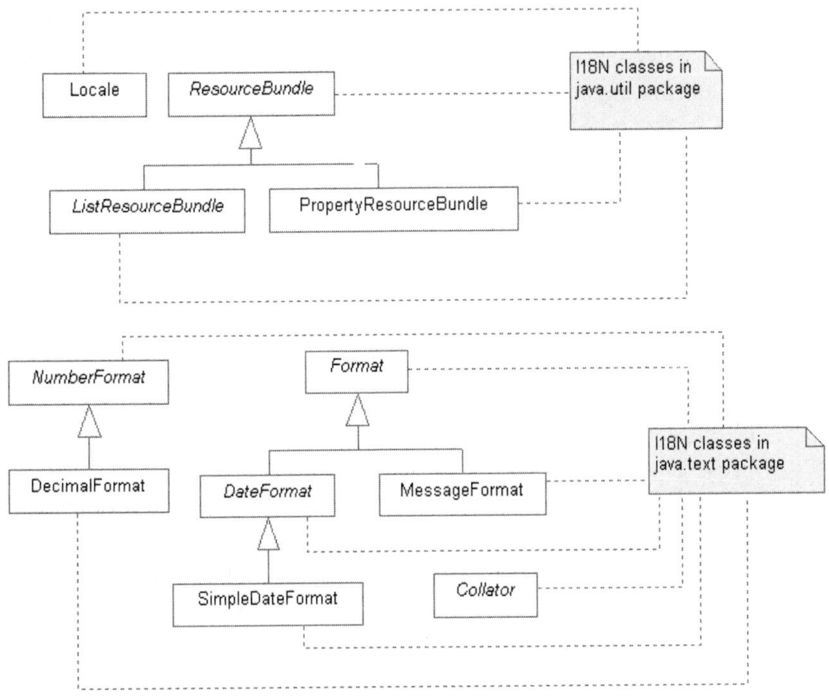

Figure 8.1 TheI18n classes provided by the Java Internationalization API

java.util.Locale

The `Locale` class represents a specific geographical or cultural region. It contains information about the region and its language and sometimes a variant specific to the user's system. The variant is vendor specific and can be WIN for a Windows system, MAC for a Macintosh etc. The following examples show you how to create a Locale object for different cases:

A Locale object that describes only a language (French):

```
Locale frenchSpeakingLocale = new Locale("fr", "");
```

A Locale object that describes both the spoken language and the country (French Canada):

```
Locale canadaLocale = new Locale("fr", "CA");
```

A Locale object that describes the spoken language, country and a variant representing the user's operating system (French Canada and Windows Operating system):

```
Locale canadaLocaleWithVariant = new Locale("fr", "CA", "WIN");
```

Accessing Locale in Servlet Container

On every request the client's locale preference is sent to the web server as part of the HTTP Header. The "Accept-Language" header contains the preferred Locale or Locales. This information is also available to the servlet container and hence in your web tier through the `HttpServletRequest`. `ServletRequest`, the interface that `HttpServletRequest` extends defines the following two methods to retrieve Locale

```
public java.util.Locale getLocale();
public java.util.Enumeration getLocales();
```

The second method contains a set of Locales in the descending order of preference. You can set the request's Locale preference in the browser. For instance in Internet Explorer, you can add, remove or change the Locales using Tools → Internet Options → Languages.

The `<controller>` (`RequestProcessor`) setup in the Struts Config file has a `locale` attribute. If this is set to true, then Struts retrieves the Locale information from the request only the first time and stores it in the `HttpSession` with the key `org.apache.struts.action.LOCALE` (Don't get confused. This is not a class name. It is the actual String used as the Session key.) The default value of the locale attribute is false for which Struts does not store the Locale information in the `HttpSession`.

A tip from usability perspective: Although it is possible to change the Locale preference from the browser, I18N usability experts suggest that it might still be valuable to explicitly provide the choice to the users and let them decide. Every web site has a navigation bar or menu or something of that sort. You can provide a

HTML choice or drop down to let the user's choose the Locale that shall override all other settings. This is easy from a Struts perspective because the Locale from the `HttpServletRequest` can be overridden with the setting in the `HttpSession` and Struts will never bother about the request header.

java.util.ResourceBundle

`ResourceBundle` is an abstract base class that represents a container of resources. It has two subclasses: `ListResourceBundle` and `PropertiesResourceBundle`. When you are localizing your application, all the locale specific resources like text-messages, icons and labels are stored in subclasses of the `ResourceBundle`. There will be *one* instance of the `ResourceBundle` per locale. The `getBundle()` method in this class retrieves the appropriate `ResourceBundle` instance for a given locale. The location of the right bundle is implemented using an algorithm explained later.

Listing 8.1 Extracting data from a ResourceBundle

```
Locale myLocale = new Locale("fr","FR");
// Get the resource bundle for myLocale
ResourceBundle mybankBundle = ResourceBundle.getBundle(
                                        "MybankResources",
                                         myLocale);
// Get the localized strings from this resource bundle
String myHeader = mybankBundle.getString("header.title");
System.out.println(myHeader);
```

Let us see how a resource bundle instance is retrieved with a simple example. Consider a custom `ResourceBundle` subclass called `MybankResources` that will contain data specific to your application. In this example, you will see how to use `PropertyResourceBundles` assuming that all the resources to be localized are strings. In order to use `PropertyResourceBundle`, you will have to create Java Properties files that will hold the data in key = value format. The file name itself identifies the Locale. For instance, if *MybankResources.properties* contains strings to be localized for the language English in the United States (en_US), then *MybankResources_fr_FR..properties* contains strings to be localized for the language "fr" (French) and region of "FR" (France). In order to use the data in these files, you have to get the ResourceBundle instance as shown in Listing 8.1.

In order to understand Listing 8.1, assume that the English properties file, *MybankResources.properties* contains a key value pair: `header.title=My Bank`. Next assume that the French properties file, *MybankResources_fr_FR.properties* also contains a key value pair: `header.title= Ma Banque`. The code snippet in Listing 8.1 produces an output "Ma Banque". What happens if the *MybankResources_fr_FR.properties* file was missing? Just to see what happens, rename the file to something else and run the program again. This time the output will be *My Bank*. But the locale was "fr_FR"!

Here's what happened. Because the locale was "fr_FR", the `getBundle()` method looked up *MybankResources_fr_FR.properties*. When it did not find this file, it looked for the "next best match" *MybankResources_fr.properties*. But this file doesn't exist either. Finally the `getBundle()` found the *MybankResources.properties* file and returned an instance of `PropertiesResourceBundle` for this file. Accordingly the String `myHeader` is looked up using the *header.title* key from the *MybankResources.properties* file and returned to the user. In general, the algorithm for looking up a Properties file is:

```
MybankResources_language_country_variant.properties
MybankResources_language_country.properties
MybankResources_language.properties
MybankResources.properties
```

Java Properties files are commonly used for web tier localization in Struts web applications. Hence we have shown you how to use them for localizing string data. If your requirement involves extracting locale specific resources besides strings, you might want to use the `ListResourceBundle` class.

NOTE: When the above program runs from the command line, the properties file is located and loaded by the default command line class loader – the System Classpath Class Loader. Similarly in a web application, the properties file should be located where the web application class loader can find it.

java.text.NumberFormat

`NumberFormat` is an abstract base class that is used to format and parse numeric data specific to a locale. This class is used primarily to format numbers and currencies. A sample example that formats currencies is shown in listing 8.2. A currency format for French Locale is first obtained. Then a double is formatted and printed using the currency format for French Locale. The output is: `Salary is: 5 124,75`

In the above example, the double amount was hard coded as a decimal in en_US format and printed as in the French format. Sometime you will have to do the reverse while processing user input in your web applications. For instance, a user in France enters a currency in the French format into a text field in the web application and you have to get the `double` amount for the business logic to process it. The `NumberFormat` class has the `parse()` method to do this. Listing 8.3 shows this. The output of the program is: `Salary is: 5124.75`

Listing 8.2 Formatting currencies using NumberFormat

```
Locale frLocale = new Locale ("fr","FR");
// get instance of NumberFormat
NumberFormat currencyFormat =
       NumberFormat.getCurrencyInstance(frLocale);

double salaryAmount = 5124.75;
// Format the amount for the French locale
String salaryInFrench = currencyFormat.format(salaryAmount);
System.out.println ("Salary is: " + salaryInFrench);
```

There is a subclass of the `NumberFormat` called `DecimalFormat` that can be used to format locale specific decimal numbers with the additional capability of providing patterns and symbols for formatting. The symbols are stored in a `DecimalFormatSymbols`. When using the `NumberFormat` factory methods, the patterns and symbols are read from localized resource bundles.

Listing 8.3 Formatting currencies using NumberFormat

```
// get the amount from a text field (5 124,75  )
String salaryInFrench = salaryField.getText();
// Print it back into a regular number
System.out.println("Salary is: " +
      CurrencyFormat.parse(salaryInFrench);
```

java.text.DateFormat

`DateFormat` is an abstract class that is used to format dates and times. When a locale is specified it formats the dates accordingly. The following code formats a date independent of locale

```
Date now = new Date();
String dateString = DateFormat.getDateInstance().format(now);
```

To format a date for a given locale:

```
DateFormat dateFormat =
   DateFormat.getDateInstance(Locale.GERMANY);
dateFormat.format(now);
```

java.text.MessageFormat

`MessageFormat` is used to create concatenated messages in a language neutral way. It takes a set of input objects, formats them and inserts the formatted strings into specific places in a given pattern. Listing 8.4 shows how to create a meaningful message by inserting string objects into specific locations in the already existing message. When you run the program, you will get the following output: `John Doe logged in at 8/28/03 2:57 PM`

Listing 8.4 Using MessageFormat to create message

```
Object[] myObjects = { "John",
                       "Doe",
                  new java.util.Date(System.currentTimeMillis())
                       };
String messageToBeDisplayed = "{0} {1} logged in at {2}";
String message =
java.text.MessageFormat.format(messageToBeDisplayed, myObjects);
System.out.println(message);
```

Internationalizing Struts Applications

The I18N features of Struts framework build upon the Java I18N features. The I18N support in Struts applications is limited to the presentation of text and images.

I18N features of Struts Resource Bundle

The Struts Resource Bundle is very similar to the Java ResourceBundle. Struts has an abstract class called `org.apache.struts.util.MessageResources` and a subclass `org.apache.struts.util.PropertyMessageResources` which as the name suggests is based on property files. In spite of the similar functionalities, the above Struts classes (surprisingly) do not inherit from their `java.util` counterparts. However if you understand the working of the `java.util.ResourceBundle`, you have more or less understood how the Struts Resource Bundles work. In general, Struts applications deal with internationalization in the following way:

1. The application developer creates several properties files (one per Locale) that contain the localized text for messages, labels and image file names to be displayed to the user. The naming convention for the Locale specific properties files is same as that of `java.util.ResourceBundle`. The base properties file name (corresponding to the `en_US`) is configured in the Struts Config file (Refer to Chapter 3). For other Locales, Struts figures out the names of the properties file by the standard naming conventions.

2. The properties file should be placed so that the web application class loader can locate it. The classes in the *WEB-INF/classes* folder are loaded by the web application class loader and is an ideal place to put the properties file. Naming conventions of Java classes applies to the properties files too. Suppose that the classes in an application are packaged in mybank.app1 package. If the *App1Messages.properties* is placed in *mybank/app1* folder it finally ends up in *WEB-INF/classes/mybank/app1* directory in the WAR. Accordingly the Message

Resource Bundle is configured as follows (from Chapter 3):

```
<message-resources parameter="mybank.app1.App1Messages"/>
```

The Struts Controller Servlet is configured to look up information from these properties files (Actually the Message Resource Bundle is loaded at startup and is stored in the ServletContext and is available within the entire web application if needed).

3. When the Struts Controller Servlet receives a request, it checks the user's Locale (by looking up the HttpSession for the key `org.apache.struts.action.LOCALE`) and then looks up a resource bundle confirming to that locale and makes it available. Interested parties (read your application logic) can then lookup Locale specific messages using the Locale independent keys.

For instance, an ActionError can be constructed in the ActionsForm's `validate()` method as follows:

```
ActionError error1 = new ActionError("error.firstname.required");
```

The actual ActionError constructed has the Locale dependent message for the key `error.firstname.required`. Some of the commonly used constructors are:

```
ActionError(String key)
ActionError(String key, Object value)
ActionError(String key, Object values[])
```

The second and the third constructor are used if any parameters need to be passed in dynamically. These constructors take the key and an array of strings containing the replacement parameters to be used in the validation error messages. This is similar to the behavior of `java.text.MessageFormat`. E.g.: The properties file contains a key value pair as

```
validation.range.message={0} cannot be less than {1} characters
```

The ActionError to access this message is:

```
String[] strArray = {"First Name", "35"};
new ActionError("validation.range.message", strArray);
```

I18N features of MessageTag

You have already used the `MessageTag` (`<bean:message>`), not in the context of I18N but for externalizing the messages. We used this tag to retrieve messages from the external properties file. Now that the same properties files are put to use in internationalizing the web application, the `MessageTag` has donned the role of providing Locale specific text in the JSP. This is one of the most frequently used tags whether you are localizing the application or not. Since you already the workings of this tag, we will not bore you with more verbosity. Instead we will compare this Struts tag with the JSTL equivalents. As has been stated earlier in Chapter 6, the word on the street is that the Struts tags should be preferably replaced with JSTL equivalents.

I18N features of HTML Tag Library

Struts HTML tag library is the key to rendering JSPs as HTML and is filled with tags offering I18N features. Look for the tag attributes whose name ends with key. For instance, the `<html:img>` tag offers `srcKey` to look up the `src` of the image and `altKey` to look up the `alt` text from message resource bundle.

I18N features of LookupDispatchAction

As you already know, `LookupDispatchAction` offers excellent capability to handle the business logic in a locale independent manner. Certain restrictions apply in that it can be used only with grey buttons or html links and not with image buttons. More details are in Chapter 4.

Internationalizing Tiles Applications

In Chapter 7 you saw how to use Tiles to organize your JSP pages. The Tiles framework provides an easy way to add tiles or templates to a JSP page to present content in a dynamic fashion. The Tiles framework, just like Struts can be localized to provide different tiles based on a user's preferred locale. For example, the header tile in Chapter 7 could be replaced with a different header that corresponds to a specific locale. It could contain an area-specific flag for instance or simply a different background color.

A Tiles application has a Tiles definition file (e.g.:*/WEB-INF/tiles-defs.xml*) that defines the structure of a JSP page using various tiles, for the header, menu, body, footer etc. In the case of a localized Tiles application, there will one such file *per locale* along with the default *tiles-defs.xml* file. For example, if your application supports US English and French, there will be two definition files, one for each locale as well as a default one – *tiles-defs_fr.xml*, *tiles-defs_en.xml* and *tiles-defs.xml*

The naming conventions for the Tiles definition files are the same as for a `java.util.ResourceBundle` class as explained earlier in the chapter. Again, just as in a localized Struts application, the session attribute `Action.LOCALE_KEY` is looked up for a user's preferred or default locale and the appropriate definition file are loaded. For instance, if the default file *tiles-defs.xml* is:

```
<tiles-definitions>
  <definition name="foo.bar" path="MybankLayout.jsp">
```

```
      <put name="title"  value="My Bank example" />
      <put name="header" value="/header.jsp" />
      <put name="menu"   value="/menu.jsp" />
      <put name="footer" value="/footer.jsp" />
      <put name="body"   value="/body.jsp" />
  </definition>
</tiles-definitions>
```

Then the localized Tiles definition file for French is:

```
<tiles-definitions>
  <definition name="foo.bar" path="MybankLayout.jsp">
      <put name="title"  value="Mon exemple de ma banque"/>
      <put name="header" value="/header.jsp" />
      <put name="menu"   value="/menu.jsp" />
      <put name="footer" value="/footer.jsp" />
      <put name="body"   value="/body.jsp" />
  </definition>
</tiles-definitions>
```

This approach is justified if you use different JSPs per locale. However if the JSPs themselves are fully I18N capable, meaning the single JSP can adapt itself to render local sensitive UI, then the only difference between the two tiles definition for the two locales, is the title. The need for different definition files in that case could be eliminated if there was a mechanism to specify the key to the message resource bundle in the `<put>` element above. Unfortunately such a mechanism doesn't seem to exist at the time of writing and hence you are left with creating definitions for each locale.

Processing Localized Input

Localized input is data input in a native language using locale specific formats. How does your back-end Java code process data input in a native language? Let us consider a simple form with two fields, `fullName` and `monthlySalary` as shown below.

```
public class CustomerForm extends ActionForm {
   private String fullName = null;
   private double monthlySalary = 0.0;
...
}
```

John Doe enters his monthly salary as 5431.52 and submits the form. That's it, the form fields are populated nicely and the application works without a hitch. The conversion of the monthly salary from a String to a double is automatically taken care of by Struts and John Doe won't have any problems with the application.

What happens if the same application is viewed by a user in France and he decides to enter the same amount in the French format as 5 431,52? When the French user submits the application, the `monthlySalary` attribute in `CustomerForm` ends up being populated with 0.0 instead of 5431.52. Why so? When the form is submitted, the RequestProcessor populates the JavaBeans properties of the ActionForm with the request parameters by using the `RequestUtils` and `BeanUtils` classes. The actual population is done by the `BeanUtils.populate()` method. That method tries to parse the String "5 431,52" and assign it to `monthlySalary` – a double field without caring much for the Locale of the user. This obviously throws an exception on which the default action is to set 0.0 in the `monthlySalary` field.

What is the solution then? How can you make the Struts applications process localized input? Since the `BeanUtils` class does not check the locale at the time of populating the form, the only way out of this situation is to make the `monthlySalary` field a `String` instead of a `double`. Now, the `BeanUtils` does not try to parse a double from the String. Instead the value is assigned AS IS. A customized routine has to be written to convert the String into a double in a Locale dependent manner.

Character encodings

Earlier, when applications were built, they were built for one language. Those were the days of "code pages". Code pages described how binary values mapped to human readable characters. A currently executing program was considered to be in a single code page. These approaches were fine until Internationalization came along. Then came the issue of how to represent multiple character sets and encodings for an application. Hence came character sets and encodings.

Character sets are sets of text and graphic symbols mapped to positive integers. ASCII was one of the first character sets to be used. ASCII though efficient, was good at representing only US English.

A Character encoding, as mentioned earlier, maps a character to fixed width units. It also defines ordering rules and byte serializing guidelines. Different character sets have multiple encodings. For example, Java programs represent Cyrillic character sets using KO18-R or KO18-U encodings. Unicode enables us to write multilingual applications.

Other examples of encodings include ISO 8859, UTF-8 etc. UTF or Unicode Transformation Format is used to encode 16 bit Unicode characters as one to four bytes. A UTF byte is equivalent to 7-bit ASCII if its higher order bit is zero. You might have come across many JSP pages, which have a line that looks like:

```
<%@ page contentType="text/html;charset=UTF-8" language="java" %>
```

Here, charset=UTF-8 indicates that the page uses a response encoding of UTF-8. When internationalizing the web tier, you need to consider three types of encodings:

- Request encoding
- Page encoding
- Response encoding

Request encoding deals with the encoding used to encode request parameters. Browsers typically send the request encoding with the *Content-type* header. If this is not present, the Servlet container will use ISO-8859-1 as the default encoding.

Page encoding is used in JSP pages to indicate the character encoding *for that file.* You can find the page encoding from:

- The Page Encoding value of a JSP property group whose URL pattern matches the page. To see how JSP property groups work, you can go to the following URL:
  http://java.sun.com/j2ee/1.4/docs/tutorial/doc/JSPIntro13.html#wp72193
- The `pageEncoding` attribute in a JSP page specified along with the page directive. If the value `pageEncoding` attribute differs from the value specified in the JSP property group, a translation error can occur.
- The CHARSET value of the `contentType` attribute in the page directive.

If none of these encodings are mentioned, then the default encoding of ISO-8859-1 is used.

Response encoding is the encoding of the text response sent by a Servlet or a JSP page. This encoding governs the way the output is rendered on a client's browser and based on the client's locale. The web container sets a response encoding from one of the following:

- The CHARSET value of the `contentType` attribute in the page directive.
- The encoding in the `pageEncoding` attribute of the page directive
- The Page Encoding value of a JSP property group whose URL pattern matches the page

If none of these encodings are mentioned, then the default encoding of ISO-8859-1 is used.

Early on, when internationalization of computer applications became popular, there was a boom in the number of encodings available to the user. Unfortunately these encodings were unable to cover multiple languages. For instance, the European Union was not able to cover all the European languages in one encoding, resulting in having to create multiple encodings to cover them. This further worsened the problem as multiple encodings could use the *same* number to represent *different characters* in different languages. The result: higher chances of data corruption.

A big company had its applications working great with a default locale of US English, until it decided to go global. One of the requirements was to support Chinese characters. The application code was modified accordingly but each time the application ran, it was just not able to produce meaningful output, as the text seemed to be distorted. The culprit was the database encoding.

Chinese characters, just like Korean and Japanese, have writing schemes that cannot be represented by single byte code formats such as ASCII and EBCDIC. These languages need at least a Double Byte Character Set (DBCS) encoding to handle their characters. Once the database was updated to support DBCS encoding, the applications worked fine. These problems led to the creation of a universal character-encoding format called Unicode.

Unicode is a 16 bit character encoding that assigns a unique number to each character in the major languages of the world. Though it can officially support up to 65,536 characters, it also has reserved some code points for mapping into additional 16-bit planes with the potential to cope with over a million unique characters. Unicode is more efficient as it defines a standardized character set that represents most of the commonly used languages. In addition, it can be extended to accommodate any additions. Unicode characters are represented as escape sequences of type \u*XXXX* where XXXX is a character's 16 bit representation in hexadecimal in cases where a Java program's source encoding is not Unicode compliant.

Struts and character encoding

Setting the character encoding in the web application requires the following steps:

1. Configure the servlet container to support the desired encoding. For instance, you have to set the servlet container to interpret the input as UTF-8 for Unicode. This configuration is vendor dependent.
2. Set the response content type to the required encoding (e.g. UTF-8). In Struts 1.1, this information is specified in the `<controller>` element in struts-config.xml using the `contentType` attribute.
3. This can also be set in the JSPs with the `@page` directive as follows:

```
<%@ page contentType="text/html; charset=UTF-8" %>.
```

4. Next add the following line in the HTML <head>:

```
<meta http-equiv="content-type"
            content="text/html; charset=UTF-8">
```

5. Make sure you are using the I18N version rather than the US version of the JRE. (If you are using JDK, this problem may ot arise)
6. Make sure that the database encoding is also set to Unicode.

NOTE: Setting `<html:html locale="true">` doesn't set the encoding stream. It is only a signal to Struts to use the locale-specific resource bundle

native2ascii conversion

Java programs can process only those files that are encoded in Latin-1 (ISO 8859-1) encoding or files in Unicode encoding. Any other files containing different encodings besides these two will not be processed. The `native2ascii` tool is used to convert such non Latin-1 or non-Unicode files into a Unicode encoded file. Any characters that are not in ISO 8859-1 will be encoded using Unicode escapes. For example, if you have a file encoded in a different language, say *myCyrillicFile* in Cyrillic, you can use the native2ascii tool to convert it into a Unicode encoded file as follows:

```
native2ascii -encoding UTF-8 myCyrillicFile myUnicodeFile
```

You can use other encodings besides UTF-8 too. Use the above tool on the Struts prorperties files (message resource bundles) containing non Latin-1 encoding. Without this conversion, the Struts application (or java for that matter) will not be able to interpret the encoded text. Consequently the `<bean:message>` and `<html:errors/>` will display garbage.

Summary

In this chapter you started with what I18N and L10N are, their need and their advantages. You also got a quick overview of the Java and Struts Internationalization API. Then you looked at the various ways to internationalize the web tier using the features in Struts and Tiles. You also saw how to process localized input using Struts applications.

Chapter 9

Struts and Exception Handling

In this chapter:

1. *You will learn about basics of Exception Handling*
2. *You will understand the exception handling from servlet specification perspective*
3. *You will understand exception handling facilities in Struts1.1*
4. *We will develop a simple yet robust utility to log exceptions*
5. *We will cover strategies to centralize logging in production environments*

Exception handling is very crucial part often overlooked in web application development that has ramifications far beyond deployment. You know how to handle exceptions using the built-in Java construct to catch one and handle it appropriately. But what is appropriate? The basic rationale behind exception handling is to catch errors and report them. What is the level of detail needed in reporting the exception? How should the user be notified of the exception? How should customer support handle problem reports and track and trace the exception from the logs? As a developer where do you handle the exceptions? These are some of the major questions we will answer in this chapter first from a generic way and then as applicable to Struts applications.

Under normal circumstances when you catch the exception in a method, you print the stack trace using the `printStacktrace()` method or declare the method to throw the exception. In a production system, when an exception is thrown it's likely that the system is unable to process end user's request. When such an exception occurs, the end user normally expects the following:

- A message indicating that an error has occurred
- A unique error identifier that he can use while reporting it to customer support.
- Quick resolution of the problem.

The customer support should have access to back-end mechanisms to resolve the problem. The customer service team should, for example, receive immediate error notification, so that the service representative is aware of the problem before the customer calls for resolution. Furthermore, the service representative should be able to use the unique error identifier (reported by the user) to lookup the production log files for quick identification of the problem – preferably up to the exact line number (or at least the exact method). In order to provide both the end user and the support team with the tools and services they need, you as a developer must have a clear picture, as you are building a system, of everything that can go wrong with it once it is deployed.

Exception Handling Basics

It is common usage by the developers to put `System.out.println()` to track the exception and flow through the code. While they come in handy, they have to be avoided due to the following reasons:

1. `System.out.println` is expensive. These calls are synchronized for the duration of disk I/O, which significantly slows throughput.
2. By default, stack traces are logged to the console. But browsing the console for an exception trace isn't feasible in a production system.
3. In addition, they aren't guaranteed to show up in the production system, because system administrators can map `System.out` and `System.errs` to ' ' `[>nul]` on NT and `dev/nul` on UNIX. Moreover, if you're running the J2EE app server as an NT service, you won't even have a console.
4. Even if you redirect the console log to an output file, chances are that the file will be overwritten when the production J2EE app servers are restarted.
5. Using `System.out.println` during testing and then removing them before production isn't an elegant solution either, because doing so means your production code will not function the same as your test code.

What you need is a mechanism to declaratively control logging so that your test code and your production code are the same, and performance overhead incurred in production is minimal when logging is declaratively turned off. The obvious solution here is to use a logging utility. It is pretty customary these days to use a utility like Log4J (http://jakarta.apache.org/log4j) for logging. With the right coding conventions in place, a logging utility will pretty much take care of recording any type of messages, whether a system error or some warning. However it is up to you as a developer to make the best use of the utilities. It requires a lot of forethought to handle exceptions effectively. In this chapter we will use Log4J to log exceptions effectively. Hence we will review Log4J before proceeding to look at some commonly accepted principles of Exception handling in Java.

Log4J crash course

Log4J is the logging implementation available from Apache's Jakarta project and has been around long before JDK Logging appeared and quite naturally has a larger developer base. Lot of material is freely available online if you want to dig deeper into Log4J and we have held back from such a detailed treatment here. As with any Logging mechanisms, this library provides powerful capabilities to declaratively control logging and the level of logging.

In Log4J, all the logging occurs through the `Logger` class in `org.apache.log4j` package. The `Logger` class supports five levels for logging. They are FATAL, ERROR, WARNING, INFO, DEBUG. Without Log4J, you would perhaps use a Boolean flag to control the logging. With such a boolean flag, there are only two states – logging or no logging. In Log4J the levels are defined to fine tune the amount of logging. Here is how you would user the Log4J.

```
Logger logger = Logger.getLogger ("foo.bar");
logger.debug ("This is a debug message");
```

The code above first obtains the Logger instance named foo.bar and logs a message at DEBUG level. You can declaratively turn off the logging for messages at lower level than WARNING. This means the messages logged at INFO and DEBUG level will not be logged.

Logged messages always end up in a destination like file, database table etc. The destination of the log message is specified using the *`Appender`*. The `Appender` can represent a file, console, email address or as exotic as a JMS channel. If you need a destination that is not supported by the classes out of the box you can write a new class that implements the `Appender` interface. Appenders can be configured at startup in a variety of ways. One way to configure them is through an XML file. A XML file is shown below.

```
<appender name="Mybank-Warn"
         class="org.apache.log4j.FileAppender">
  <param name="Threshold" value="WARN" />
  <param name="File"   value="./logs/mybank-warnings.log" />
  <param name="Append" value="false" />
  <layout class="org.apache.log4j.PatternLayout">
     <param name="ConversionPattern"
            value="%d [%x][%t] %-5p %c{2} - %m%n"/>
  </layout>
</appender>

<category name="foo.bar" additivity="false">
```

```
  <appender-ref ref="Mybank-Warn" />
  <appender-ref ref="Developer-Console" />
</category>
```

The above XML when translated to simple English reads as follows: The Appender named *Mybank-Warn* logs the messages to a file *mybank-warnings.log*. Only messages with a threshold of WARN or higher are logged. The format of the message is as specified by the *PatternLayout*.

The format of the output message is specified using `Layout`. Standard classes for specifying the layout like *PatternLayout* are used most of the times and the format is declaratively specified using symbols like %d which instructs Log4J to include date time in the log and %m – the actual message itself and so on.

As you saw earlier, the logging is performed through a named `Logger` instance. If you are wondering how the `Logger` would know which `Appender` to log to, it is the `<category>` element in the above XML that provides the link between the two. The `Logger` uses the `<category>` setting in the XML to get this information. The `<category>` in the above XML is called *foo.bar*. Recall that we tried to log using a Logger named *foo.bar*. The *foo.bar* Logger gets the FileAppender *Mybank-Warn* appender through the *foo.bar* category setting in the XML. And then the messages end up in the file *mybank-warnings.log*.

There can be more than one appenders associated with a category. This implies that the messages logged with a Logger can potentially end up in multiple locations if needed.

Principles of Exception Handling

The following are some of the generally accepted principles of exception handling:

1. If you can't handle an exception, don't catch it.
2. Catch an exception as close as possible to its source.
3. If you catch an exception, don't swallow it.
4. Log an exception where you catch it, unless you plan to re-throw it.
5. Preserve the stack trace when you re-throw the exception by wrapping the original exception in the new one.
6. Use as many typed exceptions as you need, particularly for application exceptions. Do not just use java.lang.Exception every time you need to declare a throws clause. By fine graining the throws clause, it is self-documenting and becomes evident to the caller that different exceptions have to be handled.
7. If you programming application logic, use unchecked exceptions to indicate an error from which the user cannot recover. If you are creating third party

libraries to be used by other developers, use checked exceptions for unrecoverable errors too.

8. Never throw unchecked exceptions in your methods just because it clutters the method signature. There are some scenarios where this is good (For e.g. EJB Interface/Implementations, where unchecked exceptions alter the bean behavior in terms of transaction commit and rollback), but otherwise this is not a good practice.
9. Throw Application Exceptions as Unchecked Exceptions and Unrecoverable System exceptions as unchecked exceptions.
10. Structure your methods according to how fine-grained your exception handling must be.

Principle 1 is obviously in conflict with 2. The practical solution is a trade-off between how close to the source you catch an exception and how far you let it fall before you've completely lost the intent or content of the original exception.

Principles 3, 4, and 5 is a problems developers face when they catch an exception, but do not know how to handle it and hence throw a new exception of same or different type. When this happens, the original exception's stack trace is lost. Listing 9.1 shows such a scenario. The `SQLException` is caught on Line 15 and re-thrown as a application specific `UpdateException` on Line 16. In the process, the stacktrace with valuable info about the `SQLException` is lost. Thus the developer can only trace back to Line 16 where the `UpdateException` is thrown and not beyond that (This is the best case scenario with compiler debug flags turned on. If hotspot compiler was used, the stacktrace would only have the method name without any line number). Listing 9.2 shows almost similar scenario, but the actual exception is logged to the console. This is not good choice and sometimes not feasible because of reasons cited earlier in this section.

Listing 9.1 Losing Exception stack trace

```
10 public void updateDetails(CustomerInfo info)
                                                  throws
UpdateException
11 {
12     try {
13       CustomerDAO custDAO = CustDAOFactory.getCustDAO();
14       custDAO.update(info);
15     } catch (SQLException e) {
16       throw new UpdateException("Details cannot be updated");
17     }
18 }
```

Listing 9.2 Losing Exception stack trace

```
public void updateDetails(CustomerInfo info)
                                                   throws
UpdateException
{
  try {
    CustomerDAO custDAO = CustDAOFactory.getCustDAO();
    custDAO.update(info);
  } catch (SQLException e) {
    e.printStackTrace();
    throw new UpdateException("Details cannot be updated");
  }
}
```

Listing 9.3 Preserving Exception stack trace

```
public void updateDetails(CustomerInfo info)
                                                   throws
UpdateException
{
  try {
    CustomerDAO custDAO = CustDAOFactory.getCustDAO();
    custDAO.update(info);
  } catch (SQLException e) {
    throw new UpdateException(e);
  }
}
```

A better approach is shown in Listing 9.3. Here, the `SQLException` is wrapped in the `UpdateException`. The caller of the `updateDetails` can catch the `UpdateException`, and get the knowledge of the embedded `SQLException`.

Principles 7, 8 and 9 in the above list pertain to the discussion of using checked v/s unchecked exceptions. Checked Exceptions are those that extend `java.lang.Exception`. If your method throws checked exceptions, then the caller is forced to catch these exceptions at compile time or declare in the throws clause of the method. On the other hand, unchecked exceptions are those that extend `java.lang.RuntimeException`, generally referred to as runtime exceptions. If your method throws a runtime exception, the caller of the method is not forced to catch the exception or add it to the method signature at compile time.

A rule of thumb is to model application exceptions as checked exceptions and system exceptions as unchecked exceptions. The code below is an example of application exception.

```
if (withDrawalAmt > accountBalance)
{
  throw new NotEnoughBalanceException(
    "Your account does not have enough balance");
}
```

When the account does not have enough balance for requested withdrawal amount, the user gets a `NotEnoughBalanceException`. The user can decide to withdraw lesser amount. Notice that the application exception is not logged. In case of the application exceptions, the developer explicitly throws them in the code and the intent is very clear. Hence there is no need for content (log or stack trace).

Principle 10 is about the use of debug flags with compilation. At compile time it is possible to tell the JVM to ignore line number information. The byte code without the line information are optimized for hotspot or server mode and the recommended way of deployment for production systems. In such cases, the exception stack traces do not provide the line number information. You can overcome this handicap by refactoring your code during development time and creating smaller and modular methods, so that guessing the line numbers for the exceptions is relatively easier.

The cost of exception handling

In the example used earlier to illustrate application exceptions, we are checking if withdrawal amount is greater than balance to throw the exception. This is not something you should be doing every time. Exceptions are expensive and should be used exceptionally. In order top understand some of the issues involved; let us look at the mechanism used by the Java Virtual Machine (JVM) to handle the exceptions. The JVM maintains a method invocation stack containing all the methods that have been invoked by the current thread in the reverse order of invocation. In other words, the first method invoked by the thread is at the bottom of the stack and the current method is at the top. Actually it is not the actual method that is present in the stack. Instead a stack frame representing the method is added to the stack. The stack frame contains the method's parameters, return value, local variables and JVM specific information. When the exception is thrown in a method at the top of the stack, code execution stops and the JVM takes over. The JVM searches the current method for a catch clause for the exception thrown or one of the parent classes of the thrown exception. If one is not found, then the JVM pops the current stack frame and inspects the calling method (the next method in the stack), for the catch clause for the exception or its parents. The process continues until the bottom of the stack is reached. In summary, it requires a lot of time and effort on the part of JVM.

Exceptions should be thrown only when there is no meaningful way of handling the situation. If these situations (conditions) can be handled programmatically in a meaningful manner, then throwing exceptions should be avoided. For instance if it is possible to handle the problem of withdrawal amount exceeding the balance in some other way, it has to chosen over throwing an application exception.

Examples of SystemException can be a `ConfigurationException`, which might indicate that the data load during start up failed. There is really nothing a user or even the customer support could do about it, except to correct the problem and restart the server. Hence it qualifies as a System exception and can be modeled as runtime exception.

Certain exceptions like `SQLException` might indicate a system error or application problem depending on the case. In either case, it makes a lot of sense to model `SQLException` as a checked exception because that is not thrown from your application logic. Rather it is thrown in the third party library and the library developer wants you to explicitly handle such a scenario.

JDK 1.4 and exception handling

If you are modeling the `UpdateException` as a unchecked exception, you will have to extend from `RuntimeException`. In addition if you are using JDK1.3.x and lower, you will also provide the wrapped exception attribute in your own exception. JDK1.4 onwards, you can wrap the "causative exception" in the parent class `RuntimeException` as a `java.lang.Throwable` attribute thus allowing you to carry around the "causative exception". For e.g. `SQLException` is the "causative exception" in Listing 9.3. In the `Throwable` class there is a new method getCause to get the cause of any exception which returns the wrapped exception if exists. This can result in an exception chain since the cause itself can have a cause. Prior to 1.4 Exception classes had their own non-standard exception chaining mechanisms. For instance, `RemoteException` was used to carry the actual exception across different JVMs or from EJB tier to web tier. As of 1.4, all of these classes have been retrofitted to use the standard exception chaining mechanism.

Additional exception handling features in JDK1.4 include programmatic access to stack trace. This is a boon for real time error monitoring and alert facilities. Often these systems need to manually parse the stack dump for keywords. This is been made much easier. One can invoke `getStackTrace` method on the `Exception` (or `Throwable`) and get an array of `StackTraceElements` returned. Each `StackTraceElement` provides the following methods.

- getClassName
- getFileName
- getLineNumber

- getMethodName
- isNativeMethod

By calling the above methods, you can display the stack trace in any format you like. In addition, elegant error monitoring systems can be written. For instance, the error monitoring system should alert the appropriate support team for the sub system by intelligently analyzing the stack trace. This has been made easier. The following code snippet can be used with JDK 1.4

```
StackTraceElement elements[] = e.getStackTrace();
for (int i=0, n=elements.length; i<n; i++) {
   if ( elements[i].getClassName.equals("LegacyAccessEJB")
      && elements[i].getMethodName().equals("invokeCOBOL")
   {
      //Alert the COBOL support team
   }
}
```

This code snippet checks if the exception originated in `LegacyAccessEJB` during invoking a method named "`invokeCOBOL`", it will alert the COBOL support team. Obviously the decision tree is not as simple as shown, but at least it removes the headache of parsing the trace for the same information.

Exception handling in Servlet and JSP specifications

In the previous section, you looked at the general principles in exception handling without a J2EE tilt. In this section, we will cover what servlet specification has to say about exception handling. Consider the `doGet()` method signature in a `HttpServlet`.

```
public void doGet(HttpServletRequest request,
                  HttpServletResponse response) throws
                  ServletException, IOException
```

The above method signature implies that a Servlet or a JSP (and finally a web application) is only allowed to throw

- `ServletException` or its subclasses
- `IOException` or its subclasses
- RuntimeExceptions

All other checked exceptions have to be handled in the Servlet/JSP code in one of the following manner:

- Catch the checked exception and log the error message and (or) take any business related action.

- Wrap the exception in a `ServletException` and throw the `ServletException`. (`ServletException` has overloaded constructors to wrap the actual exception.)

Servlet specification provides exception-handling support through *web.xml*. In *web.xml*, you can declare `<error-page>` to handle exceptions that are thrown but not caught.

```
<error-page>
  <exception-type>UnhandledException</exception-type>
  <location>UnhandledException.jsp</location>
</error-page>
```

What this means is that if an exception of type `UnhandledException` is thrown from your web application but not caught anywhere, then the user gets to see the *UnhandledException.jsp*. This works well for `ServletException`, `IOException`, `RuntimeException` and their subclasses.

If the `UnhandledException` is a subclass of `ServletException` and none of the error-page declaration containing exception-type fit the class hierarchy of the thrown exception, then the Servlet container gets the wrapped exception using the `ServletException.getRootCause` method. Then the container attempts again to match the error-page declaration. This approach works well if the `UnhandledException` is not a subclass of `ServletException` or `IOException` (but is a checked exception). You have to throw a `ServletException` or its subclass by wrapping the `UnhandledException` in it and the servlet container does rest of the magic.

There are times when the user cannot see a page due to incorrect access rights or the page simply does not exist. The Servlet sends an error response with an appropriate HTTP error code. For instance, 404 corresponds to Page not found, 500 corresponds to Internal Server Error and so on. You can also assign JSPs for default HTTP error code as follows.

```
<error-page>
  <error-code>404</error-code>
  <location>exceptions/Page404.jsp</location>
</error-page>
```

Similarly, exceptions can occur in the JSPs in scriptlets and custom tags. These can throw runtime exceptions. In addition scriptlets can throw `ServletException` and `IOException` since a JSP gets translated into the body of `_jspService()` method and the signature of the `_jspService()` method is same as `doGet()`.

```
public void _jspService(HttpServletRequest request,
                    HttpServletResponse response) throws
                    ServletException, IOException
```

Tags however throw `JspException` in their tag callback methods (`doStartTag()`, `doEndTag()` and so on). `JspException` is a direct subclass of `java.lang.Exception` and has no relationship with `ServletException` or `IOException`. The `_jspService()` method is container dependent but its contract is to catch all those exceptions and forward the request to the `errorPage` specified by the JSP. Hence it is a best practice to assign error pages in JSPs with the declarative: `<%@ page errorPage="/error.jsp" %>`

When forwarding to the exception page as specified by `errorPage` setting shown above, the exception describing the error is stored as request attribute with the key "`javax.servlet.jsp.JspException`". If the JSP assigned to handle the exceptions has the directive `<%@ page isErrorPage="true" %>` at the top of their page, then the exception is provided as the implicit scripting variable named `exception`.

Exception handling – Struts way

`ServletException`, `IOException`, `RuntimeException` and their sub classes can be declaratively mapped to appropriate JSP files through the *web.xml* settings. What about the other Exceptions? Fortunately since Struts1.1, you can assign JSP files for other checked exceptions too. Let us start by examining the features in Struts 1.1 for exception handling.

Declarative exception handling

Consider the method signature for the execute method in the Struts Action class.

```
public ActionForward execute(ActionMapping mapping,
                            ActionForm form,
                            HttpServletRequest request,
                            HttpServletResponse response)
                      throws java.lang.Exception
```

The `execute()` method has `java.lang.Exception` in its throws clause. Hence you don't have to handle the exceptions explicitly in Action. You can let them fall through. Consider the `execute()` method from an Action class.

```
public ActionForward execute(...) throws java.lang.Exception {
   ActionForward nextPage = null;
```

```
    ..
    userControllerEJB.createUser(UserInfo info);
    ..
    mapping.findForward("success");
}
```

The execute() method invokes the createUser() method on UserControllerEJB – a Session EJB that is responsible for creating the users. The createUser() method throws two Exceptions – RemoteException and DuplicateUserException. If the user cannot be created because another user with same id exists, then the Session EJB throws DuplicateUserException. A RemoteException is thrown if the user cannot be created because of problems in looking up or creating the Session EJB. If everything goes fine, then the user is forwarded to the ActionForward identified by *success*. However we have made no attempt to catch them and handle. Instead we have deferred their handling to Struts through the declarative exception handling facility.

Listing 9.5 Declarative Exception Handling in Struts

```
<struts-config>
 <action-mappings>
  <action
    path="/submitCustomerForm"
    type="mybank.example.CustomerAction"
    name="customerForm"
    scope="request"
    input="/CustomerDetails.jsp">

    <exception
      key="database.error.duplicate"
      path="/UserExists.jsp"
      type="mybank.account.DuplicateUserException"/>

    <exception
      key="rmi.error"
      type="java.rmi.RemoteException"
      path="/rmierror.jsp"/>

  </action>
 </action-mappings>
</struts-config>
```

Listing 9.5 shows the Struts Config file with declarative exception handling for the two exceptions – `DuplicateUserexception` and `RemoteException`. For each exception, an `<exception>` element is defined in the action mapping. The `path` attribute in the `<exception>` element specifies the page shown to the user upon that exception. For instance, if a `DuplicateUserException` is thrown when submitting the modified user profile, the controller will forward control to the *UserExists.jsp* page. The `key` attribute is used to retrieve the error message template from the associated resource bundle. Since the `<exception>` is local to the action mapping, it applies only for that action invocation. As you might have already notice the J2EE and Struts way of declaratively handling exceptions are complementary to one another.

In the Listing 9.5, the declarative exception handling was local to the `CustomerAction`. You can add global declarative exception handling too. For instance, if you want to handle the `RemoteException` in the same way across the board, use the following approach:

```
<struts-config>
   <global-exceptions>
    <exception
      key="rmi.error"
      type="java.rmi.RemoteException"
      path="/rmierror.jsp"/>
   </global-exceptions>
</struts-config>
```

Before forwarding to the page indicated in the `<exception>` element, Struts sets the exception as a request attribute with name `org.apache.struts.action.EXCEPTION`. (This is the value of `Globals.EXCEPTION_KEY`. `Globals` is a Java class in `org.apache.struts` package). The exception can be retrieved in the error page by using the method: `request.getAttribute(Globals.EXCEPTION_KEY)`.

Using the ExceptionHandler

Apart from `key`, `type` and `path`, the `<exception>` element also takes several optional attributes of which `handler` is a significant one. It is the fully qualified class name of the exception handler for that exception. By default `org.apache.struts.action.ExceptionHandler` is the class used. You can create a custom handler by extending the `ExceptionHandler` and overriding the `execute()` method. The `execute()` method has the following signature:

```
public ActionForward execute(Exception ex, ExceptionConfig ae,
         ActionMapping mapping, ActionForm formInstance,
         HttpServletRequest request,
         HttpServletResponse response) throws ServletException
```

To understand the ExceptionHandler, you have to understand the RequestProcessor workings on exception. As it does everything else, RequestProcessor invokes the execute() method on the Action instance. Hence it is natural that the exception thrown in the execute() is caught by the RequestProcessor. On receiving the exception, here is what the RequestProcessor does:

- It checks to see if the exception has an associated <exception> declaration either in local or global scope.
- If none exists, then the exception is:
  - Thrown AS IS if it is ServletException, IOException or their subclasses.
  - Wrapped in a ServletException and thrown if the above criteria is not satisfied.
- If there is a <exception> element declared then it retrieves the handler class, instantiates it and invokes execute() method in it. The default exception handler returns the path attribute of the <exception> element as an ActionForward.

As you will see later in this section, you can use a custom Exception Handler to centralize exception logging in the web tier.

When not to use declarative exception handling

Very frequently you would like to generate an ActionError and display it to the user instead of an exception. Let us look back at Listing 9.5 again for a moment. When RemoteException is thrown, the user sees *rmierror.jsp*. This makes sense since RemoteException is tantamount to a system exception and the only thing you can do is to ask the user to start all over again. However, it does not make sense to ask the user to start all over when DuplicateUserException is thrown since this is an application exception from which the user has a recovery path. A better option is to show this as an ActionError and give the user a chance to change the user id. For situations like this, you have to resort to programmatic exception handling.

Listing 9.6 shows the execute() method with programmatic exception handling. It catches the DuplicateUserException and creates an ActionErrors object to hold the error. The ActionErrors is set into the HTTP request as an attribute and then the same Form is shown back. The last part of showing the same page is achieved by the line mapping.getInput(). In this case you have to remove the declarative exception handling from Struts config file since it is being explicitly handled in the code.

If you use declarative exception handling, the default ExceptionHandler will still generate an ActionErrors object. However, the ActionErrors is associated with the page rather than a particular field. If you don't have this requirement, declarative exception handling is preferred over programmatic exception handling. Just set the initial JSP as the path for the `<exception>` and use `<html:errors/>` on the JSP and you get the exception as if it was an `ActionError` without any effort from your side.

Listing 9.6 Alternative to declarative exception handling

```
public ActionForward execute(...  ...) throws java.lang.Exception
{
   ActionForward nextPage = null;
   try {
     ..
     ..
     userControllerEJB.createUser(UserInfo info);
     ..
     mapping.findForward("success");
   }
   catch (DuplicateUserException due)
   {
     ActionErrors errors = new ActionErrors();
     ActionError error = new ActionError("userid.taken",
                                    due.getUserId());
     errors.add("userid", error);

     // This saves the ActionErrors in the request attribute
     // with the key Action.ERROR_KEY
     saveErrors(request, errors);
     nextPage = mapping.getInput();
   }
   return nextPage;
}
```

Exception handling and I18N

Another important matter of concern with exception handling is I18N. Even though the exception logging can occur in the language of your operating system, the messages should still be displayed in the language of the user's choice. This is not much of a concern is the message is generic. For instance, in Listing 9.5, the message shown to the user on `RemoteException` is identified by the key `rmi.error`. The key can have a generic message in the resource bundle. However the problem starts when the message has to get specific or the message requires replacement values. There are two possible solutions to this problem neither of which is ideal.

Here is the first approach: If you want to keep the internationalization in the web tier, then the specific exceptions from the server side should encapsulate the resource bundle keys and some (if not all) replacement values in them. The key and the replacement values can be exposed through getter methods on the exception class. This approach makes the server side code dependent on the web tier resource bundle. This also requires a programmatic exception handling since you have to pass appropriate replacement values to the ActionError.

The second approach is to send the user's Locale as one of the arguments to the server side and let the server side generate the entire message. This removes the server's dependency on the web tier code, but requires the Locale to be sent as a argument on every method call to the server.

Logging Exceptions

It is common knowledge that exceptions can occur anywhere – web-tier, ejb-tier, database. Wherever they occur, they must be caught and logged with appropriate context. It makes more sense to handle a lot, if not all of the exceptions originating in the ejb tier and database tier on the client side in the web tier. Why should exception logging take place on the client side?

First, the control hasn't passed outside of the application server yet. (Assuming both the web tier and ejb tier do not belong to disparate entities). The so-called client tier, which is composed of JSP pages, servlets and their helper classes, runs on the J2EE application server itself. Second, the classes in a well-designed web tier have a hierarchy (for example, hierarchy in the *Business Delegate* classes, *Intercepting Filter* classes, JSP base class, or in the Struts Action classes) or single point of invocation in the form of a *FrontController* servlet (Business Delegate, Intercepting Filter and Front Controller are Core J2EE Patterns. Refer to Sun blueprints for more details). The base classes of these hierarchies or the central point in FrontController classes can contain the exception logging code. In the case of session EJB-based logging, each of the methods in the EJB component must have logging code. As the business logic grows, so will the number of session EJB methods, and so will the amount of logging code. A web tier system will require less logging code. You should consider this option if you have co-located web tier and EJB tiers and you don't have a requirement to support any other type of client.

To develop a full fledged exception handling strategy let us start with a simple class shown in Listing 9.7. This class, `ExceptionCategory` categorizes the exceptions into INFO, WARNING, ERROR and FATAL. This identification helps us when the notification of Support personnel depends on the severity of the exception.

Listing 9.7 Enumeration class for Exception Category

```
public class ExceptionCategory implements java.io.Serializable {

    public static final ExceptionCategory INFO =
                                 new ExceptionCategory(0);
    public static final ExceptionCategory WARNING =
                                 new ExceptionCategory(1);
    public static final ExceptionCategory GENERAL_PROBLEM =
                                 new ExceptionCategory(2);
    public static final ExceptionCategory DATA_PROBLEM =
                                 new ExceptionCategory(3);
    public static final ExceptionCategory CONFIG_PROBLEM =
                                 new ExceptionCategory(4);
    public static final ExceptionCategory FATAL =
                                 new ExceptionCategory(5);


    private int type;

    private ExceptionCategory(int aType) {
        this.type = aType;
    }
}
```

Listing 9.8 Exception Info class

```
public class ExceptionInfo implements java.io.Serializable {
   private ExceptionCategory exceptionCategory;
   private String errorCode;
   private String exceptionID;
   private boolean logged;

   public ExceptionInfo(ExceptionCategory aCategory,
                        String aErrorCode) {
    this.exceptionCategory = aCategory;
    this.errorCode = aErrorCode;
    this.logged = false;
    this.exceptionID =
    UniqueIDGeneratorFactory.
             getUniqueIDGenerator().getUniqueID();
   }
}
```

The next class to look at is the `ExceptionInfo` class as shown in Listing 9.8 This class provides information about the Exception as the name indicates. Apart from the `ExceptionCategory`, this class also holds a unique id associated with the Exception and a boolean indicating if the exception has been already logged. The `UniqueIDGeneratorFactory` is a factory class that returns a UniqueIDGenerator. UniqueIDGenerator is represented by an interface `IUniqueIDGenerator`. This interface has just one method – `getUniqueID()`. Listing 9.9 shows a simple Unique ID Generator implementation IP Address and time.

Listing 9.9 Simple Unique ID Generator

```
public class UniqueIDGeneratorDefaultImpl
             implements IUniqueIDGenerator  {

   private static IUniqueIDGenerator instance =
                       new UniqueIDGeneratorDefaultImpl();

   private long counter = 0;

   public String getUniqueID() throws UniqueIDGeneratorException
{
      String exceptionID = null;
      try {
         exceptionID = InetAddress.getLocalHost().getHostName();
      } catch(UnknownHostException ue) {
         throw new UniqueIDGeneratorException(ue);
      }

      exceptionID = exceptionID +
                    System.currentTimeMillis() +
                    counter++;
      return exceptionID;
    }
}
```

And finally Listing 9.10 shows the actual Exception class. This is the base class for all the checked exceptions originating in *MyBank*. It is always better to have a base class for all exceptions originating in a system and then create new types as required. In this way, you can decide how much fine grained you want the catch exception blocks to be.

Listing 9.10 MybankException class

```
public abstract class MybankException extends Exception {

    private ExceptionInfo exceptionInfo;

    public MybankException(ExceptionInfo aInfo) {
       super();
       this.exceptionInfo = aInfo;
    }
}
```

Similarly you can have a base class for all unchecked exceptions thrown from system. Listing 9.11 shows such a class.

Listing 9.11 MybankRuntimeException class

```
public abstract class MybankRuntimeException extends Exception {

    private ExceptionInfo exceptionInfo;
    private Throwable wrappedException;

    public MybankException(ExceptionInfo aInfo,
                              Throwable aWrappedException) {
       super();
       this.exceptionInfo = aInfo;
       this.wrappedException = aWrappedException;
    }
}
```

Notice that `MybankRuntimeException` has only one constructor that takes both `ExceptionInfo` and a `Throwable`. This is because if someone is explicitly throwing a runtime exception from his or her code, it is probably because a system error or serious unrecoverable problem has occurred. We want to get hold of the actual cause of the problem and log it. By enforcing development time disciplines like this, one can decrease the chances of exceptions in the system without a context.

Finally we also need to look at the actual Logging utility – a stack trace printing utility shown in Listing 9.12. The default `printStackTrace()` method in `java.lang.Throwable` logs an error message to the System.err. `Throwable` also has an overloaded `printStackTrace()` method to log to a `PrintWriter` or a `PrintStream`. The above method in `StackTraceUtil` wraps the `StringWriter` within a `PrintWriter`. When the `PrintWriter` contains the stack trace, it simply calls `toString()` on the `StringWriter` to get a String representation of the stack trace.

Listing 9.12 Stack Trace printing utility.

```
public final class StackTraceTool
{
  private StackTraceTool() {}

  public static String getStackTraceAsString(
                                    MybankException exception)
  {
    String message = " Exception ID : " +
                     exception.getExceptionInfo().getExceptionID()
                   + "\n " + "Message :" + exception.getMessage();
    return getStackMessage(message, exception);
  }

  public static String getStackTraceAsString(Throwable throwable)
  {
    String message = " Exception ID : " +
    UniqueIDGeneratorFactory.getUniqueIDGenerator().getUniqueID()
             + "\n " + "Message :" + exception.getMessage();
    return getStackMessage(message, exception);
  }

  private static String getStackMessage(String message,
                                        Throwable exception)
  {
        StringWriter sw = new StringWriter();
        PrintWriter pw = new PrintWriter(sw);
        pw.print(" [ " );
        pw.print(exception.getClass().getName());
        pw.print(" ] ");
        pw.print(message);
        exception.printStackTrace(pw);
        return sw.toString();
    }
}
```

The StackTraceUtil class has two overloaded methods – getStackTraceAsString() – One of them takes the MybankException as the parameter, the other takes Throwable as the parameter. All exceptions of type MybankException already have the unique id in-built. For other exceptions, to be logged the unique id has to be explicitly generated. MybankException also has the flag indicating whether the exception has been logged making it easier to prevent multiple logging, as you will see very soon. Other Exceptions don't have this capability and it is up to the caller program and called to collaborate and ensure that duplicate logging does not happen.

Armed with these knowledge let us look at a scenario that will lead to duplicate logging in the system when an exception occurs. Consider a case when a method, `foo()`, in an entity EJB component is accessed in a session EJB method, called `bar()`. A web-tier client invokes the method `bar()` on the session EJB component, and also logs the exceptions. If an exception occurs in the entity EJB method `foo()` when the session EJB method `bar()` is invoked from the web-tier, the exception will have been logged in three places: first in the entity EJB component, then in the session EJB component, and finally in the web tier.

Fortunately, addressing these problems is fairly easy to do in a generic way. All you need is a mechanism for the caller to:

- Access the unique ID
- Find out if the exception has already been logged
- If the exception has been already logged don't log it again.

We have already developed the `MybankException` and `ExceptionInfo` class that let us check if the exception is already logged. If not logged already, log the exception and set the logged flag to be true. These classes also generate a unique id for every exception. Listing 9.13 shows a sample.

Listing 9.13 Sample Exception Logging

```
try {
    CustomerDAO cDao = CustomerDAOFactory.getDAO();
    cDao.createCustomer(CustomerValue);
} catch (CreateException ce) {
    //Assume CreateException is a subclass of MybankException
    if (! ce.isLogged() ) {
      String traceStr = StackTraceTool.getStackTraceAsString(ce);
      LogFactory.getLog(getClass().getName()).error(
              ce.getUniqueID() + ":" + traceStr);
      ce.setLogged(true);
    }
    throw ce;
}
```

Listing 9.13 shows the logging scenario when the exception caught is of type `MybankException`. It is very much a fact that not all of the exceptions thrown by your application are in this hierarchy. Under such conditions it is even more important that the logging is centralized in one place since there is no mechanism to prevent duplicate logging for exceptions outside the `MybankException` hierarchy.

That brings us to the idea of centralized logging. In the beginning of this section we said that it is easy and convenient to log exceptions on web-tier since most of the web-tier classes have a hierarchy. Let us examine this claim in more detail.

Strategies for centralized logging

In the previous section, we saw how to avoid duplicate logging. But when it comes to the entire application, you also learnt that logging should not only be done once but also centralized for disparate modules of the system if possible. There are various strategies to achieve centralized logging in the web tier. This section will cover those strategies.

Consider the web-tier for *MyBank*. After the Struts Forms are populated the `RequestProcessor` invokes the execute method on Action classes. Typically, in the execute method you access enterprise data and business logic in session ejbs and legacy systems. Since you want to decouple your web tier from the business logic implementation technology (EJB for example – which forces you to catch `RemoteException`) or the legacy systems, you are most likely to introduce *Business Delegates*. (Business Delegate is a Core J2EE Pattern). The Business Delegates might throw a variety of exceptions, most of which you want to handle by using the Struts declarative exception handling. When using the declarative exception handling you are most likely to log the exceptions in the JSPs since the control passes out of your code at the end of the execute method. Instead of adding the exception logging code to every JSP declared in Struts Config file, you can create a parent of all the error JSPs and put the logging code in there. Listing 9.14 shows a sample base JSP class.

There is quite a bit going on in Listing 9.14. First the class implements the `javax.servlet.jsp.HttpJspPage` interface. All the methods in this interface except the `_jspService()` have concrete implementations. These methods represent the various methods called during the JSP life cycle. In particular you will recognize the service method that is similar to the servlet's service method. In the course of this method execution, the `_jspService()` method is also executed. `_jspService()` method is not implemented by the page author or the developer. Instead it is auto generated by the servlet container during JSP pre-compilation or run time. All the markup, tags and scriptlets contained in the JSP get transformed into Java code and form the gist of the `_jspService()` method. The page author indicates that the jsp extends from this java class by adding the directive

```
<%@ page extends="mybank.webtier.MybankBaseErrorJsp" %>
```

If all of the Error-JSPs extend from this abstract JSP class, centralized logging is achieved. Before you celebrate for having nailed down the problem, shall we remind you that this solution may not work in all servlet containers. The reason for this is `JspFactory` and `PageContext` implementations are vendor dependent. Normally the calls for `JspFactory.getDefaultFactory()` and `factory.getPageContext()` occur in the auto generated `_jspService()` method. It is possible that some of the implementations may not initialize these objects we accessed in the `service()` method until they reach the `_jspService()` method!

Listing 9.14 Base JSP class for error pages

```
public abstract class MybankBaseErrorJsp implements HttpJspPage {
  private ServletConfig servletConfig;

  public ServletConfig getServletConfig() {
    return servletConfig;
  }

  public String getServletInfo() {
    return "Base JSP Class for My Bank Error Pages";
  }

  public void init(ServletConfig config)
                              throws ServletException {
    this.servletConfig = config;
    jspInit();
  }

  public void jspInit()     {}
  public void jspDestroy() {}

  public void service(ServletRequest req, ServletResponse res)
                throws ServletException, IOException  {
     HttpServletRequest request = (HttpServletRequest)req;
     HttpServletResponse response = (HttpServletResponse)res;

     JspFactory  factory     = JspFactory.getDefaultFactory();
     PageContext pageContext = factory.getPageContext(
                               this, request, response,
                               null,  // errorPageURL
                               false, // needsSession
                               JspWriter.DEFAULT_BUFFER,
                               true   // autoFlush
                               );
     Exception exc = pageContext.getException();
```

```
        String trace =StackTraceTool.getStackTraceAsString(exc);
        Logger.getLogger(getClass().getName()).error(trace);

        //proceed with container generated code from here
        _jspService(request,response);
    }

    public abstract void _jspService(HttpServletRequest request,
                                     HttpServletResponse response)
                              throws ServletException, IOException;
}
```

Don't panic. We have an alternate solution, which is less elegant but is guaranteed to work across vendor implementations. Let us create a custom tag to be invoked from all of the Error-JSPs. Listing 9.15 shows the logic for `doStartTag()` method of this custom tag. You will notice that it is very much similar to the `service()` method in Listing 9.14. After obtaining the exception object, it is logged by obtaining the `Logger` from Log4J. Since this tag is invoked within the `_jspService()` method for the JSP, it is guaranteed to have access to all of the implicit objects including `pagecontext` and `exception` in every vendor implementation.

Listing 9.15 Custom Tag for exception logging

```
public class ExceptionLoggingTag extends TagSupport
{
    public int doStartTag() throws ServletException, IOException
    {
        Exception exc = pageContext.getException();
        String trace =StackTraceTool.getStackTraceAsString(exc);
        LogFactory.getLog(getClass().getName()).error(trace);

        return EVAL_BODY_INCLUDE;
    }
}
```

For those of you who are visualizing the big picture, you will realize that logging from the JSP is not the right way. However there is no ideal way to achieve centralized logging without taking this approach. Each mechanism has its drawbacks and tradeoffs. This is something you will experience whenever design abstractions meet reality.

Listing 9.16 Mybank Base Action

```
public class MybankBaseAction extends Action {

  public ActionForward execute(ActionMapping mapping,
          ActionForm form, HttpServletRequest request,
          HttpServletResponse response) throws Exception
  {
    ActionForward actionForward = null;
    MybankBaseForm aForm = (MybankBaseForm)form;
    try  {
      preprocess(mapping, aForm, request, response);
      process(mapping, aForm, request, response);
      postprocess(mapping, aForm, request, response);
    }
    catch(MybankException ae) {
      //Any Special Processing for Mybank goes here
      if (ae.isLogged()) {
        String trace = StackTraceTool.getStackMessage(ae);
        LogFactory.getLog(getClass().getName()).error(
                 ae.getUniqueID() + ":" + trace);
        ae.setLogged(true);
      }
      actionForward = errorPage;
    }
  }

  protected abstract void preprocess(ActionMapping mapping,
          MybankBaseForm form, HttpServletRequest request,
          HttpServletResponse response) throws Exception;

  protected abstract void process(ActionMapping mapping,
          MybankBaseForm form, HttpServletRequest request,
          HttpServletResponse response) throws Exception;

  protected abstract void postprocess(ActionMapping mapping,
          MybankBaseForm form, HttpServletRequest request,
          HttpServletResponse response) throws Exception;
}
```

Until now you have seen a JSP based approach of exception handling and logging. What if you have a requirement to handle the exceptions originating from your application differently? Let us consider the application exceptions from our very own *MyBank*. The exceptions originating from the *MyBank* are subclasses of

MybankException and MybankRuntimeException. When using Struts as the framework in your web applications, then you will most likely have a base Action class with trivial functionality common to all of the Actions factored out. The base Action class is the ideal location to centralize the special processing for the application exceptions. Listing 9.16 shows a sample base Action, MybankBaseAction for the special processing just mentioned.

This class implements the execute method, but defines three abstract methods preprocess(), process() and postprocess() which take the same arguments as the execute() method but are invoked before, during and after the actual processing of the request. In the execute method, the MybankException is caught and any special processing required is done and then re-throw the exception for the declarative exception handling to work or programmatically forward to the relevant error page.

Note that you can achieve the same result by creating a custom exception handler for the MybankException. The custom exception handler's execute() method will do exactly what the catch block in Listing 9.16 is doing.

Reporting exceptions

Until now, you have looked at various exception logging strategies. After the exception is logged, there is also a need to report the fatal and serious ones by sending out emails and pager messages to the support team. Several approaches exist and the choices are numerous, but in this chapter we would like to consolidate the logging and error reporting for better coordination and control. For this, let us look at what Log4J has to offer.

As you already know, Log4J has three main components: *Layout*, *Appender*, and *Category* (also known as *Logger*). Layout represents the format of the message to be logged. *Appender* is an alias for the physical location at which the message will be logged. And category is the named entity; you can think of it as a handle for logging. Layouts and Appenders are declared in an XML configuration file. Every category comes with its own layout and Appender definitions. When you get a category and log to it, the message ends up in all the appenders associated with that category, and all those messages will be represented in the layout format specified in the XML configuration file.

Log4J comes with several standard appenders and one of them is called SMTPAppender. By using the SMTPAppender, you can declaratively send email messages when the errors occur in your system. You can configure the SMTPAppender like any other Appender – in the Log4J configuration file. Listing 9.17 shows a sample setup for SMTPAppender. It takes a *Threshold*, beyond which the Appender is operational, a subject for the email, the From and To addresses, SMTP server name and the pattern for the email message body.

Listing 9.17 SMTP Appender setup

```
<appender name="Mybank-Mail"
        class="org.apache.log4j.net.SMTPAppender">
   <param name="Threshold" value="ERROR" />
   <param name="Subject" value="Mybank Online has problems" />
   <param name="From" value="prod-monitor@mybank.com" />

   <!-- use commas in value to separate multiple recipients -->
   <param name="To" value="prod-support@mybank.com " />

   <param name="SMTPHost" value="mail.mybank.com" />
   <layout class="org.apache.log4j.PatternLayout">
      <param name="ConversionPattern" value="%m" />
   </layout>
</appender>
```

You can set up the category for the above `SMTPAppender` as

```
<category name="com.mybank.webtier.action" additivity="false">
   <priority value="ERROR"/>
   <appender-ref ref="Mybank-Mail"/>
   <appender-ref ref="Mybank-ErrorLog"/>
</category>
```

With this setup all the exceptions that are caught in the base Struts Action – `MybankBaseAction` are reported to email address prod-support@mybank.com. This is because the category name is identified by the package name for `MybankBaseAction` and while logging in Listing 9.16, we used the category whose name is same as the fully qualified class name for `MybankBaseAction` which happens to be `com.mybank.webtier.action.MybankBaseAction`. The email address prod-support@mybank.com is generally an email group configured in the enterprise mail server to include several individual recipients. Alternatively, you can explicitly specify multiple recipients in the To param in Listing 9.17 with commas separating the recipients. You can take a similar approach if you are logging in the Base JSP class of Listing 9.14 or the custom tag class of 9.15. But what if you are logging the exception using a scriptlet in the JSP. Although this approach is not recommended, suppose that you already have it in place and want to retrofit the Log4J email feature. In this case, you still can setup the appender as in Listing 9.17. But what about the jsp? What is the fully qualified class name for the JSP? This depends on the vendor. For instance, in weblogic a JSP in a directory called mortgage will reside in package named `jsp_servlet.mortgage`. Accordingly, for WebLogic, you can setup the category as follows

```
<category name="jsp_servlet.mortgage" additivity="false">
   <priority value="ERROR"/>
   <appender-ref ref="Mybank-Mail"/>
   <appender-ref ref="Mybank-ErrorLog"/>
</category>
```

Note that this setting is vendor specific and may not be portable to other application servers. But this is a minor change and should not be a problem if you decide to port to another application server say JBoss.

If you are wondering, "Email messages are all fine. How do I send pager beeps?" The quick answer is "No problem". Pagers have email addresses too. You can ask your service provider to associate the email address with the pager. Telecommunications companies and providers can use JavaMail API to implement a PAGER transport protocol that sends email messages to alphanumeric pagers. Similar approach works for Short Message Service (SMS) too since you can email a SMS device.

Summary

In development environments, the developer can go back, fix the root cause of the exception and move on. Not so in production systems. Exception handling is a very crucial part of enterprise applications. It is the key to quick response from the support team and resolution of the problems in working systems. A delayed or no resolution can leave the customer frustrated. In the internet world, where the competitor is just a click away, the importance of exception handling, logging, reporting and resolving cannot be stressed enough. This chapter gave you the insights into various gotchas on your way, common mistakes and strategies to address them from a web tier perspective.

Chapter 10

Effectively extending Struts

In this chapter:

1. *You will learn how to extend Struts using PlugIn as an example*
2. *You will see how to construct a rudimentary page flow controller by customizing ActionMapping*
3. *You will develop a mechanism for controlling validation for image button form submission*
4. *You will see how to handle sensitive resubmissions in a generic way rather than handling in every form*
5. *You will devise a strategy to avail DispatchAction-like functionality for image button form submission*

Struts is a generic framework. It works fine without modification. But there are times when it has to be customized. And we are not talking about straightforward customizations like extending the Form, Action and custom tags. We are referring to the "hooks" that Struts provides to extend the framework. In this chapter you will see several practical uses of these hooks.

A word of caution though: The customization features are probably going to be around without modification until Struts 2.0. The main candidates for overhaul are `ActionMapping` and `RequestProcessor`. The replacements would be designed using Command, interceptor and chain of responsibility patterns. However, since the above classes is part of public API, an alternative strategy will definitely emerge to seamlessly migrate the customizations discussed in this chapter so that none of the application code is affected and only the customization code might change. Of course this is just a speculation.

To understand the hooks, consider a Struts Plugin for say, a slick menu utility (Such a utility indeed exists. Check out http://struts-menu.sourceforge.net). The menu utility needs to read the configuration data from an external file. If the PlugIn were instead implemented as a servlet, it would read the file name from an `<init-param>` in *web.xml.* The `<set-property>` can do the same task for the PlugIn. The file name is set in the struts-config.xml by using `<set-property>`.

```
<plug-in className="mybank.example.MyMenuPlugIn">
    <set-property property="fileName"
                  value="/WEB-INF/menudata.xml"/>
</plug-in>
```

A JavaBeans property with the same name (`fileName`) is then added to the PlugIn class. The `<set-property>` tells the Struts framework to set the corresponding JavaBeans property in the plugin class (or any class associated with the configuration) with the `value` attribute of the `<set-property>` element. In addition, the Struts PlugIn implements the `PlugIn` interface from `org.apache.struts.action` package. Accordingly, the `MyMenuPlugIn` class is defined as:

```
public class MyMenuPlugIn implements PlugIn {
   private String fileName;

   public String getFileName() {
      return fileName;
   }

   public void setFileName(String name) {
     this.fileName = name;
   }

   public void init(ActionServlet servlet,
       ModuleConfig config) throws ServletException {
       .. ..
   }

   public void destroy() {
      .. ..
   }
}
```

During startup, Struts sets the `fileName` property using the corresponding setter method (and other properties if exist) and finally calls the `init()` method. Since PlugIns are the last ones to be configured by Struts, all other data from the struts-config.xml is guaranteed to be loaded before the `init()` method is invoked. The `init()` method is an opportunity to override and change any other settings including the RequestProcessor! Frameworks like SAIF (stands for Struts Action Invocation Framework. Available at http://struts.sourceforge.net) utilize this to change the RequestProcessor to one of its own.

Back to <set-property>. The <set-property> is the cornerstone of hook-based customization. Its DTD entry is as follows:

```
<!ATTLIST set-property   id        ID        #IMPLIED
                         property  CDATA     #REQUIRED
                         value     CDATA     #REQUIRED>
```

Both property and value are mandatory and ID is never set explicitly. The following elements in *struts-config.xml* can be customized using <set-property>: Form-bean, Exception, DataSource, PlugIn, RequestProcessor, MessageResources, ActionForward and ActionMapping.

Customizing the action mapping

The <action mapping> is the most frequently customized element. One way to customize action mapping is by setting the className in *struts-config.xml* as shown in Listing 10.1.

Listing 10.1 struts-config.xml for custom action mapping

```
<action   path="/submitCustomerForm"
          className="mybank.struts.MyActionMapping"
          type="mybank.app1.CustomerAction"
          name="CustomerForm"
          scope="request"
          validate="true"
          input="CustomerDetails.jsp">
   <set-property property="buttons"
             value="nextButton,saveButton,cancelButton" />
   <set-property property="forwards"
                value="page2,success,cancel" />
   <forward name="page2"  path="Page2.jsp"  />
   <forward name="success"  path="success.jsp"  />
   <forward name="success"  path="cancel.jsp"  />
</action>
```

The className attribute tells Struts to use the specified class (mybank.struts.MyActionMapping) for storing the action-mapping configuration. MyActionMapping extends ActionMapping in the package org.apache.struts.action. In addition it has a JavaBeans property for each of the <set-property> elements. MyActionMapping class is shown below:

```
public class MyActionMapping extends ActionMapping {
   private String buttons;
   private String forwards;
```

```
    //getters and setters for actions and forwards

    public MyActionMapping() { }
}
```

The custom action mapping is now ready to use. During startup, Struts instantiates the subclass of ActionMapping (instead of ActionMapping itself) and sets its JavaBeans properties to the values specified in the corresponding `<set-property>` element. As you know, the `execute()` method in the Action accepts `ActionMapping` as one of the arguments. When the `execute()` method in the `CustomerAction` is invoked at runtime, `MyActionMapping` is passed as the `ActionMapping` argument due to the setting in Listing 10.1. It can then be cast to `MyActionMapping` to access its JavaBeans properties as follows:

```
public ActionForward execute(ActionMapping mapping,
        ActionForm form, HttpServletRequest request,
        HttpServletResponse response) throws Exception {
    MyActionMapping customMapping =
                        (MyActionMapping) mapping;

    String actions = customMapping.getButtons();
      ..
    ..
}
```

Listing 10.2 struts-config.xml with global custom action mapping

```
<action-mappings type="mybank.struts.MyActionMapping">
    <action   path="/submitCustomerForm"
              type="mybank.app1.CustomerAction"
              name="CustomerForm"
              scope="request"
              validate="true"
              input="CustomerDetails.jsp">
      <set-property property="buttons"
              value="nextButton,saveButton,cancelButton" />
      <set-property property="forwards"
              value="page2,success,cancel" />
      <forward name="page2"   path="Page2.jsp"   />
      <forward name="success"  path="success.jsp"  />
      <forward name="success"  path="cancel.jsp"  />
    </action>
  </action-mappings>
```

There are several uses of simple customizations like this. As you will see later in this chapter, a lot of code that needs to be often repeated everywhere can be eliminated by simple customizations. While doing so, a single customized ActionMapping will be used for all the action mappings in the application. Setting the `className` for individual action mapping as shown in Listing 10.1 is painful. The alternative is to specify the `type` attribute on the `<action-mappings>` element as shown in Listing 10.2. This tells Struts to use the corresponding ActionMapping class for all the `<action>` elements. Listing 10.2 forms the basis for some of the utilities we develop in this chapter – a rudimentary page flow controller, auto-validation feature for image based form submissions, a generic mechanism to handle sensitive form resubmissions and a DispatchAction-like facility for image based form submissions. All of these will use the base Action class and base form conceived in Chapter 4 in conjunction with the *HtmlButton* described in Chapter 6 for form submission.

A rudimentary page flow controller

In the last section you have seen how ActionMapping can be customized. Let us use the customized action mapping to build a rudimentary page flow controller. Every Action has to render the next view to the user after successful business logic invocation. This would mean that a standard `mapping.findForward()` in every method of yours. The rudimentary page flow controller eliminates this by providing this information in a declarative manner in struts-config.xml utilizing `MyActionMapping`. That information is used at runtime to automatically decide which page to forward to. The reason why the page flow controller is called rudimentary is because it has a serious limitation. If the page transitions are dynamic, then it cannot work. The controller serves as an example for customized action mapping usage. Some of the groundwork for the page flow controller is already done in Listing 10.2, in case you didn't know it already!). In particular pay attention to the two lines:

```
<set-property property="buttons"
          value="nextButton,saveButton,cancelButton" />
<set-property property="forwards"
             value="page2,success,cancel" />
```

This first property (`buttons`) is a comma-separated name of all the buttons in the form. The second property (`forwards`) is a comma-separated name of the views rendered to the user when the corresponding buttons are selected. The view names refer to the forwards instead of the actual JSPs. Since the `forwards` is provided declaratively, the task of deciding the next view can be refactored into the base Action. This functionality has been added to the `MybankBaseAction` from Chapter 4. The code is shown in Listing 10.3 with the changes highlighted in bold.

Listing 10.3 The new and modified methods in MybankBaseA tion

```
public MybankBaseAction extends Action {
  public ActionForward execute(ActionMapping mapping,
            ActionForm form, HttpServletRequest request,
            HttpServletResponse response) throws Exception {
           ...
    MybankBaseForm myForm = (MybankBaseForm) form;
    MyActionMapping myMapping = (MyActionMapping) mapping;
    String selectedButton =
              getSelectedButton(myForm, myMapping);
    preprocess(myMapping, myForm, request, response);
    // Returns a null forward if the page controller is used.
    ActionForward forward =
        process(myMapping, myForm, request, response);
    postprocess(myMapping, myForm, request, response);
      ...
    if (forward == null) { // For page controller only
      String forwardStr = mapping.getForward(selectedButton);
      forward = mapping.findForward(forwardStr);
    }
    return forward;
  }

  protected String getSelectedButton(MyActionForm form,
                                     MyActionMapping mapping) {
    String selectedButton = null;
    String[] buttons = mapping.getButtons();
    for (int i=0;i<buttons.length;i++) {
      HtmlButton button = (HtmlButton)
           PropertyUtils.getProperty(form, buttons[i]);
      if (button.isSelected()) {
        selectedButton = buttons[i];
        break;
      }
    }
    return selectedButton;
  }
}
```

First notice that the `ActionMapping` is cast to `MyActionMapping`. Also notice that the signature of the three abstract methods – `process()`, `preprocess()` and `postprocess()` have been changed to accept `MyActionMapping` as the argument instead of `ActionMapping`. The page flow controller logic is implemented at the end of `execute()` method. The logic is simple: The code first checks which button has been selected. This is done in the `getSelectedButton()` method. It then retrieves the corresponding ActionForward and returns it. The RequestProcessor subsequently renders the view as usual. Since the code has been refactored into the base Action class, the child classes need not worry about `mapping.findFoward()`. They can simply return null. `MybankBaseAction` is now capable of automatically selecting the appropriate ActionForward.

Controlling the validation

The default mechanism in Struts to skip validations when a button is pressed is by using `<html:cancel>` in the JSP. Behind the scenes, this tag creates a button with a name – `org.apache.struts.taglib.html.CANCEL`. When the page is finally submitted, one of the first things RequestProcessor does is to check if the request has a parameter with the name `org.apache.struts.taglib.html.CANCEL`. If so, the validation is cancelled and the processing continues. While this may be acceptable for grey buttons (even those pages with multiple buttons), image buttons cannot be named as `org.apache.struts.taglib.html.CANCEL` due to their peculiar behavior. When images are used for form submission, the browsers do not submit the name and value, but the X and Y coordinates of the image. This is in accordance with the W3C specification. Even though an image corresponding to Cancel was pressed, the RequestProcessor is oblivious to this fact. It innocently requests the page validation and the end user is only but surprised to see the validation pop up! This is an area where some minor customization goes a long way. Let us start by customizing the action mapping in the struts-config.xml. Listing 10.4 shows the new addition in bold.

In addition to the existing `<set-property>` elements, a new `<set-property>` is added for a property called `validationFlags`. This is a comma-separated list of `true` and `false` telling Struts if validation needs to be performed when corresponding `buttons` (also comma-separated values) are selected on the browser. The `validationFlags` in the Listing are interpreted as: "When next and cancel buttons are selected, no validation is necessary. When save button is selected, validation is required". In addition another interesting change you will find in Listing 10.4 is that the validation is turned off by setting `validate=false`. With this setting, the validation in RequestProcessor is completely turned off for all buttons. The validation will be explicitly invoked in the base Action's `execute()` method. Listing 10.5 shows the `execute()` method. The changes are shown in bold.

Listing 10.4 struts-config.xml with global custom action mapping

```
<action-mappings type="mybank.struts.MyActionMapping">
   <action    path="/submitCustomerForm"
              type="mybank.app1.CustomerAction"
              name="CustomerForm"
              scope="request"
              validate="false"
              input="CustomerDetails.jsp">
     <set-property property="buttons"
                value="nextButton,saveButton,cancelButton" />
     <set-property property="validationFlags"
                value="false,true,false" />
     <forward name="page2"  path="Page2.jsp"  />
     <forward name="success"  path="success.jsp"  />
     <forward name="success"  path="cancel.jsp"  />
   </action>
</action-mappings>
```

The new `validationFlags` setting requires some minor code changes to the in `MyBankBaseAction`. The changes involve explicitly running the form validation and saving the ActionErrors. The key logic deciding if the validation is required for the selected button is in `MyActionMapping` class in `isValidationRequired()` method. The method requires the selected button name as an argument. A sample implementation for the `isValidationRequired()` method is as follows:

```
public boolean isValidationRequired(String selectedButton) {
  String validationStr = validationFlagMap.get(selectedButton);
  return Boolean.valueOf(validationStr);
}
```

The above method uses the selected button name to lookup a `HashMap` named `validationFlagMap`. As you know, the JavaBeans properties – `buttons` and `validationFlags` were provided as comma separated values. Parsing through the comma separated values at runtime for every user is a sheer waste of time and resources. Hence the comma-separated values are parsed in their corresponding setters to create a `HashMap` with the button name as the key. This ensures a fast retrieval of the values.

Listing 10.5 execute() method for controlling validation

```
Public MybankBaseAction extends Action {
  public ActionForward execute(ActionMapping mapping,
            ActionForm form, HttpServletRequest request,
            HttpServletResponse response) throws Exception {
           ...
    MybankBaseForm myForm = (MybankBaseForm) form;
       ...
    MyActionMapping myMapping = (MyActionMapping) mapping;
    String selectedButton =
              getSelectedButton(myForm, myMapping);

    boolean validationReqd =
                myMapping.isValidationRequired(buttons[i]);
    if (validationReqd) {
      ActionErrors errors =
               myForm.validate(myMapping, request);
      if (errors != null && ! errors.isEmpty()) {
        saveErrors(request, errors);
        return myMapping.getInput();
      }
    }

    preprocess(myMapping, myForm, request, response);
    ActionForward forward =
        process(myMapping, myForm, request, response);
    postprocess(myMapping, myForm, request, response);
       ...
    return forward;
  }
}
```

A sample implementation of the setters and the `resolve()` method is shown below:

```
public void setButtons(String buttonNames) {
  this.buttons = buttonNames;
  resolve();
}

public void setValidationFlags(String flags) {
  this.validationFlags = flags;
  resolve();
```

```
}

public void resolve() {
  if (buttons != null && validationFlags != null) {
    validationFlagMap = new HashMap();

    StringTokenizer stButtons = new StringTokenizer(buttons ",");
    StringTokenizer stFlags =
                    new StringTokenizer(validationFlags, ",");

    while (stButtons.hasMoreTokens()) {
      String buttonName = stbuttons.nextToken();
      String flagValue = stFlags.nextToken();
      validationFlagMap.put(buttonName, flagValue);
    }
  }
}
```

As seen above, every setter invokes the `resolve()` method. When the final setter is invoked, all the attributes are non-null and the `if` block in `resolve()` is entered. At this point every instance variable is guaranteed to be set by the Struts start up process. The `resolve()` method creates a `StringTokenizer` and parses the comma-delimited values to create a `HashMap` with button name as the key and the validation flag as the value. This `HashMap` thus created is utilized at runtime for a faster retrieval of flag values in the `isValidationRequired()` method.

Controlling duplicate form submissions

In chapter 4, you looked at how duplicate form submission can be handled effectively at individual form level. Here is a recap.

- The `isTokenValid()` is invoked in the `execute()` method (or one its derivatives).
- If the page is the last in a multi-page form, the token is reset.
- After processing, the user is forwarded or redirected to the next page.
- If the next page thus shown also has a form with sensitive submission, the `saveToken()` is called to set the token in session just before forwarding to the page.

Page after page, the logic remains the same as above with two blanks to be filled. They are:

1. Should the `execute()` (or any equivalent method in Action) method check if

the submission was valid for the current page? (through the `isTokenValid()` method)?

2. Does the page rendered after processing (in `execute()` or any equivalent method in Action) has sensitive submissions needs?

Two approaches emerge to fill in the blanks. The first is to use *Template Method* pattern and encapsulate the logic of handling sensitive resubmissions in the base class and delegate the task of filling the two blanks to the child classes by declaring two abstract methods in the base Action. While this sounds as the logical thing to do, there is an even better way. You got it – customizing Struts.

For a moment consider what would the two methods do if you chose the former option? The first method would simply provide a boolean value (without any logic) indicating whether the page should handle duplicate submission or not. The second method would decide (a simple if logic) whether the next view rendered needs the token in session. This information is best provided as configuration information and that is exactly what the forthcoming customization does.

Listing 10.6 struts-config.xml for duplicate form submission handling

```
<action-mappings type="mybank.struts.MyActionMapping">
  <action   path="/submitCustomerForm"
              type="mybank.app1.CustomerAction"
              name="CustomerForm"
              scope="request"
              validate="true"
              input="CustomerDetails.jsp">
    <set-property property="validateToken" value="true" />
    <set-property property="resetToken" value="true" />
    <forward name="success"
               className="mybank.struts.MyActionForward"
               path="success.jsp">
      <set-property property="setToken" value="true" />
    /forward>
     <forward name="success"  path="cancel.jsp"  />
  </action>
</action-mappings>
```

Listing 10.6 shows all the customizations needed to achieve what is needed. The application flow that is used is the same flow as before: `CustomerForm` is a single page form. On submit, a success page is shown. On Cancel, *cancel.jsp* is shown. However the only twist is that *success.jsp* is treated as a JSP with a form that needs to avoid duplicate submission (For simplicity purposes, we are not showing the `redirect=true` setting).

The action mapping in listing 10.6 provides all the information needed for sensitive resubmission logic to be retrieved in a generic manner in the base Action class. Before looking at the actual code in MybankBaseAction, let us look at what Listing 10.6 conveys. It has two new <set-property> elements. The first setting, validateToken is used to determine if token validation is necessary on entering the execute(). The second setting, resetToken is useful for the multi-page form scenario when the token has to be reset only on the final page (See chapter 4 for more information). These two settings fill in the first blank.

Next, there is a new kind of ActionForward called mybank.struts.MyActionForward. This is an example of extending the ActionForward class to add custom settings. The <forward> itself now contains a <set-property> for a JavaBeans property called setToken on MyActionForward. This setting fills the second blank.

Now, let us look at the actual code that handles form submission. This code goes into the base Action class and is shown in Listing 10.7. The new code is shown in bold. In addition, the listing includes all the useful code discussed so far that should make into the base Action (except page flow Controller). You can use this Listing as the template base Action for real world applications.

The getValidateToken() method retrieves the validateToken (<set-property>) from MyActionMapping. This setting tells the framework whether to check for sensitive resubmissions on the current page. After the check is done, duplicate form submissions need to be handled as prescribed by your business. For regular submissions, retrieve the ActionForward for the next page. If the next page happens to be one of those requiring a token in the Http Session, saveToken() is invoked and then the ActionForward is returned.

Listing 10.7 The complete base Action class

```
public class MybankBaseAction extends Action {
  public ActionForward execute(ActionMapping mapping,
           ActionForm form, HttpServletRequest request,
          HttpServletResponse response) throws Exception   {
    // Add centralized logging here (Entry point audit)

    // Check here if the user has rights to this application
    // or retrieve app specific profile for the user

    ActionForward forward = null;
    MybankBaseForm myForm = (MybankBaseForm) form;

    // Set common MybankBaseForm variables using request &
    // session attributes for type-safe access in subclasses.
    // For e.g. myForm.setUserProfile(
    //                request.getAttribute("profile"));
```

```
    MyActionMapping myMapping = (MyActionMapping) mapping;
    String selectedButton =
              getSelectedButton(myForm, myMapping);

    boolean validationReqd =
                myMapping.isValidationRequired(buttons[i]);
    if (validationReqd) {
      ActionErrors    errors    =    myForm.validate(myMapping,
request);
      if (errors != null && ! errors.isEmpty()) {
        saveErrors(request, errors);
        return myMapping.getInput();
      }
    }

    boolean tokenIsValid = true;
    if (myMapping.getValidateToken()) { // validate token
      if (myMapping.getResetToken()) {
        tokenIsValid = isTokenValid(request, true);
      }
      else {
        tokenIsValid = isTokenValid(request, false);
      }
    }

    if (tokenIsValid) {
      preprocess(myMapping, myForm, request, response);
      forward = process(myMapping, myForm, request, response);
      postprocess(myMapping, myForm, request, response);
    }
    else { //duplicate submission
      //Adopt a strategy to handle duplicate submissions
      //This is up to you and unique to your business
    }

    if (forward.getClass().equals(
                mybank.struts.MyActionForward.class) {
      MyActionForward myForward = (MyActionForward) forward;
      if(myForward.getSetToken()) {
        // next page is a form with sensitive resubmission
        saveToken(request);
      }
```

```
    }

    // Add centralized logging here (Exit point audit)

    return forward;
  }
}
```

DispatchAction for Image Button form submissions

DispatchAction and LookupDispatchAction work by invoking a method on the Action whose name matches a predefined request parameter. This works fine for form submissions when all the buttons have the same name but does not work for image button form submissions. In this section, we will further customize the ActionMapping to support a DispatchAction like feature for image based form submissions. This can be used in an enterprise application without a second thought. It will definitely prove useful timesaver.

As before, a new <set-property> needs to be added to the struts-config.xml as follows:

```
<set-property property="methods"
              value="doNext,saveCustInfo,cancelTx" />
```

This setting works in conjunction with the <set-property> for buttons property in MyActionMapping. The methods is a comma-separated list of method names to be invoked for every button name defined in the comma-separated buttons <set-property>. A subclass of MybankBaseAction called MyDispatchAction is created to provide the DispatchAction-like features. This class has concrete implementation for MybankBaseAction's process() method. To use this class, you should subclass the MyDispatchAction. At runtime, the MyDispatchAction invokes appropriate method from your subclass via reflection. The process() method is shown in Listing 10.8.

The underlying logic is almost similar to previous utilities. In the process() method, the method to be invoked for the currently selected button is retrieved from MyActionMapping. Then, using the MethodUtils (another helper class from *BeanUtils* package), the actual method is invoked. The actual method name to be invoked is specified in the action mapping. These methods are similar to any method you would write had it been a regular DispatchAction. The methods have the fixed signature:

```
public ActionForward methodName(MyActionMapping mapping,
            MybankBaseForm form, HttpServletRequest request,
            HttpServletResponse response) throws Exception
```

Listing 10.8 Base Action class with DispatchAction like featur(s

```
public class MyDispatchAction extends MybankBaseAction {
   protected ActionForward process(MyActionMapping mapping,
            MybankBaseForm form, HttpServletRequest request,
            HttpServletResponse response) throws Exception
   {
      ActionForward forward = null;
      String selectedButton =
                  getSelectedButton(myForm, mapping)
      String methodName = mapping.getMethod(button);
      Object[] args = {mapping, form, request, response};

      // this invokes the appropriate method in subclass
      forward = (ActionForward)
         MethodUtils.invokeMethod(this, ,methodName, args);
      return forward;
   }
}
```

Summary

In this chapter you looked at how to effectively customize Struts to reap maximum benefit and minimize the burdens while developing web applications. Hopefully you were able to realize the strengths of extending Struts and its hidden potential for making your application cleaner and better.

INDEX

ISBN: 0-9748488-1-6 (paperback)

Errata

Chapter 2

1. Page 36, last line mentions Appendix A. Appendix A is not present in the book.
2. Page 38, Listing 2.3 – The JSP names in the ActionMapping (`<action>`) for "/submitDetailForm" are not prefixed with a "/". It is required as shown below to function correctly.

```
input="/CustomerDetailForm.jsp"
<forward name="success" path="/ThankYou.jsp"
                         redirect="true" />
<forward name="failure" path="/Failure.jsp" />
```

3. Page 38, Listing 2.3 – The correct package for ForwardAction is org.apache.struts.actions.ForwardAction
4. Page 40, Listing 2.4 – The action attribute for the <html:form> does not require a .do. It is automatically added. The correct form is <html:form action="/submitDetailForm" />
5. Page 42, last line has errors.suffix=<li>. It should be errors.prefix=<li>

Chapter 3

Page 59, Point 6 and 7 are the same. Only one of them is sufficient

Chapter 4

1. Page 66, In Section "MVC compliant usage of LinkTag", the package name for and xml syntax for ForwardAction is incorrect. Instead, it should be `type="org.apache.struts.actions.ForwardAction"`.
2. Page 67, Section "Using LinkTag's action attribute" – Same error as 1)
3. Page 67, Section "Using LinkTag's forward attribute" – Same error as 1)
4. Page 68, Section "Using ForwardAction for Integration" – Same error as 1)
5. Page 70, Last line – Same error as 1). In addition the `<action name="..."` should be replaced with `<action path="..."`.
6. Page 73, third line. IncludeAction package name should be `org.apache.struts.actions.IncludeAction`
7. Page 86, Section "Handling Duplicate Form Submissions". The three

paragraphs starting from "The method generates a random token....." should read as follows:

The method generates a random token using session id, current time and a MessageDigest and stores it in the session using a key name `org.apache.struts.action.TOKEN` (This is the value of the static variable TRANSACTION_TOKEN_KEY in `org.apache.struts.Globals` class.

The Action class that renders the form invokes the `saveToken()` method to create a session attribute with the above name. In the JSP, you have to use the token as a hidden form field as follows:

```
<input type="hidden"
name="<%=org.apache.struts.taglib.html.Constants.TOKEN_KEY%>"
value="<bean:write name="<%=Globals.TRANSACTION_TOKEN_KEY%>"/>">
```

The embedded `<bean:write>` tag shown above, looks for a bean named `org.apache.struts.action.TOKEN` (which is the the value of Globals. TRANSACTION_TOKEN_KEY) in session scope and renders its value as the `value` attribute of the hidden input variable. The name of the hidden input variable is `org.apache.struts.taglib.html.TOKEN` (This is nothing but the value of the static variable TOKEN_KEY in the class `org.apache.struts.taglib.html.Constants`).

Chapter 6

Page 132, Section "Struts Logic Tags" subsection "Iterate Tag" has some errors. It is completely rewritten for better understanding as follows:

The iterate tag is used to iterate over a collection (or a bean containing collection) in any of the four scopes (page, request, session and application) and execute the body content for every element in the collection. For instance, the following tag iterates over the collection named `customers`.

```
<logic:iterate name="customers">
   //execute for every element in the collection
</logic:iterate>
```

Another alternative is to use a bean and iterate over its property identified by the attribute `property`. The following tag accesses the `company` bean from one of the scope and then invokes `getCustomers()` on it to retrieves a collection and iterates over it.

```
<logic:iterate name="company" property="customers">
   // Execute for every element in the customers
   // collection in company bean
```

```
</logic:iterate>
```

Most of the times a collection is iterated over to display the contents of that collection, perhaps in the table format. This requires the individual element of the collection is exposed as a scripting variable to the inner tags and scriptlets. This is done using the id attribute as follows:

```
<logic:iterate id="customer" name="company" name="customers">
   // Execute for every element in the customers
   // collection in company bean.
   // Use the scripting variable named customer
   <bean:write name="customer" property="firstName" />
</logic:iterate>
```

Chapter 10

Listing 10.7 has a error. When there are validation errors in the final page of a multipage form, the base Action class behavior is affected. The following changes are needed:

1. Replace myMapping.getInput() with mapping.findForward(mapping.getInput())
2. Replace

```
if (myMapping.getValidateToken()) { // validate token
  if (myMapping.getResetToken()) {
    tokenIsValid = isTokenValid(request, true);
  } else {
    tokenIsValid = isTokenValid(request, false);
  }
}
```

   with

```
if (myMapping.getValidateToken()) { // validate token
    tokenIsValid = isTokenValid(request);
}
```

3. Replace the code block setting the Token for MyActionForward with following

```
if (forward.getClass().equals(MyActionForward.class) {
   MyActionForward myForward = (MyActionForward) forward;
  /* Reset the token if there are no errors and
     resetToken attribute in ActionMapping is true.
     Note that in multipage scenarios, resetToken is
     false in the ActionMapping */
   if (!hasErrors(request) && myMapping.getResetToken()) {
       resetToken(request);
   }
```

```
    /* If there are no errors and next page requires
       a new token, set it. The setToken is false
       in the ActionForwards for that ActionMapping.
       Hence a multipage form flow has a single token
       a unique identifier for the biz transaction */
    if (myForward.getSetToken() && !hasErrors(request)) {
      // next page is a form with sensitive resubmission
      saveToken(request);
    }
}
```